Introduction to Computational Neuroscience

Introduction to Computational Neuroscience

Madison White

WILLFORD PRESS
www.willfordpress.com

Published by Willford Press,
118-35 Queens Blvd., Suite 400,
Forest Hills, NY 11375, USA

ISBN: 978-1-64728-029-1

Cataloging-in-Publication Data

Introduction to computational neuroscience / Madison White
    p. cm.
Includes bibliographical references and index.
ISBN 978-1-64728-029-1
1. Computational neuroscience. 2. Computational biology.
3. Neurosciences--Data processing. I. White, Madison.
QP357.5 .I58 2022
612.8--dc23

For information on all Willford Press publications
visit our website at www.willfordpress.com

Table of Contents

Preface

This book is a culmination of my many years of practice in this field. I attribute the success of this book to my support group. I would like to thank my parents who have showered me with unconditional love and support and my peers and professors for their constant guidance.

The branch of neuroscience that uses theoretical analysis, mathematical models and abstractions of the brain for understanding the nervous system is known as computational neuroscience. It is involved in studying the development, structure, physiology and cognitive abilities of the nervous system. The models within this field seek to capture the essential features of the biological system at multi-spatial temporal scales. These models are used to develop hypotheses which can be tested through biological or psychological experiments. The major topics that are studied under computational neuroscience are single-neuron modeling, sensory processing, motor control, computational clinical neuroscience, cognition, discrimination and learning, memory, and synaptic plasticity. This book outlines the processes and applications of computational neuroscience in detail. The various studies that are constantly contributing towards advancing technologies and evolution of this field are examined in detail. This book will provide comprehensive knowledge to the readers.

The details of chapters are provided below for a progressive learning:

Chapter – What is Computational Neuroscience?

The branch of neuroscience which deals with the utilization of computer approaches to study the nervous system is known as computational neuroscience. It is also involved in building models for understanding the working of neurons, axons and dendrites. This chapter will briefly introduce all the significant aspects of computational neuroscience as well as neuroinformatics.

Chapter – Nervous System

The highly complex part of an animal which coordinates its action and sensory information by transmitting the signals to and from different body parts of the body is known as the nervous system. Some of its basic parts are neurons, spinal cord and brain. This chapter has been carefully written to provide an easy understanding of the nervous system.

Chapter – Models used in Computational Neuroscience

There are various types of models used in computational neuroscience. Some of these include FitzHugh-Nagumo model, Hindmarsh-Rose model, Galves–Löcherbach model, Dehaene-Changeux model, Wilson–Cowan model and Morris–Lecar model. The diverse applications of these models in computational neuroscience have been thoroughly discussed in this chapter.

Chapter – Artificial Intelligence and Artificial Neural Network

The computing systems that are inspired by the biological neural networks which constitute animal brains are referred to as artificial neural networks. They contribute significantly to the field of artificial intelligence by replicating the working of the brain. This chapter closely examines the key concepts and types of artificial neural network and artificial intelligence to provide an extensive understanding of the subject.

Chapter – Softwares and Technologies used in Computational Neuroscience

Various software and technologies are used in computational neuroscience. The most common of them are GENESIS, NEURON, BRIAN, neurocomputational speech processing and artificial brain. The topics elaborated in this chapter will help in gaining a better perspective about these software and technologies used in computational neuroscience.

Madison White

1

What is Computational Neuroscience?

The branch of neuroscience which deals with the utilization of computer approaches to study the nervous system is known as computational neuroscience. It is also involved in building models for understanding the working of neurons, axons and dendrites. This chapter will briefly introduce all the significant aspects of computational neuroscience as well as neuroinformatics.

Computational neuroscience is the science of studying brain function with computer science modeling, and looking at all of the activity of the human brain through the lens of computer science. Scientists engaged in computational neuroscience might build models to understand how neurons, axons and dendrites work. The field of computational neuroscience blends aspects of computer science and electrical engineering with traditional studies of biology. Computational neuroscience is also known as theoretical neuroscience.

Although computational neuroscience uses models to look at brain activity, it is different from some of the other models that are most useful in artificial intelligence today. A common explanation is that computational neuroscience is different from psychological connectionism because it emphasizes the biology of neurons and not just their function. Another way to say this is that computational neuroscience is focused on more fully realizing the biology of the brain, and not on the simulation of intelligence primarily.

Computational neuroscience can be applied in many ways. It can be applied to look at the ways that the brain processes information, for example, in advanced analysis of human or animal vision or in other senses, such as the sense of smell. It may be applied to models assessing basic motor skills or mobile development. It may be applied to either active or involuntary aspects of the central nervous system. Computational neuroscience seeks to understand the brain and how it works through direct application of new high-tech sciences.

Brain science seeks to understand the myriad functions of the brain in terms of principles that lead from molecular interactions to behavior. Although the complexity of the brain is daunting and the field seems brazenly ambitious, painstaking experimental efforts have made impressive progress. While investigations, being dependent on methods of measurement, have frequently been driven by clever use of the newest technologies, many diverse phenomena have been rendered comprehensible through interpretive analysis, which has often leaned heavily on mathematical and statistical ideas. These ideas are varied, but a central framing of the problem has been to "elucidate the representation and transmission of information in the nervous system" (Perkel and Bullock 1968). In addition, new and improved measurement and storage devices have enabled increasingly detailed recordings, as well as methods of perturbing neural circuits, with many scientists feeling at once excited and overwhelmed by opportunities of learning from the ever-larger and more complex data sets they are collecting. Thus, computational neuroscience has come to encompass not only a program of modeling neural activity and brain function at all levels of detail and abstraction, from sub-cellular biophysics to human behavior, but also advanced methods for analysis of neural data.

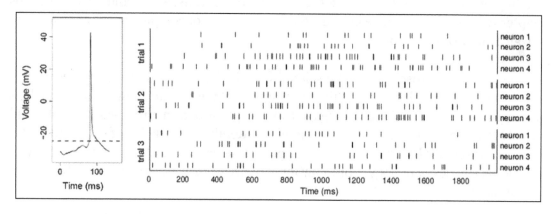

In a living organism, each neuron is connected to many others through synapses, with the totality forming a large network. We discuss both mechanistic models formulated with differential equations and statistical models for data analysis, which use probability to describe variation. Mechanistic and statistical approaches are complementary, but their starting points are different, and their models have tended to incorporate different details. Mechanistic models aim to explain the dynamic evolution of neural activity based on hypotheses about the properties governing the dynamics. Statistical models aim to assess major drivers of neural activity by taking account of indeterminate sources of variability labeled as noise. These approaches have evolved separately, but are now being drawn together. For example, neurons can be either excitatory, causing depolarizing responses at downstream (post-synaptic) neurons (i.e., responses that push the voltage toward the firing threshold, as illustrated in Figure), or inhibitory, causing hyperpolarizing post-synaptic responses (that push the voltage away from threshold). This detail has been crucial for mechanistic models but, until relatively recently, has been largely ignored in statistical models. On the other hand, during experiments, neural activity changes while an animal reacts to a stimulus or produces a behavior. This kind of non-stationarity has been seen as a fundamental challenge in the statistical work, while mechanistic approaches have tended to emphasize emergent behavior of the system. In current research, as the two perspectives are being combined increasingly often, the distinction has become blurred.

The left panel shows the voltage drop recorded across a neuron's cell membrane. The voltage fluctuates stochastically, but tends to drift upward, and when it rises to a threshold level (dashed line) the neuron fires an action potential, after which it returns to a resting state; the neuron then responds to inputs that will again make its voltage drift upward toward the threshold. This is often modeled as drifting Brownian motion that results from excitatory and inhibitory Poisson process inputs. The right panel shows spike trains recorded from 4 neurons repeatedly across 3 experimental replications, known as trials. The spike times are irregular within trials, and there is substantial variation across trials, and across neurons.

The Brain-as-computer Metaphor

The modern notion of computation may be traced to a series of investigations in mathematical logic in the 1930s, including the Turing machine. Although we now understand logic as a mathematical subject existing separately from human cognitive processes, it was natural to conceptualize the rational aspects of thought in terms of logic (as in Boole's 1854 *Investigation of the Laws of Thought* which "aimed to investigate those operations of the mind by which reasoning is performed"), and this led to the 1943 proposal by Craik that the nervous system could be viewed "as a calculating machine capable of modeling or paralleling external events" while McCulloch and Pitts provided what they called "A logical calculus of the ideas immanent in nervous activity". In fact, while it was an outgrowth of preliminary investigations by a number of early theorists, the McCulloch and Pitts paper stands as a historical landmark for the origins of artificial intelligence, along with the notion that mind can be explained by neural activity through a formalism that aims to define the brain as a computational device; see Figure 2. In the same year another noteworthy essay, by Norbert Wiener and colleagues, argued that in studying any behavior its purpose must be considered, and this requires recognition of the role of error correction in the form of feedback. Soon after, Wiener consolidated these ideas in the term *cybernetics*. Also, in 1948 Claude Shannon published his hugely influential work on information theory which, beyond its technical contributions, solidified information (the reduction of uncertainty) as an abstract quantification of the content being transmitted across communication channels, including those in brains and computers.

The first computer program that could do something previously considered exclusively the product of human minds was the *Logic Theorist* of Newell and Simon, which succeeded in proving 38 of the 52 theorems concerning the logical foundations of arithmetic in Chapter 2 of *Principia Mathematica*. The program was written in a list-processing language they created (a precursor to LISP), and provided a hierarchical symbol manipulation framework together with various heuristics, which were formulated by analogy with human problem-solving. It was also based on serial processing, as envisioned by Turing and others.

A different kind of computational architecture, developed by Rosenblatt, combined the McCulloch-Pitts conception with a learning rule based on ideas artic, now known as *Hebbian learning*. Hebb's rule was, "When an axon of cell A is near enough to excite a cell B and repeatedly or persistently takes part in firing it, some growth process or metabolic change takes place in one or both cells such that A's efficiency, as one of the cells firing B, is increased, that is, the strengths of the synapses connecting the two neurons increase, which is sometimes stated colloquially as, "Neurons that fire together, wire together." Rosenblatt called his primitive neurons *perceptrons*, and he created a rudimentary classifier, aimed at imitating biological decision making, from a network of perceptrons, see Figure. This was the first artificial neural network that could carry out a non-trivial task.

As the foregoing historical outline indicates, the brain-as-computer metaphor was solidly in place by the end of the 1950s. It rested on a variety of technical specifications of the notions that logical thinking is a form of information processing, information pro- cessing is the purpose of computer programs, while, information processing may be implemented by neural systems (explicitly in the case of McCulloch-Pitts model and its de- scendents, but implicitly otherwise). A crucial recapitulation of the information-processing framework, given later by David Marr, distinguished three levels of analysis: *computation* ("What is the goal of the computation, why is it appropriate, and what is the logic of the strategy by which it can be carried out?"), *algorithm* ("What is the repre- sentation for the input and output, and what is the algorithm for the transformation?"), and *implementation* ("How can the representation and algorithm be realized physically?"). This remains a very useful way to categorize descriptions of brain computation.

Neurons as Electrical Circuits

A rather different line of mathematical work, more closely related to neurobiology, had to do with the electrical properties of neurons. So-called "animal electricity" had been observed by. The idea that the nervous system was made up of individual neurons was put forth by Cajal in 1886, the synaptic basis of communication across neurons was established by Sherrington in 1897, and the notion that neurons were electrically excitable in a manner similar to a circuit involving capacitors and resistors in parallel was proposed by Hermann in 1905. In 1907, Lapique gave an explicit solution to the resulting differential equation, in which the key constants could be determined from data, and he compared what is now known as the leaky integrate-and-fire model (LIF) with his own experimental results. This model, and variants of it, remain in use today. Then, a series of investigations by Adrian and colleagues established the "all or nothing" nature of the AP, so that increasing a stimulus intensity does not change the voltage profile of an AP but, instead, increases the neural firing rate. The conception that stimulus or behavior is related to firing rate has become ubiquitous in neurophysiology. It is often called rate coding, in contrast to temporal coding, which involves the information carried in the precise timing of spikes.

Following these fundamental descriptions, remaining puzzles about the details of action potential generation led to investigations by several neurophysiologists and, ultimately, to one of the great scientific triumphs, the Hodgkin-Huxley model. Published in, the model consisted of a differential equation for the neural membrane potential (in the squid giant axon) together with three subsidiary differential equations for the dynamic properties of the sodium and potassium ion channels. This work produced accurate predictions of the time courses of membrane conductances; the form of the action potential; the change in action potential form with varying concentrations of sodium; the number of sodium ions involved in inward flux across the membrane; the speed of action potential propagation; and the voltage curves for sodium and potassium ions. Thus, by the time the brain-as-computer metaphor had been established, the power of biophysical modeling had also been demonstrated. Over the past 60 years, the Hodgkin-Huxley equations have been refined, but the model's fundamental formulation has endured, and serves as the basis for many present-day models of single neuron activity.

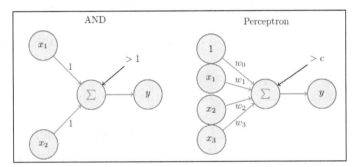

In the left diagram, McCulloch-Pitts neurons x_1 and x_2 each send binary activity to neuron y using the rule $y = 1$ *if* $x_1 + x_2 > 1$ and $y = 0$ otherwise; this corresponds to the logical AND operator; other logical operators NOT, OR, NOR may be similarly implemented by thresholding. In the right diagram, the general form of output is based on thresholding linear combinations, i.e., $y = 1$ when $\sum w_i x_i > c$ and $y = 0$ otherwise. The values w_i are called synaptic weights. However, because networks of perceptrons (and their more modern artificial neural network descendents) are far simpler than networks in the brain, each artificial neuron corresponds conceptually not to an individual neuron in the brain but, instead, to large collections of neurons in the brain.

Receptive Fields and Tuning Curves

In early recordings from the optic nerve of the *Limulus* (horseshoe crab), Hartline found that shining a light on the eye could drive individual neurons to fire, and that a neuron's firing rate increased with the intensity of the light. He called the location of the light that drove the neuron to fire the neuron's *receptive field*. In primary visual cortex (known as area V1), the first part of cortex to get input from the retina, Hubel and Wiesel showed that bars of light moving across a particular part of the visual field, again labeled the receptive field, could drive a particular neuron to fire and, furthermore, that the orientation of the bar of light was important: many neurons were driven to fire most rapidly when the bar of light moved in one direction, and fired much more slowly when the orientation was rotated 90 degrees away. When firing rate is considered as a function of orientation, this function has come to be known as a *tuning curve*. More recently, the terms "receptive field" and "tuning curve" have been generalized to refer to non-spatial features that drive neurons to fire. The notion of tuning curves, which could involve many dimensions of tuning simultaneously, is widely applied in computational neuroscience.

Networks

Neuron-like artificial neural networks, advancing beyond perceptron networks, were developed during the 1960s and 1970s, especially in work on associative memory where a memory is stored as a pattern of activity that can be recreated by a stimulus when it provides even a partial match to the pattern. To describe a given activation pattern, Hopfield applied statistical physics tools to introduce an energy function and showed that a simple update rule would decrease the energy so that the network would settle to a patternmatching "attractor" state. Hopfield's network model is an example of what statisticians call a two-way interaction model for N binary variables, where the energy function becomes the negative log-likelihood function. Hinton and Sejnowski provided a stochastic mechanism for optimization and the interpretation that a posterior distribution was being maximized, calling their method a Boltzmann machine because the probabilities they used were those of the Boltzmann distribution in statistical mechanics . Geman and Geman then provided a rigorous analysis together with their reformulation in terms of the Gibbs sampler. Additional tools from statistical mechanics were used to calculate memory capacity and other properties of memory retrieval.

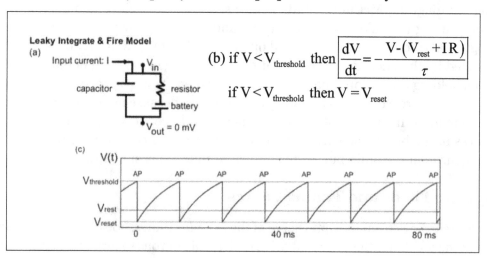

(a)The LIF model is motivated by an equivalent circuit. The capacitor represents the cell membrane through which ions cannot pass. The resistor represents channels in the membrane (through which ions can pass) and the battery a difference in ion concentration across the membrane. (b) The equivalent circuit motivates the differential equation that describes voltage dynamics (gray box). When the voltage reaches a threshold value ($V_{threshold}$), it is reset to a smaller value (V_{reset}). In this model, the occurrence of a reset indicates an action potential; the rapid voltage dynamics of action potentials are not included in the model. (c) An example trace of the LIF model voltage (blue). When the input current (I) is large enough, the voltage increases until reaching the voltage threshold (red horizontal line), at which time the voltage is set to the reset voltage (green horizontal line). The times of reset are labeled as "AP", denoting action potential. In the absence of an applied current ($I = 0$) the voltage approaches a stable equilibrium value (V_{rest}).

Artificial neural networks gained traction as models of human cognition through a series of developments in the 1980s, producing the paradigm of parallel distributed processing (PDP). PDP models are multi-layered networks of nodes resembling those of their perceptron precursor, but they are interactive, or recurrent, in the sense that they are not necessarily feed-forward: connections between nodes can go in both directions, and they may have structured inhibition and excitation. In addition, training (i.e., estimating parameters by minimizing an optimization criterion such as the sum of squared errors across many training examples) is done by a form of gradient descent known as back propagation (because iterations involve steps backward from output errors toward input weights). While the nodes within these networks do not correspond to individual neurons, features of the networks, including back propagation, are usually considered to be biologically plausible. For example, synaptic connections between biological neurons are plastic, and change their strength following rules consistent with theoretical models (e.g., Hebb's rule). Furthermore, PDP models can reproduce many behavioral phenomena, famously including generation of past tense for English verbs and making childlike errors before settling on correct forms. Currently, there is increased interest in neural network models through deep learning.

Hodgkin-Huxley Model

(a)

(b) K^+ current, Na^+ current, Leak current

$$C\frac{dV}{dt} = I(t) - \overline{g}_k n^4 (V - V_k) - \overline{g}_{Na} m^3 h (V - V_{Na}) - \overline{g}_L (V - V_L)$$

$$\frac{dn}{dt} = -\frac{n - n_\infty(V)}{\tau_n(V)}, \quad \frac{dm}{dt} = -\frac{m - m_\infty(V)}{\tau_m(V)}, \quad \frac{dh}{dt} = -\frac{h - h_\infty(V)}{\tau_h(V)}$$

The Hodgkin-Huxley model provides a mathematical description of a neuron's voltage dynamics in terms of changes in sodium (Na^+) and potassium (K^+) ion concentrations. The cartoon in (a) illustrates a cell body with membrane channels through which (Na^+) and (K^+) may pass. The model consists of four coupled nonlinear differential equations

(b) that describe the voltage dynamics (V), which vary according to an input current (I), a potassium current, a sodium current, and a leak current. The conductances of the potassium (n) and sodium currents (m, h) vary in time, which controls the flow of sodium and potassium ions through the neural membrane. Each channel's dynamics depends on (c) a steady state function and a time constant. The steady state functions range from 0 to 1, where 0 indicates that the channel is closed (so that ions cannot pass), and 1 indicates that the channel is open (ions can pass). One might visualize these channels as gates that swing open and closed, allowing ions to pass or impeding their flow; these gates are indicated in green and red in the cartoon (a). The steady state functions depend on the voltage; the vertical dashed line indicates the typical resting voltage value of a neuron. The time constants are less than 10ms, and smallest for one component of the sodium channel (the sodium activation gate m). (d) During an action potential, the voltage undergoes a rapid depolarization (V increases) and then less rapid hyperpolarization (V decreases), supported by the opening and closing of the membrane channels.

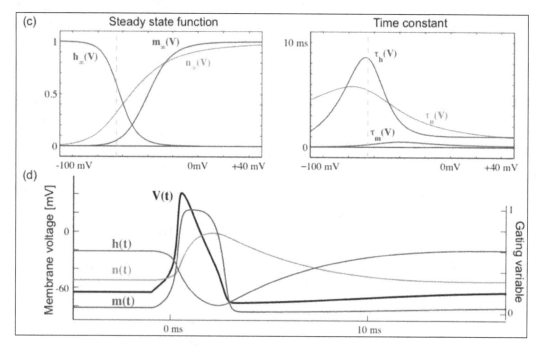

Analysis of the overall structure of network connectivity, exemplified in research on social networks (see Fienberg for historical overview), has received much attention following the 1998 observation that several very different kinds of networks, including the neural connectivity in the worm C. elegans, exhibit "small world" properties of short average path length between nodes, together with substantial clustering of nodes, and that these properties may be described by a relatively simple stochastic model. This style of network description has since been applied in many contexts involving brain measurement, mainly using structural and functional magnetic resonance imaging (MRI), though cautions have been issued regarding the difficulty of interpreting results physiologically.

Statistical Models

Stochastic considerations have been part of neuroscience since the first descriptions of neural activity, outlined briefly above, due to the statistical mechanics underlying the flow of ions across channels and synapses. Spontaneous fluctuations in a neuron's membrane potential are believed to arise from the random opening and closing of ion channels, and this spontaneous variability has been analyzed using a variety of statistical methods. Such analysis provides information about the numbers and properties of the ion channel populations responsible for excitability. Probability has also been used extensively in psychological theories of human behavior for more than 100 years, e.g., Stigler. Especially popular theories used to account for behavior include Bayesian inference and reinforcement learning, which we will touch on below. A more recent interest is to determine signatures of statistical algorithms in neural function. For example, drifting diffusion to a threshold, which is used with LIF models, has also been used to describe models of decision making based on neural recordings. However, these are all examples of ways that statistical models have been used to describe neural activity, which is very different from the role of statistics in data analysis.

Recording Modalities

Efforts to understand the nervous system must consider both anatomy (its constituents and their connectivity) and function (neural activity and its relationship to the apparent goals of an organism). Anatomy does not determine function, but does strongly constrain it. Anatomical methods range from a variety of microscopic methods to static, wholebrain MRI. Functional investigations range across spatial and temporal scales, beginning with recordings from ion channels, to action potentials, to local field potentials (LFPs) due to the activity of many thousands of neural synapses. Functional measurements outside the brain (still reflecting electrical activity within it), come from electroencephalography (EEG) and magnetoencephalography (MEG), as well as indirect methods that measure a physiological or metabolic parameter closely associated with neural activity, including positron emission tomography (PET), functional MRI (fMRI), and nearinfrared resonance spectroscopy (NIRS). These functional methods have timescales spanning milliseconds to minutes, and spatial scales ranging from a few cubic millimeters to many cubic centimeters.

While interesting mathematical and statistical problems arise in nearly every kind of neuroscience data, we focus here on neural spiking activity. Spike trains are sometimes recorded from individual neurons in tissue that has been extracted from an animal and maintained over hours in a functioning condition (in vitro). In this setting, the voltage drop across the membrane is nearly deterministic; then, when the neuron is driven with the same current input on each of many repeated trials, the timing of spikes is often replicated precisely across the trials, as seen in portions of the spike trains in Figure. Recordings from brains of living animals (in vivo) show substantial irregularity in spike timing, as in Figure. These recordings often come from electrodes that have been inserted into brain tissue near, but not on or in, the neuron generating a resulting spike train; that is, they are extracellular recordings. The data could come from one up to dozens, hundreds, or even thousands of electrodes. Because the voltage on each electrode is due to activity of many nearby neurons, with each neuron contributing its own voltage signature repeatedly, there is an interesting statistical clustering problem known as spike sorting, but we will ignore that here. Another important source of activity, recorded from many individual neurons simultaneously, is calcium imaging, in which light is emitted by fluorescent indicators in response to the flow of calcium ions into neurons when they fire. Calcium dynamics, and the nature of the indicator, limit temporal resolution to between tens and several hundred milliseconds. Signals can be collected using one-photon microscopy even from deep in the brain of a behaving animal; two-photon microscopy provides significantly higher spatial resolution but at the cost of limiting recordings to the brain surface. Due to the temporal smoothing, extraction of spiking data from calcium imaging poses its own set of statistical challenges.

Neural firing rates vary widely, depending on recording site and physiological circumstances, from quiescent (essentially 0 spikes per second) to as many as 200 spikes per second. The output of spike sorting is a sequence of spike times, typically at time resolution of 1 millisecond (the approximate width of an AP). While many analyses are based on spike counts across relatively long time intervals (numbers of spikes that occur in time bins of tens or hundreds of milliseconds), some are based on the more complete precise timing information provided by the spike trains.

In some special cases, mainly in networks recorded in vitro, neurons are densely sampled and it is possible to study the way activity of one neuron directly influences the activity of other neurons (Pillow et al. 2008). However, in most experimental settings to date, a very small proportion of the neurons in the circuit are sampled.

Data Analysis

In experiments involving behaving animals, each experimental condition is typically repeated across many trials. On any two trials, there will be at least slight differences in behavior, neural activity throughout the brain, and contributions from molecular noise, all of which results in considerable variability of spike timing. Thus, a spike train may be regarded as a point process, i.e., a stochastic sequence of event times, with the events being spikes. We discuss point process modeling below, but note here that the data are typically recorded as sparse binary time series in 1 millisecond time bins (1 if spike, 0 if no spike). When spike counts within broader time bins are considered, they may be assumed to form continuous-valued time series, and this is the framework for some of the methods referenced below. It is also possible to apply time series methods directly to the binary data, or smoothed versions of them, but see the caution in Kass et al. A common aim is to relate an observed pattern of activity to features of the experimental stimulus or behavior. However, in some settings predictive approaches are used, often under the rubric of decoding, in the sense that neural activity is "decoded" to predict the stimulus or behavior. In this case, tools associated with the field of statistical machine learning may be especially useful. We omit many interesting questions that arise in the course of analyzing biological neural networks, such as the distribution of the post-synaptic potentials that represent synaptic weights.

Data analysis is performed by scientists with diverse backgrounds. Statistical approaches use frameworks built on probabilistic descriptions of variability, both for inductive reasoning and for analysis of procedures. The resulting foundation for data analysis has been called the statistical paradigm.

Components of the Nervous System

When we speak of neurons, or brains, we are indulging in sweeping generalities: properties may depend not only on what is happening to the organism during a study, but also on the component of the nervous system studied, and the type of animal being used. Popular organisms in neuroscience include worms, mollusks, insects, fish, birds, rodents, non-human primates, and, of course, humans. The nervous system of vertebrates comprises the brain, the spinal cord, and the peripheral system. The brain itself includes both the cerebral cortex and sub-cortical areas. Textbooks of neuroscience use varying organizational rubrics, but major topics include the molecular physiology of neurons, sensory systems, the motor system, and systems that support higher-order functions associated with complex and flexible behavior. Attempts at understanding computational properties of the nervous system have often focused on sensory systems: they are more easily accessed experimentally, controlled inputs to them can be based on naturally occurring inputs, and their response properties are comparatively simple. In addition, much attention has been given to the cerebral cortex, which is involved in higher-order functioning.

Single Neurons

Mathematical models typically aim to describe the way a given phenomenon arises from some architectural constraints. Statistical models typically are used to describe what a particular data set can say concerning the phenomenon, including the strength of evidence.

LIF Models and their Extensions

Originally proposed more than a century ago, the LIF model continues to serve an important role in neuroscience research. Although LIF neurons are deterministic, they often mimic the variation in spike trains of real neurons recorded in vitro, such as those in Figure 5. In the left panel of that figure, the same fluctuating current is applied repeatedly as input to the neuron, and this creates many instances of spike times that are highly precise in the sense of being replicated across trials; some other spike times are less precise. Precise spike times occur when a large slope in the input current leads to wide recruitment of ion channels. Temporal locking of spikes to high frequency inputs also can be seen in LIF models. Many extensions of the original leaky integrate-and-fire model have been developed to capture other features of observed neuronal activity (Gerstner et al. 2014), including more realistic spike initiation through inclusion of a quadratic term, and incorporation of a second dynamical variable to simulate adaptation and to capture more diverse patterns of neuronal spiking and bursting. Even though these models ignore the biophysics of action potential generation (which involve the conductances generated by ion channels, as in the Hodgkin-Huxley model), they are able to capture the nonlinearities present in several biophysical neuronal models. The impact of stochastic effects due to the large number of synaptic inputs delivered to an LIF neuron has also been extensively studied using diffusion processes.

Biophysical Models

These include models that capture additional biological features, such as additionalionic currents, and aspects of the neuron's extracellular environment, both of which introduce new fast and slow timescales to the dynamics. Contributions due to the extensive dendrites (which receive inputs to the neuron) have been simulated in detailed biophysical models. While increased biological realism necessitates additional mathematical complexity, especially when large populations of neurons are considered, the Hodgkin-Huxley model and its extensions remain fundamental to computational neuroscience research.

Simplified mathematical models of single neuron activity have facilitated a dynamical understanding of neural behavior. The Fitzhugh-Nagumo model is a purely phenomenological model, based on geometric and dynamic principles, and not directly on the neuron's biophysics. Because of its low dimensionality, it is amenable to phase-plane analysis using dynamical systems tools (e.g., examining the nullclines, equilibria and trajectories).

An alternative approach is to simplify the equations of a detailed neuronal model in ways that retain a biophysical interpretation. For example, by making a steady-state approximation for the fast ionic sodium current activation in the Hodgkin-Huxley model, and recasting two of the gating variables (n and h), it is possible to simplify the original Hodgkin-Huxley model to a two-dimensional model, which can be investigated more easily in the phase plane. The de velopment of simplified models is closely interwoven with bifurcation theory and the theory of normal forms within dynamical systems. One well-studied reduction of the Hodgkin-Huxley equations to a 2-dimensional conductance-based model was developed by John. In this case, the geometries of the phenomenological Fitzhugh-Nagumo model and the simplified Rinzel model are qualitatively similar. Yet another approach to dimensionality reduction consists of neglecting the spiking currents (fast sodium and delayed-rectifying potassium) and considering only the currents that are active in the sub-threshold regime. This cannot be done in the original Hodgkin-Huxley model, because the only ionic currents are those that lead to spikes, but it is useful in models that include additional ionic currents in the sub-threshold regime.

Point Process Regression Models of Single Neuron Activity

Mathematically, the simplest model for an irregular spike train is a homogeneous Poisson process, for which the probability of spiking within a time interval $(t, t + \Delta t]$, for small Δt, may be written:

$$P \text{ spike in } (t, t + \Delta t)| \approx \lambda \Delta t,$$

where λ represents the firing rate of the neuron and where disjoint intervals have independent spiking. This model, however, is often inadequate for many reasons. For one thing, neurons have noticeable refractory periods following a spike, during which the probability of spiking goes to zero (the absolute refractory period) and then gradually increases, often over tens of milliseconds (the relative refractory period). In this sense neurons exhibit memory effects, often called spike history effects. To capture those, and many other physiological effects, more general point processes must be used. We outline the key ideas underlying point process modeling of spike trains.

A fundamental result in neurophysiology is that neurons respond to a stimulus or contribute to an action by increasing their firing rates. The measured firing rate of a neuron within a time interval would be the number of spikes in the interval divided by the length of the interval (usually in units of seconds, so that the ratio is in spikes per second, abbreviated as Hz, for Hertz). The point process framework centers on the theoretical instantaneous firing rate, which takes the expected value of this ratio and passes to the limit as the length of the time interval goes to zero, giving an intensity function for the process. To accurately model a neuron's spiking behavior, however, the intensity function typically must itself evolve over time depending on changing inputs and experimental conditions, the recent past spiking behavior of the neuron, the behavior of other neurons, the behavior of local field potentials, etc. It is therefore called a conditional intensity function and may be written in the form:

$$\lambda(t \mid x_t) = \lim_{\Delta t \to 0} \frac{E\left(N_{(t, t+\Delta t]} \mid X_t = x_t\right)}{\Delta t}$$

where, $N_{(t, t+\Delta t]}$ is the number of spikes in the interval $(t, t + \Delta t]$ and where the vector X_t includes both the past spiking history H_t prior to time t and also any other quantities that affect the neuron's current spiking behavior. In some special cases, the conditional intensity will be deterministic, but in general, because X_t is random, the conditional intensity is also random. If X_t includes unobserved random variables, the process is often called doubly stochastic. When the conditional intensity depends on the history H_t, the process is often called self-exciting (though the effects may produce an inhibition of firing rate rather than an excitation). The vector X_t may be high-dimensional. A mathematically tractable special case, where contributions to the intensity due to previous spikes enter additively in terms of a fixed kernel function, is the Hawkes process.

As a matter of interpretation, in sufficiently small time intervals the spike count is either zero or one, so we may replace the expectation with the probability of spiking and get:

$$P\left(\text{spike in } (t, t + \Delta t) \mid X_t = x_t\right) \approx \lambda\left(t \mid x_t\right) \Delta t$$

A statistical model for a spike train involves two things: a simple, universal formula for the probability density of the spike train in terms of the conditional intensity function (which we omit here and a specification of the way the conditional intensity function depends on variables X_t. An analogous statement is also true for multiple spike trains, possibly involving multiple neurons. Thus, when the data are resolved down to individual spikes, statistical analysis is primarily concerned with modeling the conditional intensity function in a form that can be implemented efficiently and that fits the data adequately well. That is, writing:

$$\lambda\left(t \mid x_t\right) = f\left(x_t\right),$$

The challenge is to identify within the variable x_t all relevant effects, or features, in the terminology of machine learning, and then to find a suitable form for the function f, keeping in mind that, in practice, the dimension of x_t may range from 1 to many millions. This identification of the components of x_t that modulate the neuron's firing rate is a key step in interpreting the function of a neural system. Details may be found in Kass et al, but see Amarasingham et al. for an important caution about the interpretation of neural firing rate through its representation as a point process intensity function.

A statistically tractable non-Poisson form involves log-additive models, the simplest case being:

$$\log \lambda\left(t \mid x_t\right) = \log \lambda\left(t \mid H_t\right) = \log g_0\left(t\right) + \log g_1\left(t - s_*\left(t\right)\right)$$

where, $s_*\left(t\right)$ is the time of the immediately preceding spike, and g_0 and g_1 are functions that may be written in terms of some basis. To include contributions from spikes that are earlier than the immediately preceding one, the term $\log g_1(t - s_*\left(t\right))$ is replaced by a sum of terms of the form $\log g_{1j}(t - s_j(t))$, where $s_j\left(t\right)$ is the j - th spike back in time preceding t, and a common simplification is to assume the functions g_{1j} are all equal to a single function g_1. The resulting probability density function for the set of spike times (which defines the likelihood function) is very similar to that of a Poisson generalized linear model (GLM) and, in fact, GLM software may be used to fit many point process models. The use of the word "linear" may be misleading here because highly nonlinear functions may be involved, e.g., in Equation $\log \lambda(t \mid x_t) = \log \lambda(t \mid H_t) = \log g_0(t) + \log g_1(t - s_*(t))$, g_0 and g_1 are typically nonlinear. An alternative is to call these point process regression models. Nonetheless, the model is often said to specify a GLM neuron, as are other point process regression models.

Point Process Regression and Leaky Integrate-and-fire Models

Assuming excitatory and inhibitory Poisson process inputs to an LIF neuron, the distribution of waiting times for a threshold crossing, which corresponds to the inter-spike interval (ISI), is found to be inverse Gaussian and this distribution often provides a good fit to experimental data when neurons are in steady state, as when they are isolated in vitro and spontaneous activity is examined. The inverse Gaussian distribution, within a biologically-reasonable range of coefficient of variations, turns out to be qualitatively very similar to ISI distributions generated by processes given by Equation $\log \lambda(t \mid x_t) = \log \lambda(t \mid H_t) = \log g_0(t) + \log g_1(t - s_*(t))$. Furthermore, spike trains generated from LIF models can be fitted well by these GLM-type models.

An additional connection between LIF and GLM neurons comes from considering the response of neurons to injected currents, as illustrated in Figure. In this context, the first term in Equation ($\log \lambda(t \mid x_t) = \log \lambda(t \mid H_t) = \log g_0(t) + \log g_1(t - s_*(t))$) may be rewritten as a convolution with the current $I(t)$ at time t, so that becomes:

$$\log \lambda(t \mid x_t) = \log \lambda(t \mid H_t, I_t) = \int_0^\infty g_0(s) I(t-s) ds + \log g_1(t - s_*(t))$$

The estimate of g_o that results from fitting this model to data illustrated in that figure. Here, the function g_o is often called a stimulus filter. On the other hand, following Gerstner et al, we may write a generalized version of LIF in integral form,

$$V(t) = V_{\text{rest}} + \int_0^\infty g_0(s) I(t-s) ds + \log g_1(t - s_*(t))$$

which those authors call a Spike Response Model (SRM). By equating the log conditional intensity to voltage in,

$$\log \lambda(t \mid H_t, I_t) = V(t) - V_{\text{rest}}$$

we thereby get a modified LIF neuron that is also a GLM neuron. Thus, both theory and empirical study indicate that GLM and LIF neurons are very similar, and both describe a variety of neural spiking patterns.

It is interesting that these empirically-oriented SRMs, and variants that included an adaptive threshold, performed better than much more complicated biophysical models in a series of international competitions for reproducing and predicting recorded spike times of biological neurons under varying circumstances.

Multidimensional Models

The one-dimensional LIF dynamic model in Figure is inadequate when interactions of sub-threshold ion channel dynamics cause a neuron's behavior to be more complicated than integration of inputs. Neurons can even behave as differentiators and respond only to fluctuations in input. Furthermore, features that drive neural firing can be multidimensional. Multivariate dynamical systems are able to describe the ways that interacting, multivariate effects can bring the system to its firing threshold, as in the Hodgkin-Huxley model. A number of model variants that aim to account for such multidimensional effects have been compared in predicting experimental data from sensory areas.

Statistical Challenges in Biophysical Modeling

Conductance-based biophysical models pose problems of model identifiability and parameter estimation. The original Hodgkin-Huxley equations contain on the order of two dozen numerical parameters describing the membrane capacitance, maximal conductances for the sodium and potassium ions, kinetics of ion channel activation and inactivation, and the ionic equilibrium potentials (at which the flow of ions due to imbalances of concentration across the cell membrane offsets that due to imbalances of electrical charge). Hodgkin and Huxley arrived at estimates of these parameters through a combination of extensive experimentation, biophysical reasoning, and regression techniques. Others have investigated the experimental information necessary to identify the model. In early work, statistical analysis of nonstationary ensemble fluctuations was used to estimate the conductances of individual ion channels. Following the introduction of single-channel recording techniques, which typically report a binary projection of a multistate underlying Markovian ion channel process, many researchers expanded the theory of aggregated Markov processes to handle inference problems related to identifying the structure of the underlying Markov process and estimating transition rate parameters.

More recently, parameter estimation challenges in biophysical models have been tackled using a variety of techniques under the rubric of "data assimilation," where data results are combined with models algorithmically. Data assimilation methods illustrate the interplay of mathematical and statistical approaches in neuroscience. For example, in Meng et al, the authors describe a state space modeling framework and a sequential Monte Carlo (particle filter) algorithm to estimate the parameters of a membrane current in the Hodgkin-Huxley model neuron. They applied this framework to spiking data recorded from rat layer V cortical neurons, and correctly identified the dynamics of a slow membrane current. Variations on this theme include the use of synchronization manifolds for parameter estimation in experimental neural systems driven by dynamically rich inputs , combined statistical and geometric methods, and other state space models.

Networks

Mechanistic Approaches for Modeling Small Networks

While biological neural networks typically involve anywhere from dozens to many millions of neurons, studies of small neural networks involving handfuls of cells have led to remarkably rich insights. We describe three such cases here, and the types of mechanistic models that drive them.

First, neural networks can produce rhythmic patterns of activity. Such rhythms, or oscillations, play clear roles in central pattern generators (CPGs) in which cell groups produce coordinated firing for, e.g., locomotion or breathing. Small network models have been remarkably successful in describing how such rhythms occur. For example, models involving pairs of cells have revealed how delays in connections among inhibitory cells, or reciprocal interactions between excitatory and inhibitory neurons, can lead to rhythms in the gamma range (30-80 Hz) associated with some aspects of cognitive processing. A general theory, beginning with two-cell models of this type, describes how synaptic and intrinsic cellular dynamics interact to determine when the underlying synchrony will and will not occur. Larger models involving three or more interacting cell types describe the origin of more complex rhythms, such as the triphasic rhythm in the stomatogastric ganglion (for digestion in certain invertebrates). This system in particular has revealed a rich interplay between the intrinsic dynamics in multiple cells and the synapses that connect them. There turn out to be many highly distinct parameter combinations, lying in subsets of parameter space, that all produce the key target rhythm, but do so in very different ways. Understanding the origin of this flexibility, and how biological systems take advantage of it to produce robust function, is a topic of ongoing work.

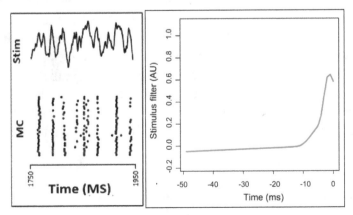

Left panel displays the current ("Stim," for stimulus, at the top of the panel) injected into a mitral cell from the olfactory system of a mouse, together with the neural spiking response (MC) across many trials (each row displays the spike train for a particular trial). The response is highly regular across trials, but at some points in time it is somewhat variable. The right panel displays a stimulus filter fitted to the complete set of data using model (3), where the stimulus filter, i.e., the function $g_o(s)$, represents the contribution to the firing rate due to the current $I(t - s)$ at s milliseconds prior to time t.

The underlying mechanistic models for rhythmic phenomena are of Hodgkin-Huxley type, involving sodium and potassium channels. For some phenomena, including respiratory and stomatogastric rhythms, additional ion channels that drive bursting in single cells play a key role. Dynamical systems tools for assessing the stability of periodic orbits may then be used to determine what patterns of rhythmic activity will be stably produced by a given network. Specifically, coupled systems of biophysical differential equations can often be reduced to interacting circular variables representing the phase of each neuron. Such phase models yield to very elegant stability analyses that can often predict the dynamics of the original biophysical equations.

A second example concerns the origin of collective activity in irregularly spiking neural circuits. To understand the development of correlated spiking in such systems, stochastic differential equation models, or models driven by point process inputs, are typically used. This yields Fokker-Planck or population density equations and these can be iterated across multiple layers or neural populations. In many cases, such models can be approximated using linear response approaches, yielding analytical solutions and considerable mechanistic insight. A prominent example comes from the mechanisms of correlated firing in feedforward networks. Here, stochastically firing cells send diverging inputs to multiple neurons downstream. The downstream neurons thereby share some of their input fluctuations, and this, in turn, creates correlated activity that can have rich implications for information transmission.

A third case of highly influential small circuit modeling concerns neurons in the early visual cortex (early in the sense of being only a few synapses from the retina), which are responsive to visual stimuli (moving bars of light) with specific orientations that fall within their receptive field. Neurons having neighboring regions within their receptive field in which a stimulus excites or inhibits activity were called simple cells, and those without this kind of sub-division were complex cells. Hubel and Wiesel famously showed how simple circuit models can account for both the simple and complex cell responses. Later work described this through one or several iterated algebraic equations that map input firing rates x_i into outputs $y = f(\sum_i w_i x_i)$ where $w = (w_1, ..., w_N)$ is a synaptic weight vector.

Statistical Methods for Small Networks

Point process models for small networks begin with conditional intensity specifications similar to that in Equation ($\log \lambda(t \mid x_t) = \log \lambda(t \mid H_t) = \log g_0(t) + \log g_1(t - s_*(t))$ and include coupling terms and references therein).

Mechanistic Models of Large Networks across Scales and Levels of Complexity

There is a tremendous variety of mechanistic models of large neural networks. We here describe these in rough order of their complexity and scale.

Binary and firing rate models: At the simplest level, binary models abstract the activity of each neuron as either active (taking the value 1) or silent (0) in a given time step. As mentioned in the Introduction, despite their simplicity, these models capture fundamental properties of network activity and explain network functions such as associative memory. The proportion of active neurons at a given time is governed by effective rate equations. Such firing rate models feature a continuous range of activity states, and often take the form of nonlinear ordinary or stochastic differential equations. Like binary models, these also implement associative memory (Hopfield 1984), but are widely used to describe broader dynamical phenomena in networks, including predictions of oscillations in excitatory-inhibitory networks, transitions from fixed point to oscillatory to chaotic dynamics in randomly connected neural networks, amplified selectivity to stimuli, and the formation of line attractors (a set of stable solutions on a line in state space) that gradually store and accumulate input signals.

Firing rate models have been a cornerstone of theoretical neuroscience. Their second order statistics can analytically be matched to more realistic spiking and binary models. We next describe how trial-varying dynamical fluctuations can emerge in networks of spiking neuron models.

Stochastic spiking activity in networks: A beautiful body of work summarizes the network state in a population-density approach that describes the evolution of the probability density of states rather than individual neurons. The theory is able to capture refractoriness and adaptation. Furthermore, although it loses the identity of individual neurons, it can faithfully capture collective activity states, such as oscillations. Small synaptic amplitudes and weak correlations further reduce the time-evolution to a Fokker-Planck equation. Network states beyond such diffusion approximations include neuronal avalanches, the collective and nearly synchronous firing of a large fraction of cells, often following power-law distributions. While early work focused on the firing rates of populations, later work clarified how more subtle patterns of correlated spiking develop. In particular, linear fluctuations about a stationary state determine population-averaged measures of correlations.

At an even larger scale, a continuum of coupled population equations at each point in space lead to neuronal field equations. They predict stable "bumps" of activity, as well as traveling waves and spirals. Intriguingly, when applied as a model of visual cortex and rearranged to reflect spatial layout of the retina, patterns induced in these continuum equations can resemble visual hallucinations.

Analysis has provided insight into the ways that spiking networks can produce irregular spike times like those found in cortical recordings from behaving animals, as in. Suppose we have a network of N^E excitatory and N^I inhibitory LIF neurons with connections occurring at random according to independent binary (Bernoulli) random variables, i.e., a connection exists when the binary random variable takes the value 1 and does not exist when it is 0. We denote the binary connectivity random variables by $\kappa_{ij}^{\alpha\beta}$, where α and β take the values E or I, with $\kappa_{ij}^{\alpha\beta} = 1$ when the output of neuron j in population β injects current into neuron i in population α. We let $J^{\alpha\beta}$ be the coupling strength (representing synaptic current) from a neuron in population β to a neuron in population α. Thus, the contribution to the current input of a neuron in population α generated at time t by a spike from neuron in population β at time s will be $J^{\alpha\beta}\kappa_{ij}^{\alpha\beta}\delta(t-s)$, where $\delta(t-s)$ is the Dirac delta function. The behavior of the network can be analyzed by letting $N^E \to \infty$ and $N^I \to \infty$. Based on reasonable simplifying assumptions, the mean $M\alpha$ and variance V^α of the total current for population α have been derived, and these determine the regularity or irregularity in spiking activity.

We step through three possibilities, under three different conditions on the network, using a modification of the LIF equation found in Figure 3. The set of equations, for all the neurons in the network, includes terms defined by network connectivity and also terms defined by external input fluctuations. Because the connectivity matrix may contain cycles (there may be a path from any neuron back to itself), network connectivity is called recurrent. Let us take the membrane potential of neuron i from population α to be:

$$\tau^\alpha \frac{dV_i^\alpha}{dt} = -V_i^\alpha + \underbrace{\mu_0^\alpha + \sqrt{\tau^\alpha}\sigma_0^\alpha\ \xi_i^\alpha(t)}_{\text{external inputs}}$$

$$\underbrace{\tau^\alpha J^{\alpha E}\sum_{j=1}^{N^E}\kappa_{ij}^{\alpha E}\delta\left(t-t_{jk}^E\right)}_{\text{recurrent excitation}} - \underbrace{\tau^\alpha J^{\alpha I}\sum_{j=1}^{N^I}\kappa_{ij}^{\alpha I}\delta\left(t-t_{jk}^I\right)}_{\text{recurrent inhibition}}$$

where t_{ik}^α is the kth spike time from neuron i of population α, τ^α is the membrane dynamics time constant, and the external inputs include both a constant μ_0 and a fluctuating source $\sigma_0\xi(t)$ where $\xi(t)$ is white noise (independent across neurons). This set of equations is supplemented with the spike reset rule that when $V_i^\alpha(t)=V_T$ the voltage resets to $V_R < V_T$.

The firing rate of the average neuron in population α is $\lambda^\alpha = \sum_j\sum_\kappa \delta\left(t-t_{jk}^\alpha\right)/N^\alpha$. For the network to remain stable, we take these firing rates to be bounded, i.e., $\lambda^\alpha \sim \mathcal{O}(1)$. Similarly, to assure that the current input to each neuron remains bounded, some assumption must be made about the way coupling strengths J $\alpha\beta$ scale as the number of inputs K increases. Let us take the scaling to be $J^{\alpha\beta} = j^{\alpha\beta} / K^\gamma$, with $j^{\alpha\beta} \sim \mathcal{O}(1)$ as $K \to \infty$, where γ is a scaling exponent. We describe the resulting spiking behavior under scaling conditions $\gamma = 1$ and $\gamma = 1/2$.

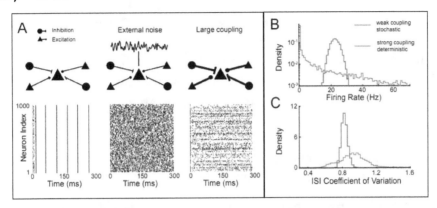

Panel A displays plots of spike trains from 1000 excitatory neurons in a network having 1000 excitatory and 1000 inhibitory LIF neurons with connections determined from independent Bernoulli random variables having success probability of 0.2; on average $K = 200$ inputs per neuron with no synaptic dynamics. Each neuron receives a static depolarizing input; in absence of coupling each neuron fires repetitively. Left: Spike trains under weak coupling, current $J \propto K^{-1}$. Middle: Spike trains under weak couplng, with additional uncorrelated noise applied to each cell. Right: Spike trains under strong coupling, $J \propto K^{-\frac{1}{2}}$. Panel B shows the distribution of firing rates across cells, and panel C the distribution of interspike interval (ISI) coefficient of variation across cells.

If we set $\gamma = 1$ then we have $J \sim 1/K$, so that $JK = j \sim \mathcal{O}(1)$. In this case we get $M^\alpha \sim \mathcal{O}(1)$ and $V^\alpha = \left[\sigma_0^\alpha\right]^2 + \mathcal{O}(1\sqrt{K})$. If we further set σ α 0 = 0, so that all fluctuations must be internal, then V^α vanishes for large K. In such networks, after an initial transient, the neurons synchronize, and each fires with perfect rhythmicity (left part of panel A in Figure). This is very different than the irregularity seen in cortical recordings. Therefore, some modification must be made.

The first route to appropriate spike train irregularity keeps $\gamma = 1$ while setting $\left[\sigma_0^\alpha\right]^2 \sim \mathcal{O}(1)$ so that V α no longer vanishes in the large K limit. Simulations of this network maintain realistic rates, but also show realistic irregularity, as quantified in Figure by the coefficient of variation (CV) of the inter-spike intervals. Treating irregular spiking activity as the consequence of stochastic inputs has a long history.

The second route does not rely on external input stochasticity, but instead increases the synaptic connection strengths by setting $\gamma = 1/2$. As a consequence we get $V^\alpha \sim \mathcal{O}(1)$

even if $\sigma_0^\alpha = 0$ so that variability is internally generated through recurrent interactions, but to get $M^\alpha \sim \mathcal{O}(1)$, an additional condition is needed. If the recurrent connectivity is dominated by inhibition, so that the network recurrence results in negative current, the activity dynamically settles into a state in which:

$$M^\alpha = \sqrt{K} \; \underbrace{\left(\mu^\alpha + j^{\alpha E} \tau^\alpha \lambda^E - j^{\alpha I} \tau^\alpha \lambda^I \right)}_{\mathcal{O}(1/\sqrt{K}):\; \text{balance condition}} \sim \mathcal{O}(1)$$

where μ_0^α has been replaced by the constant μ^α using $\mu_0^\alpha = \sqrt{K} \mu^\alpha$ so that the mean external input is of order $\mathcal{O}(\sqrt{K})$. The scaling $\gamma = 1/2$ now makes the total excitatory and the total inhibitory synaptic inputs individually large, i.e., $\mathcal{O}(\sqrt{K})$ so that the V^α is also large. However, given the balance condition in, excitation and inhibition mutually cancel and V^α remains moderate. Simulations of the network with $\gamma = 1/2$ and $\sigma_0^\alpha = 0$ shows an asynchronous network dynamic. Further, the firing rates stabilize at low mean levels, while the inter-spike interval CV is large.

These two mechanistic routes to high levels of neural variability differ strikingly in the degree of heterogeneity of the spiking statistics. For the weak coupling with $\gamma = 1$ the resulting distribution of firing rates and inter-spike interval CVs are narrow. At strong coupling with $\gamma = 1/2$, however, the spread of firing rates is large: over half of the neurons fire at rates below 1 Hz (Figure 6B, blue curve), in line with observed cortical activity. The approximate dynamic balance between excitatory and inhibitory synaptic currents has been confirmed experimentally and is usually called balanced excitation and inhibition.

Asynchronous dynamics in recurrent networks. The analysis above focused only on M^α and V^α, ignoring any correlated activity between the currents neurons in the network. The original justification for such asynchronous dynamics in relied on a sparse wiring assumption, i.e, $K / N^\alpha \to 0$ as $N^\alpha \to \infty$ for $\alpha \in (E, I)$. However, more recently it has been shown that the balanced mechanism required to keep firing rates moderate also ensures that network correlations vanish. Balance arises from the dominance of negative feedback which suppresses fluctuations in the population-averaged activity and hence causes small pairwise correlations. As a consequence, fluctuations of excitatory and inhibitory synaptic currents are tightly locked so that Equation $M^\alpha = \sqrt{K} \; \underbrace{\left(\mu^\alpha + j^{\alpha E} \tau^\alpha \lambda^E - j^{\alpha I} \tau^\alpha \lambda^I \right)}_{\mathcal{O}(1/\sqrt{K}):\; \text{balance condition}} \sim \mathcal{O}(1)$ is satisfied. The excitatory and inhibitory cancellation mechanism therefore extends to pairs of cells and operates even in networks with dense wiring, i.e., $K / N^\alpha \sim \mathcal{O}(1)$, so that input correlations are much weaker than expected by the number of shared inputs. This suppression and cancellation of correlations holds in the same way for intrinsically-generated fluctuations that often even dominate the correlation structure. Recent work has shown that the asynchronous state is more robustly realized in nonrandom networks than normally distributed random networks.

There is a large literature on how network connectivity, at the level of mechanistic models, leads to different covariance structures in network activity Highly local connectivity features scale up to determine global levels of covariance. Moreover, features of that connectivity that point specifically to low-dimensional structures of neural covariability can be isolated. An outstanding problem is to create model networks that mimic the low-dimensional covariance structure reported in experiments.

Statistical Methods for Large Networks

New recording technologies should make it possible to track the flow of information across very large networks of neurons, but the details of how to do so have not yet been established. One tractable component of the problem involves co-variation in spiking activity among many neurons (typically dozens to hundreds), which leads naturally to dimensionality reduction and to graphical representations (where neurons are nodes, and some definition of correlated activity determines edges). However, two fundamental complications affect most experiments. First, co-variation can occur at multiple timescales. A simplification is to consider either spike counts in coarse time bins (20 milliseconds or longer) or spike times with precision in the range of 1-5 milliseconds. Second, experiments almost always involve some stimuli or behaviors that create evolving conditions within the network. Thus, methods that assume stationarity must be used with care, and analyses that allow for dynamic evolution will likely be useful. Fortunately, many experiments are conducted using multiple exposures to the same stimuli or behavioral cues, which creates a series of putatively independent replications (trials). While the responses across trials are variable, sometimes in systematic ways, the setting of multiple trials often makes tractable the analysis of non-stationary processes.

After reviewing techniques for analyzing co-variation of spike counts and precisely-timed spiking we will also briefly mention three general approaches to understanding network behavior: reinforcement learning, Bayesian inference, and deep learning. Reinforcement learning and Bayesian inference use a decision-theoretic foundation to define optimal actions of the neural system in achieving its goals, which is appealing insofar as evolution may drive organism design toward optimality.

Correlation and dimensionality reduction in spike counts. Dimensionality reduction methods have been fruitfully applied to study decision-making, learning, motor control, olfaction, working memory, visual attention, audition, rule learning, speech, and other phenomena. Dimensionality reduction methods that have been used to study neural population activity include principal component analysis, factor analysis, latent dynamical systems, and non-linear methods such as Isomap and locally-linear embedding. Such methods can provide two types of insights. First, the time course of the neural response can vary substantially from one experimental trial to the next, even though the presented stimulus, or the behavior, is identical on each trial. In such settings, it is of interest to examine population activity on individual trials. Dimensionality reduction provides a way to summarize the population activity time course on individual experimental trials by leveraging the statistical power across neurons. One can then study how the latent variables extracted by dimensionality reduction change across time or across experimental conditions. Second, the multivariate statistical structure in the population activity identified by dimensionality reduction may be indicative of the neural mechanisms underlying various brain functions. For example, one study suggested that a subject can imagine moving their arms, while not actually moving them, when neural activity related to motor preparation lies in a space orthogonal to that related to motor execution. Furthermore, the multivariate structure of population activity can help explain why some tasks are easier to learn than others and how subjects respond differently to the same stimulus in different contexts.

Correlated spiking activity at precise time scales. In principle, very large quantities of information could be conveyed through the precise timing of spikes across groups of neurons. The idea that the nervous system might be able to recognize such patterns of precise timing is therefore an intriguing possibility. However, it is very difficult to obtain strong experimental evidence in favor of a widespread computational role for precise timing (e.g., an accuracy within 1-5 milliseconds), beyond the influence of the high arrival rate of synaptic impulses when multiple input neurons fire nearly synchronously. Part of the issue is experimental, because precise timing may play an important role only in specialized circumstances, but part is statistical: under plausible point process models, patterns such as nearly synchronous firing will occur by chance, and it may be challenging to define a null model that captures the null concept without producing false positives. For example, when the firing rates of two neurons increase, the number of nearly synchronous spikes will increase even when the spike trains are otherwise independent; thus, a null model with constant firing rates could produce false positives for the null hypothesis of independence. This makes the detection of behaviorally-relevant spike patterns a subtle statistical problem.

A strong indication that precise timing of spikes may be relevant to behavior came from an experiment involving hand movement, during which pairs of neurons in motor cortex fired synchronously (within 5 milliseconds of each other) more often than predicted by an independent Poisson process model and, furthermore, these events, called Unitary Events, clustered around times that were important to task performance. While this illustrated the potential role of precisely timed spikes, it also raised the issue of whether other plausible point process null models might lead to different results. Much work has been done to refine this methodology. Related approaches replace the null assumption of independence with some order of correlation, using marked Poisson processes.

There is a growing literature on dependent point processes. Some models do not include a specific mechanism for generating precise spike timing, but can still be used as null models for hypothesis tests of precise spike timing. On a coarse time scale, point process regression models as in Equation ($\lambda(t \mid x_t) = f(x_t),$) can incorporate effects of one neuron's spiking behavior on another. On a fine time scale, one may instead consider multivariate binary processes (multiple sequences of 0s and 1s where 1s represent spikes). In the stationary case, a standard statistical tool for analyzing binary data involves loglinear models, where the log of the joint probability of any particular pattern is represented as a sum of terms that involve successively higher-order interactions, i.e., terms that determine the probability of spiking within a given time bin for individual neurons, pairs of neurons, triples, etc. Two-way interaction models, also called maximum entropy models, which exclude higher than pairwise interactions, have been used in several studies and in some cases higher-order interactions have been examined, sometimes using information geometry, though large amounts of data may be required to find small but plausibly interesting effects. Extensions to non-stationary processes have also been developed. Dichotomized Gaussian models, which instead produce binary outputs from threshold crossings of a latent multivariate Gaussian random variable, have also been used, as have Hawkes processes. A variety of correlation structures may be accommodated by analyzing cumulants.

To test hypotheses about precise timing, several authors have suggested procedures akin to permutation tests or nonparametric bootstrap. The idea is to generate re-sampled data, also called pseudo-data or surrogate data, that preserves as many of the features of the original data as possible, but that lacks the feature of interest, such as precise spike timing. A simple case, called dithering or jittering, modifies the precise time of each spike by some random amount within a small interval, thereby preserving all coarse temporal structure and removing all fine temporal structure. Many variations on this theme have been explored, and connections have been made with the well-established statistical notion of conditional inference.

Reinforcement Learning

Reinforcement learning (RL) grew from attempts to describe mathematically the way organisms learn in order to achieve repeatedly-presented goals. The motivating idea was spelled out in 1911 by Thorndike: when a behavioral response in some situation leads to reward (or discomfort) it becomes associated with that reward (or discomfort), so that the behavior becomes a learned response to the situation. While there were important precursors, the basic theory reached maturity with the 1998 publication of the book by Sutton and Barto . Within neuroscience, a key discovery involved the behavior of dopamine neurons in certain tasks: they initially fire in response to a reward but, after learning, fire in response to a stimulus that predicts reward; this was consistent with predictions of RL. (Dopamine is a neuromodulator, meaning a substance that, when emitted from the synapses of neurons, modulates the synaptic effects of other neurons; a dopamine neuron is a neuron that emits dopamine; dopamine is known to play an essential role in goal-directed behavior).

In brief, the mathematical framework is that of a Markov decision process, which is an action-dependent Markov chain (i.e., a stochastic process on a set of states where the probability of transitioning from one state to the next is action-dependent) together with rewards that depend on both state transition and action. When an agent (an abstract entity representing an organism, or some component of its nervous system) reaches stationarity after learning, the current value V_t of an action may be represented in terms of its futurediscounted expected reward:

$$V_t = E(R_t + \gamma R_{t+1} + \gamma^2 R_{t+2} + \gamma^3 R_{t+3} + \cdots)$$
$$= E\left(R_t + \gamma V_{t+1}\right)$$

where R_t is the reward at time t. Thus, to drive the agent toward this stationarity condition, the current estimate of value $\hat{V}_t$ should be updated in such a way as to decrease the estimated magnitude of $E\left(R_t + \gamma V_{t+1}\right) - V_t$, which is known as the reward prediction error (RPE),

$$\delta_t = \hat{E}\left(R_t + \gamma V_{t+1}\right) - \hat{V}_t = r_t + \gamma \hat{V}_{t+1} - \hat{V}_t.$$

This is also called the temporal difference learning error. RL algorithms accomplish learning by sequentially reducing the magnitude of the RPE. The essential interpretation of Schultz et al. which remains widely influential, was that dopamine neurons signal RPE.

The RL-based description of the activity of dopamine neurons has been considered one of the great success stories in computational neuroscience, operating at the levels of computation and algorithm in Marr's framework. A wide range of further studies have elaborated the basic framework and taken on topics such as the behavior of other neuromodulators; neuroeconomics; the distinction between model-based learning, where transition probabilities are learned explicitly, and model-free learning; social behavior and decision-making; and the role of time and internal models in learning.

Bayesian inference - Although statistical methods based on Bayes' Theorem now play a major role in statistics, they were, until relatively recently, controversial. In neuroscience, Bayes' Theorem has been used in many theoretical constructions in part because the brain must combine prior knowledge with current data somehow, and also because evolution may have led to neural network behavior that is, like Bayesian inference (under well specified conditions), optimal, or nearly so. Bayesian inference has played a prominent role in theories of human problem-solving (Anderson, visual perception, sensory and motor integration, and general cortical processing.

Deep learning - Deep learning is an outgrowth of PDP modeling. Two major architectures came out of the 1980's and 1990's, convolutional neural networks (CNNs) and long short term memory (LSTM). LSTM enables neural networks to take as input sequential data of arbitrary length and learn long-term dependencies by incorporating a memory module where information can be added or forgotten according to functions of the current input and state of the system. CNNs, which achieve state of the art results in many image classification tasks, take inspiration from the visual system by incorporating receptive fields and enforcing shift-invariance (physiological visual object recognition being invariant to shifts in location). In deep learning architectures, receptive fields identify a very specific input pattern, or stimulus, in a small spatial region, using convolution to combine inputs. Receptive fields induce sparsity and lead to significant computational savings, which prompted early success with CNNs. Shift invariance is achieved through a spatial smoothing operator known as pooling (a weighted average, or often the maximum value, over a local neighborhood of nodes). Because it introduces redundancies, pooling is often combined with downsampling. Many layers, each using convolution and pooling, are stacked to create a deep network, in rough analogy to multiple anatomical layers in the visual system of primates. Although artificial neural networks had largely fallen out of widespread use by the end of the 1990s, faster computers combined with availability of very large repositories of training data, and the innovation of greedy layer-wise training brought large gains in performance and renewed attention, especially when ALEXNET was applied to the ImageNet database. Rapid innovation has enabled the application of deep learning to a wide variety of problems of increasing size and complexity.

The success of deep learning in reaching near human-level performance on certain highly constrained prediction and classification tasks, particularly in the area of computer vision, has inspired interest in exploring the connections between deep neural networks and the brain. Studies have shown similarities between the internal representations of convolutional neural networks and representations in the primate visual system. Furthermore, the biological phenomenon of hippocampal replay during memory consolidation prompted innovation in artificial intelligence, in part through the incorporation of reinforcement learning into deep learning architectures. On the other hand, some studies have shown cases in which biological vision and deep networks diverge in performance Even though they are not biologically realistic, deep learning architectures may suggest new scientific hypotheses.

Neuroinformatics

Neuroinformatics refers to a research field that focuses on organizing neuroscience data through analytical tools and computational models. It combines data across all scales and levels of neuroscience in order to understand the complex functions of the brain and work toward treatments for brain-related illness. Neuroinformatics involves the techniques and tools for acquiring, sharing, storing, publishing, analyzing, modeling, visualizing and simulating data.

Neuroinformatics helps researchers to work together and share data across different facilities and different countries through the exchange of approaches and tools for integrating and analysing data. This field makes it possible to integrate any type of data across various biological organization levels.

The advancement of neuroinformatics technology facilitates the research done in this field and helps in the free exchange of data and ideas among neurological researchers worldwide.

Neuroinformatics has the following key functions:

- The creation of tools and technologies that help neuroscience researchers to effortlessly manage, communicate and share the overall data load in real time. This helps the researchers use the time effectively and make sure that they are working on the most up-to-date data.

- The creation of up-to-date tools and software for analyzing the neuroscience data in the best possible way and developing complicated models based on that data.

- The development of complicated models of the central nervous system, which helps researchers to understand the functioning of computational processes and perform direct experiments on a model to understand its reaction to different situations and stimulations.

The benefits of neuroinformatics include:

- Advancement in neuroscience and improvement in the treatment of several neurological disorders.

- The enhancement of researchers' knowledge. Neuroinformatics enables them to understand the working pattern of some particular neurological functions by permitting the researchers to trace some specific functions inside the computerized models.

- The accomplishment of huge volumes of new data for creating more sophisticated models for testing.

Neuroinformatics combines neuroscience and informatics research to develop and apply advanced tools and approaches essential for a major advancement in understanding the structure and function of the brain. The field covers three primary areas:

- Neuroscience data and knowledge bases, increasingly capable of handling the full complexity and organization of the nervous system, from molecular to behavioral levels. e.g. see activities of the Nottingham Brain & Body Center – "an interdisciplinary setting for studies of environmental and genetic factors that are shaping structure and function of the human brain and body."

- Tools for data-acquisition, analysis, visualization and distribution of nervous system data.

- Theoretical, computational and simulation environments for modeling and understanding the brain (Computational Neuroscience).

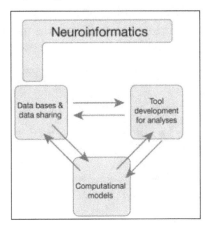

Informatics

Informatics includes the science of information and the practice of information processing. Bioinformatics is a specialised example, targetted at sequence alignment, gene finding, genome assembly, protein structure alignment, protein structure prediction, prediction of gene expression and protein-protein interactions.

A common thread in informatics specialisations (neuro-, bio-) is the use of mathematical tools to extract useful information from high dimensional data sets (e.g. the genome, spike-trains, fMRI).

CoCoMac (Collations of Connectivity Data on the Macaque Brain)

This is a systematic record of the known wiring of the primate brain. The main database contains details of hundreds of tracing studies in their original descriptions. Further data are continuously added.

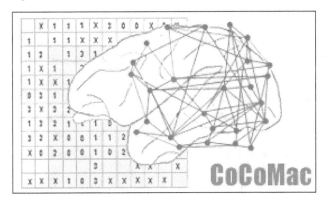

NeuroMorpho

NeuroMorpho is a centrally curated inventory of digitally reconstructed neurons. It contains contributions from over two-dozen labs and is continuously updated as new morphological reconstructions are collected, published, and shared, with the goal of densely covering all available data. Morphological data are essential for understanding the cellular complexity of the nervous system, and are used for analysis, visualization, and modeling. It allows for neuronal morphologies to be saved in NEURON format.

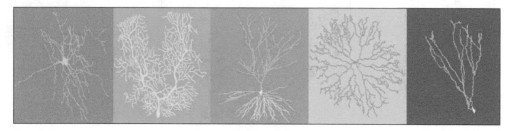

The Scaleable Brain Atlas

Visualization of neuroscientific data is important for a number of reasons. For purposes of presentation, a well-designed visualization has the capability to provide an intuitive illustration of modelled phenomena where words can fall short. It is also quite useful to the researcher to have a visual means of interpreting his or her model and the data obtained from it. The Scaleable Brain Atlas is a visualization tool for portraying a brain atlas in 3D space.

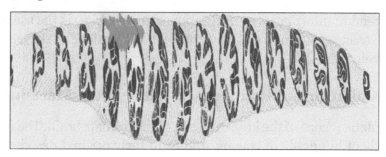

Single Neuron Modeling

Even single neurons have complex biophysical characteristics. In Hodgkin and Huxley's original model only employed two voltage-sensitive currents, the fast-acting sodium and the inwardrectifying potassium. Though successful in predicting the timing and qualitative features of the action potential, it nevertheless failed to predict such things important as adaptation. We now know that there is a zoo of voltage-sensitive currents, and the implications of the differing dynamics, modulations and sensitivity of these currents is an important topic of computational neuroscience.

- Hodgkin-Huxley model output (train of action potentials).

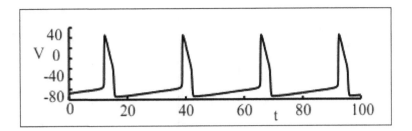

- Wang-Buzsaki model (of hippocampal and neocortical fast-spiking inter-neurons).

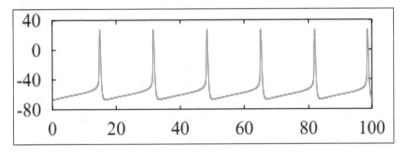

- Aplysia R-15 neuron model, showing calcium mediated (parabolic) bursting.

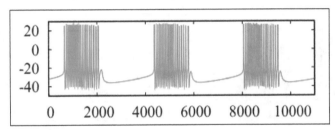

The above plots were obtained using XPP - software that can evolve ordinary differential equation (ODE) models forward in time. Most single neuron modelling is based around the notion of current balance.

Current through capacitor = Current through resistive pathways + Injected Current

The computational functions of complex dendrite are also under intense investigation. There is a large body of literature regarding how different currents interact with geometric properties of neurons.

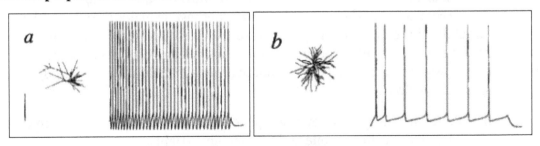

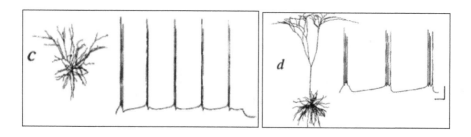

Development, Axonal Patterning and Guidance

How do axons and dendrites form during development? How do axons know where to target and how to reach these targets? How do neurons migrate to the proper position in the central and peripheral systems? How to synapses form? We know from molecular biology that distinct parts of the nervous system release distinct chemical cues, from growth factors to hormones that modulate and influence the growth and development of functional connections between neurons. Theoretical investigations into the formation and patterning of synaptic connection and morphology is still nascent. One hypothesis that has recently garnered some attention is the minimal wiring hypothesis, which postulates that the formation of axons and dendrites effectively minimizes resource allocation while maintains maximal information storage.

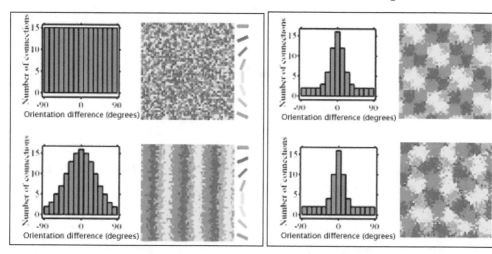

Statistics of inter-neuronal connections in the visual cortex (left column) and corresponding maps of orientation preference (right column) obtained by minimizing the length of these connections. The minimal wiring hypothesis explains the observed inter species variability in map appearance as a result of the variability in inter-neuronal connectivity. Several features of the orientation maps, such as pinwheels and fractures (two bottom rows), could be evolutionary adaptations that minimize the length of inter-neuronal connections.

Orientation Preference in Tree Shrew: Complete map of orientation preference (left) and detail of singularities, linear zone and saddlepoints (right).

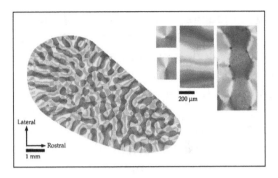

Sensory Processing

Models of sensory processing understood within a theoretical framework is credited to Horace Barlow. Barlow understood the processing of the early sensory systems to be a form of efficient coding, where the neurons encoded information which minimized the number of spikes. Experimental and computational work have since supported this hypothesis in one form or another. Current research in sensory processing is divided among biophysical modelling of different subsystems and more theoretical modelling function of perception. Current models of perception have suggested that the brain performs some form of Bayesian inference and integration of different sensory information in generating our perception of the physical world (and borrows from the field of machine learning).

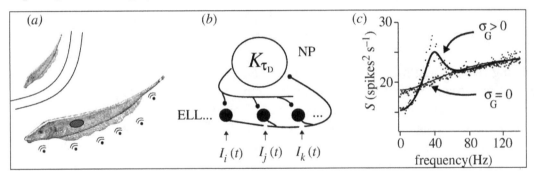

a: An electric fish experiences global electrosensory inputs from a communicating fish (upper left), and local inputs from swarm of prey Daphnia (bottom right). The filled circle on the body is the approximate size of the receptive field of an electrosensory lateral line lobe (ELL) pyramidal neuron. b: Schematic of the ELL pyramidal cell population and global inhibitory feedback from populations of bipolar cells in the NP nucleus. c: The spike train power spectrum S of a representative neuron in an integrate-and-fire model network. Simulations of the system are circles and solid lines are from a linear response calculation.

Memory and Synaptic Plasticity

Earlier models of memory are primarily based on the postulates of Hebbian learning (neurons that fire together wire together). Biologically relevant models such as the Hopfield net have been developed to address the properties of associative, rather than content-addressable style of memory that occur in biological systems. These attempts are primarily focusing on the formation of medium-term and long-term memory, localising in the hippocampus. Models of working memory, relying on theories of network oscillations and persistent activity, have been built to capture some features of the prefrontal cortex in context-related memory. One of the major problems in biological memory is how it is maintained and changed through multiple time scales. Unstable synapses are easy to train but also prone to stochastic disruption. Stable synapses forget less easily, but they are also harder to consolidate. It is likely that computational tools will contribute greatly to our understanding of how synapses function and change in relation to external stimulus in the coming decades.

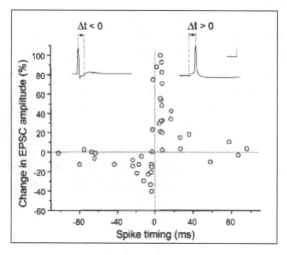

Timing requirements between pre- and postsynaptic spikes. Synaptic changes occur only if presynaptic firing and postsynaptic activity occur sufficiently close to each other. Experimentally measured weight changes (circles) as a function of relative pre- and post-synaptic firing times (showing a two-phase learning window). A positive change (LTP) occurs if the presynaptic spike precedes the postsynaptic one; for a reversed timing, synaptic weights are decreased.

Behaviors of Networks

Biological neurons are connected to each other in a complex, recurrent fashion. These connections are, unlike most artificial neural networks, sparse and most likely, specific. It is not known how information is transmitted through such sparsely connected networks. It is also unknown what the computational functions, if any, of these specific connectivity pattern are. The interactions of neurons in a small network can be often reduced to simple models such as the Ising model (of a magnet). The statisical mechanics of such simple systems are well-characterized theoretically.

Central Pattern Generators

One of the fundamental problems in neuroscience is understanding how circuit function arises from the intrinsic properties of individual neurons and their synaptic connections. Of particular interest is the extent to which similar circuit outputs can be generated by multiple mechanisms, both in different individual animals, or in the same animal over its life-time. The Marder lab[5] is actively pursuing this for central pattern generating circuits in the crusctacean stomatogastric nervous system. Central pattern generators are groups of neurons found in vertebrate and invertebrate nervous systems responsible for the generation of specific rhythmic behaviors such as walking, swimming, and breathing. The central pattern generators in the stomatogastric ganglion (STG) of lobsters and crabs are ideal for many analyses because the STG has only about 30 large neurons, the connectivity is established, the neurons are easy to record from, and when the stomatogastric ganglion is removed from the animal, it continues to produce rhythmic motor patterns.

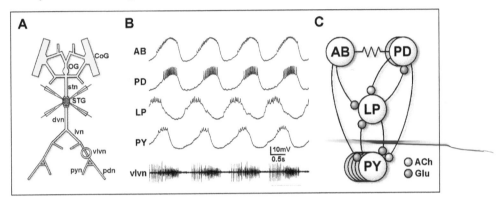

Cultures

With the emergence of two-photon microscopy and calcium imaging, there are now powerful experimental methods with which to test new theories regarding neuronal networks, particularly for neuronal cultures. Cultures of dissociated neurons from rat embryos can rapidly form synapses in culture and develop complex patterns of spontaneous activity. Moreover, more traditional electrophysiology can be used to both record and stimulate cells. Interestingly cells may be cultured on multi-electrode arrays (MEAs), to form a long-term, two-way interface between the cultured networks and a computer. The cultured nets can serve as the 'brain' of simulated animats or robotic creatures.

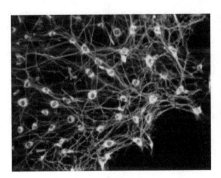 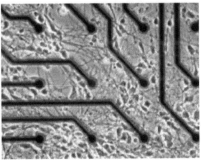

Cognition, Discrimination and Learning

Computational modeling of higher cognitive functions has only begun recently. Experimental data comes primarily from single unit recording in primates. The frontal lobe and parietal lobe function as intergrators of information from multiple sensory modalities. There are some tentative ideas regarding how simple mutually inhibitory functional circuits in these areas may carry out biologically relevant computation. The brain seems to be able to discriminate and adapt particularly well in certain contexts. For instance, human beings seem to have an enormous capacity for memorizing and recognizing faces. One of the key goals of computational neuroscience is to dissect how biological systems carry out these complex computations efficiently and potentially replicate these processes in building intelligent machines.

2

Nervous System

The highly complex part of an animal which coordinates its action and sensory information by transmitting the signals to and from different body parts of the body is known as the nervous system. Some of its basic parts are neurons, spinal cord and brain. This chapter has been carefully written to provide an easy understanding of the nervous system.

NEURONS

Neuron, also called nerve cell, is the basic cell of the nervous system in vertebrates and most invertebrates from the level of the cnidarians (e.g., corals, jellyfish) upward. A typical neuron has a cell body containing a nucleus and two or more long fibres. Impulses are carried along one or more of these fibres, called dendrites, to the cell body; in higher nervous systems, only one fibre, the axon, carries the impulse away from the cell body. Bundles of fibres from neurons are held together by connective tissue and form nerves. Some nerves in large vertebrates are several feet long. A sensory neuron transmits impulses from a receptor, such as those in the eye or ear, to a more central location in the nervous system, such as the spinal cord or brain. A motor neuron transmits impulses from a central area of the nervous system to an effector, such as a muscle.

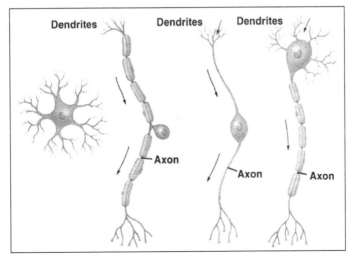

1. A neuron is a type of cell that receives and transmits information in the Central Nervous System (CNS – brain and spinal cord) and the Peripheral Nervous System (PNS – afferent & efferent nerves).

2. Parts of the neuron: cell body (soma), dendrites, axon, axon hillock, synaptic boutons.

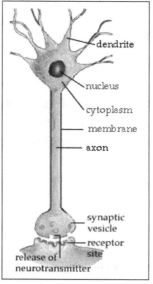

The Nerve Impulse.

The Resting Potential

1. When a neuron is at rest, the neuron maintains an electrical polarization (i.e., a negative electrical potential exists inside the neuron's membrane with respect to the outside). This difference in electrical potential or voltage is known as the resting potential. At rest, this potential is around -70mV.

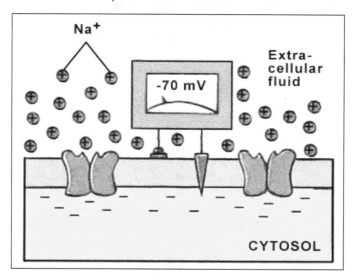

2. Concentration gradient (difference in distribution of ions between the inside and the outside of the membrane): During the resting potential, a difference in the distribution of ions is established with sodium (Na^+) 10 times more concentrated outside the membrane than inside and potassium (K^+) 20 times more concentrated inside than outside.

Because the body has far more sodium ions than potassium ions, the concentration of sodium ions outside is greater then the potassium ions inside making the outside more positively charged than the inside.

3. The neuron membrane has selective permeability, which allows some molecules to pass freely (e.g., water, carbon dioxide, oxygen, etc).

4. During the resting potential, K^+ and (chloride) Cl^- gates (channels) remain open along the membrane, which allows both ions to pass through; Na^+ gates remain closed restricting the passage of Na^+ ions.

5. Sodium-potassium pump: Protein mechanism found along the neuron membrane which transports 3 Na^+ ions outside of the cell while also drawing 2 K^+ ions into the cell; this is an active transport mechanism (requires energy (ATP) to function).

6. Electrical gradient (difference in positive and negative charges across the membrane): Due to the negative charge inside the membrane, K^+ (a positively-charged ion) is attracted into the neuron; Na^+ is also attracted to the negative charge, but remains mostly outside of the neuron due to the sodiumpotassium pump and the closing of sodium gates.

7. The advantage of the resting potential is to allow the neuron to respond quickly to a stimulus.

The Action Potential

1. Hyperpolarization (increased polarization): Occurs when the negative charge inside the axon increases (e.g., -70mV becomes -80mV).

2. Depolarization (decreasing polarization towards zero): Occurs when the negative charge inside the axon decreases (e.g., -70mV becomes -55mV).

3. Threshold of excitation (threshold): The level that a depolarization must reach for an action potential to occur. In most neurons the threshold is around -55mV to -65mV.

4. Action potential: A rapid depolarization and slight reversal of the usual membrane polarization. Occurs when depolarization meets or goes beyond the threshold of excitation.

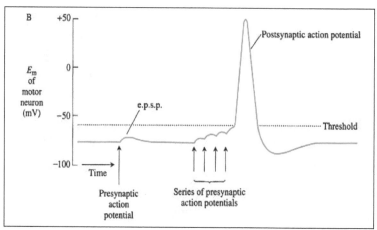

Response of the postsynaptic motor to action potentials in the presynaptic sensory neuron. At the upward arrows, action potential are triggered in the presynaptic neuron by an electrical stimulus.

5. When the potential across an axon membrane reaches threshold, voltage-activated
(membrane channels whose permeability depends on the voltage difference across the
membrane) Na+ gates open and allow sodium ions to enter; this causes the membrane
potential to depolarize past zero to a reversed polarity (e.g., -70mV becomes +50mV at
highest amplitude of the action potential).

6. When the action potential reaches its peak, voltage-activated Na+ gates close, but K+
ions flow outside of the membrane due to their high concentration inside the neuron as
opposed to outside.

7. A temporary hyperpolarization occurs before the membrane returns to its normal
resting potential (this is due to K+ gates opening wider than usual, allowing K+ to continue to exit past the resting potential).

8. After the action potential, the neuron has more Na+ and fewer K+ ions inside for
a short period (this is soon adjusted by the sodium-potassium pumps to the neuron's
original concentration gradient).

9. Local anesthetic drugs (e.g., Novocain, Xylocaine, etc.) hinder the occurrence of action potentials by blocking voltage-activated Na+ gates (preventing Na+ from entering
a membrane).

10. General anesthetics (e.g., ether and chloroform) cause K+ gates to open wider, allowing K+ to flow outside of a neuron very quickly, thus preventing an action potential
from occurring (no pain signal).

11. Action potentials only occur in axons as cell bodies and dendrites do not have voltage-dependent channels.

12. All-or-none law: The size, amplitude, and velocity of an action potential are independent of the intensity of the stimulus that initiated it. If threshold is met or exceeded

an action potential of a specific magnitude will occur, if threshold is not met, an action potential will not occur.

13. Refractory period: A period of immediately after an action potential occurs when the neuron will resist the production of another action potential.

- Absolute refractory period: Na$^+$ gates are incapable of opening; hence, an action potential cannot occur regardless of the amount of stimulation.

- Relative refractory period: Na$^+$ gates are capable of opening, but K$^+$ channels remain open; a stronger than normal stimulus (i.e., exceeding threshold) will initiate an action potential.

Propagation Movement of the Action Potential

- The action potential begins at the axon hillock (a swelling located where an axon exits the cell body).

- The action potential is regenerated due to Na$^+$ ions moving down the axon, depolarizing adjacent areas of the membrane.

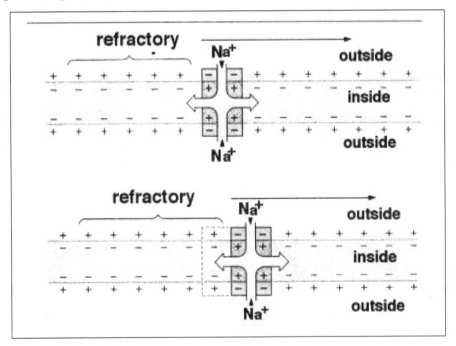

- Propagation of the action potential: Transmission (movement) of an action potential down an axon. The action potential moves down the axon by regenerating itself at successive points on the axon.

- The refractory periods prevent the action potentials from moving in the opposite direction (i.e., back toward the axon hillock).

Myelin Sheath and Saltatory Conduction

- Myelinated axons: Axons covered with a myelin sheath. The myelin sheath is found only in vertebrates and is composed mostly of fats.

- Nodes of Ranvier: Short unmyelinated sections on a myelinated axon.

- Saltatory conduction: The jumping of the action potential from node to node.

- Multiple sclerosis: A disease characterized by the loss of myelin along axons; the loss of the myelin sheath prevents the propagation of action potentials down the axon.

The Concept of the Synapse

A. Synapse: A gap between neurons where a specialized type of communication occurs.

B. Sherrington discovered that:

- Reflexes are slower than conduction along an axon; thus, there must be a delay at the synapse.

- Synapses are capable of summating stimuli.

- Excitation of one synapse leads to a decreased excitation or inhibition of others.

C. Temporal summation: Repeated stimulation of one presynaptic neuron (the neuron that delivers the synaptic potential) occurring within a brief period of time having a cumulative effect on the postsynaptic neuron (the neuron that receives the message).

D. Graded potentials: Either depolarization (excitatory) or hyperpolarization (inhibitory) of the postsynaptic neuron. A graded depolarization is known as an excitatory postsynaptic potential (EPSP) and occurs when Na^+ ions enter the postsynaptic neuron. EPSP'S are not action potentials: The EPSP's magnitude decreases as it moves along the membrane.

E. Spatial summation: Several synaptic inputs originating from separate locations exerting a cumulative effect on a postsynaptic neuron.

F. Inhibitory postsynaptic potential (IPSP): A temporary hyperpolarization of a postsynaptic cell (this occurs when K^+ leaves the cell or Cl^- enters the cell after it is stimulated).

G. Spontaneous firing rate: The ability to produce action potentials without synaptic input (EPSP's and IPSP's increase or decrease the likelihood of firing action potentials).

Chemical Events at the Synapse

A. In most cases, synaptic transmission depends on chemical rather than electrical stimulation. This was demonstrated by Otto Loewi's experiments where fluid from a stimulated frog heart was transferred to another heart. The fluid caused the new heart to react as if stimulated.

B. The major events at a synapse are:

- Neurons synthesize chemicals called neurotransmitters.

- Neurons transport these chemicals to the axon terminal.

- Action potentials travel down the axon.

- At the axon or presynaptic terminal, the action potentials open voltage-gated calcium channels to open, allowing calcium to enter the cell. This leads to the release of the neurotransmitters from the terminal into the synaptic cleft (space between the presynaptic and postsynaptic neuron).

- Neurotransmitters, once released into the synaptic cleft, attach to receptors and alter activity of the postsynaptic neuron.

- The neurotransmitters will separate from their receptors and (in some cases) are converted into inactive chemicals.

- In some cells much of the released neurotransmitters are taken back into the presynaptic neuron for recycling. This is called reuptake.

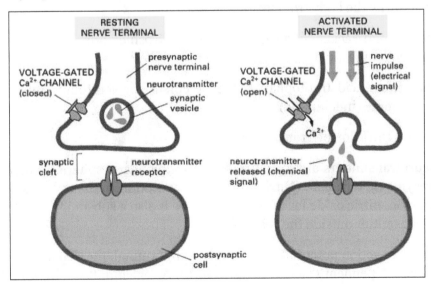

C. Chemicals released by one neuron at the synapse and affect another neuron are neurotransmitters.

D. Types of neurotransmitters include:

- Amino acids: Acids containing an amine group (NH_2), e.g., gamma-aminobutyric acid (GABA).

- Neuropeptides: A peptide is a chain of amino acids. A long chain is called a polypeptide; a still longer chain is a protein. Endorphins (endogenous opiates) are neuropeptides.

- Acetylcholine: A chemical similar to an amino acid, with the NH_2 group replaced by an $N(CH_3)_3$ group.

- Monoamines: Nonacidic neurotransmitters containing an amine group (NH_2) formed by a metabolic change of an amino acid. Catecholamines are a type of monoamine.

- Purines: Adenosine and several of its derivatives.

- Gases: Specifically nitric oxide (NO) and possibly others.

E. Synthesis of neurotransmitters: Neurons synthesize neurotransmitters from precursors derived originally from food or else from old neurotransmitters recycled via reuptake.

- Catecholamines (Dopamine (DA), Epinephrine (E) and Norepinephrine (NE)): Three closely related compounds containing a catechol and an amine group.

- Choline is the precusor for acetylcholine. Choline is obtained from certain foods or made by the body from lecithin.

- The amino acids phenylalanine and tyrosine are precursors for the catecholamines.

- The amino acid tryptophan is the precursor for serotonin, another type of monoamine (indolamine).

F. Release and Diffusion of Transmitters:

- Neurotransmitters are stored in vesicles (tiny nearly spherical packets) in the presynaptic terminal. (Nitric oxide is an exception to this rule, as neurons do not store nitric oxide for future use). There is also a substantial amount of neurotransmitter outside the vesicles.

- When an action potential reaches the axon terminal, the depolarization causes voltage-dependent calcium gates to open. As calcium flows into the terminal, the neuron releases neurotransmitters into the synaptic cleft for 1-2 milliseconds. This process of neurotransmitter release is called exocytosis.

- After being released by the presynaptic neuron, the neurotransmitter diffuses across the synaptic cleft to the postsynaptic membrane where it will attach to receptors.

- The brain uses dozens of neurotransmitters, but no single neuron releases them all.

G. Activation of Receptors of the Postsynaptic Cell:

- A neurotransmitter can have three types of major effects when it attaches to the active site of the receptor: ionotropic, metabotropic, and modulatory.

- Ionotropic effects: Neurotransmitter attaches to the receptor causing the immediate opening of an ion gate (e.g., glutamate opens Na^+ gates).

- Metabotropic effects: Neurotransmitter attaches to a receptor and alters the configuration of the rest of the receptor protein; enabling a portion of the protein inside the neuron to react with other molecules. Activation of the receptor by the neurotransmitter leads to activation of G-proteins which are attached to the receptor.

- G-proteins: A protein coupled to the energy-storing molecule, guanosine triphosphate (GTP).

- Metabotropic effects are slower and longer lasting than ionotropic effects and depend on the actions of second messengers.

- Second messenger: Chemicals that carry a message to different areas within a postsynaptic cell; the activation of a G-protein inside a cell increases the amount of a second messenger.

- Neurotransmitters can interact with several different kinds of receptors. Some neurotransmitters can interact with both ionotropic and metabotropic receptors.

H. Inactivation and Reuptake of Neurotransmitters:

- Neurotransmitters become inactive shortly after binding to postsynaptic receptors.

  Various neurotransmitters are inactivated in different way.

- Acetylcholinesterase (AchE): Found in acetylcholine (Ach) synapses; AchE quickly breaks down Ach after it releases from the postsynaptic receptor.

- Myasthenia gravis: Motor disorder caused by a deficit of acetylcholine transmission. This disease is treated with drugs which block AchE activity (thus allowing more Ach to stay in the synapse).

- Serotonin and the catecholamines are taken up by the presynaptic neuron which released them after they separated from postsynaptic receptors. This process is called reuptake; it occurs through specialized proteins called transporters.

- Some serotonin and catecholamine molecules are converted into inactive chemicals by enzymes such as COMT (converts catecholamines) and MAO (converts both catecholamines and serotonin).

Neurons may be classified according to polarity: bipolar neuron – a neuron in which the processes extend from opposite ends of the soma (pseudo)unipolar neuron – a neuron in which the process extends from one end of the soma multipolar neuron – a neuron in which an axon and several dendrites extend from the soma.

Sensory Neurons

Sensory neurons are the nerve cells that are activated by sensory input from the environment - for example, when you touch a hot surface with your fingertips, the sensory neurons will be the ones firing and sending off signals to the rest of the nervous system about the information they have received.

The inputs that activate sensory neurons can be physical or chemical, corresponding to all five of our senses. Thus, a physical input can be things like sound, touch, heat, or light. A chemical input comes from taste or smell, which neurons then send to the brain. Most sensory neurons are pseudounipolar, which means they only have one axon which is split into two branches.

Motor Neurons

Motor neurons of the spinal cord are part of the central nervous system (CNS) and connect to muscles, glands and organs throughout the body. These neurons transmit impulses from the spinal cord to skeletal and smooth muscles (such as those in your stomach), and so directly control all of our muscle movements. There are in fact two types of motor neurons: those that travel from spinal cord to muscle are called lower motor neurons, whereas those that travel between the brain and spinal cord are called upper motor neurons.

Motor neurons have the most common type of 'body plan' for a nerve cell they are multipolar, each with one axon and several dendrites.

Interneurons

As the name suggests, interneurons are the ones in between - they connect spinal motor and sensory neurons. As well as transferring signals between sensory and motor neurons, interneurons can also communicate with each other, forming circuits of various complexity. They are multipolar, just like motor neurons.

Neurons in the Brain

In the brain, the distinction between types of neurons is much more complex. Whereas in the spinal cord we could easily distinguish neurons based on their function, that isn't the case in the brain. Certainly, there are brain neurons involved in sensory processing like those in visual or auditory cortex and others involved in motor processing like those in the cerebellum or motor cortex.

However, within any of these sensory or motor regions, there are tens or even hundreds of different types of neurons. In fact, researchers are still trying to devise a way to neatly classify the huge variety of neurons that exist in the brain.

Looking at which neurotransmitter a neuron uses is one way that could be a useful for classifying neurons.

However, within categories we can find further distinctions. Some GABA neurons, for example, send their axon mostly to the cell bodies of other neurons; others prefer to target the dendrites.

Furthermore, these different neurons have different electrical properties, different shapes, different genes expressed, different projection patterns and receive different inputs. In other words, a particular combination of features is one way of defining a neuron type.

The thought is that a single neuron type should perform the same function, or suite of functions, within the brain. Scientists would consider where the neuron projects to, what it connects with and what input it receives.

STRUCTURE OF NEURONS

In addition to having all the normal components of a cell (nucleus, organelles, etc.) neurons also contain unique structures for receiving and sending the electrical signals that make neuronal communication possible.

Dendrite

Dendrites are branch-like structures extending away from the cell body, and their job is to receive messages from other neurons and allow those messages to travel to the cell body. Although some neurons do not have any dendrites, other types of neurons have multiple dendrites. Dendrites can have small protrusions called dendritic spines, which further increase surface area for possible connections with other neurons.

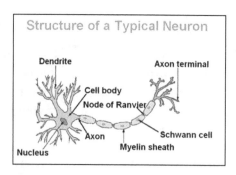

The structure of a neuron: The above image shows the basic structural components of an average neuron, including the dendrite, cell body, nucleus, Node of Ranvier, myelin sheath, Schwann cell, and axon terminal.

Cell Body

Like other cells, each neuron has a cell body (or soma) that contains a nucleus, smooth and rough endoplasmic reticulum, golgi apparatus, mitochondria, and other cellular components.

Axon

An axon, at its most basic, is a tube-like structure that carries an electrical impulse from the cell body (or from another cell's dendrites) to the structures at opposite end of the neuron axon terminals, which can then pass the impulse to another neuron. The cell body contains a specialized structure, the axon hillock, which serves as a junction between the cell body and the axon.

Synapse

The synapse is the chemical junction between the axon terminals of one neuron and the dendrites of the next. It is a gap where specialized chemical interactions can occur, rather than an actual structure.

Function of a Neuron

The specialized structure and organization of neurons allows them to transmit signals in the form of electric impulses from the brain to the body and back. Individually, neurons can pass a signal all the way from their own dendrites to their own axon terminals; but at a higher level neurons are organized in long chains, allowing them to pass signals very quickly from one to the other. One neuron's axon will connect chemically to another neuron's dendrite at the synapse between them. Electrically charged chemicals flow from the first neuron's axon to the second neuron's dendrite, and that signal will then flow from the second neuron's dendrite, down its axon, across a synapse, into a third neuron's dendrites, and so on.

This is the basic chain of neural signal transmission, which is how the brain sends signals to the muscles to make them move, and how sensory organs send signals to the brain. It is important that these signals can happen quickly, and they do. Think of how fast you drop a hot potato before you even realize it is hot. This is because the sense organ (in this case, the skin) sends the signal "This is hot" to neurons with very long axons that travel up the spine to the brain. If this didn't happen quickly, people would burn themselves.

Other Structures

Dendrites, cell bodies, axons, and synapses are the basic parts of a neuron, but other important structures and materials surround neurons to make them more efficient.

Myelin Sheath

Some axons are covered with myelin, a fatty material that wraps around the axon to form the myelin sheath. This external coating functions as insulation to minimize dissipation of the electrical signal as it travels down the axon. Myelin's presence on the axon greatly increases the speed of conduction of the electrical signal, because the fat prevents any electricity from leaking out. This insulation is important, as the axon from a human motor neuron can be as long as a meter from the base of the spine to the toes. Periodic gaps in the myelin sheath are called nodes of ranvier. At these nodes, the signal is "recharged" as it travels along the axon.

Glial Cells

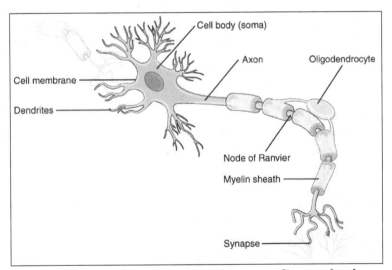

Neuron in the central nervous system: This neuron diagram also shows the oligodendrocyte, myelin sheath, and nodes of Ranvier.

The myelin sheath is not actually part of the neuron. Myelin is produced by glial cells, which are non-neuronal cells that provide support for the nervous system. Glia function to hold neurons in place supply them with nutrients, provide insulation, and remove pathogens and dead neurons. In the central nervous system, the glial cells that form the myelin sheath are called oligodendrocytes; in the peripheral nervous system, they are called Schwann cells.

Stages of the Action Potential

Neural impulses occur when a stimulus depolarizes a cell membrane, prompting an action potential which sends an "all or nothing" signal.

Neural Impulses in the Nervous System

The central nervous system (CNS) goes through a three-step process when it functions: sensory input, neural processing, and motor output. The sensory input stage is when the neurons (or excitable nerve cells) of the sensory organs are excited electrically. Neural impulses from sensory receptors are sent to the brain and spinal cord for processing. After the brain has processed the information, neural impulses are then conducted from the brain and spinal cord to muscles and glands, which is the resulting motor output.

A neuron affects other neurons by releasing a neurotransmitter that binds to chemical receptors. The effect upon the postsynaptic (receiving) neuron is determined not by the presynaptic (sending) neuron or by the neurotransmitter itself, but by the type of receptor that is activated. A neurotransmitter can be thought of as a key, and a receptor as a lock: the key unlocks a certain response in the postsynaptic neuron, communicating a particular signal. However, in order for a presynaptic neuron to release a neurotransmitter to the next neuron in the chain, it must go through a series of changes in electric potential.

Stages of Neural Impulses

Resting potential is the name for the electrical state when a neuron is not actively being signaled. A neuron at resting potential has a membrane with established amounts of sodium (Na^+) and potassium (K^+) ions on either side, leaving the inside of the neuron negatively charged relative to the outside.

The action potential is a rapid change in polarity that moves along the nerve fiber from neuron to neuron. In order for a neuron to move from resting potential to action potential a short-term electrical change that allows an electrical signal to be passed from one neuron to another the neuron must be stimulated by pressure, electricity, chemicals, or another form of stimuli. The level of stimulation that a neuron must receive to reach action potential is known as the threshold of excitation, and until it reaches that threshold, nothing will happen. Different neurons are sensitive to different stimuli, although most can register pain.

The action potential has several stages.

1. Depolarization: A stimulus starts the depolarization of the membrane. Depolarization, also referred to as the "upswing," is caused when positively charged sodium ions rush into a nerve cell. As these positive ions rush in, the membrane of the stimulated cell reverses its polarity so that the outside of the membrane is negative relative to the inside.

2. Repolarization: Once the electric gradient has reached the threshold of excitement, the "downswing" of repolarization begins. The channels that let the positive sodium ion channels through close up, while channels that allow positive potassium ions open, resulting in the release of positively charged potassium ions from the neuron. This expulsion acts to restore the localized negative membrane potential of the cell, bringing it back to its normal voltage.

3. Refractory Phase: The refractory phase takes place over a short period of time after the depolarization stage. Shortly after the sodium gates open, they close and go into an inactive conformation. The sodium gates cannot be opened again until the membrane is repolarized to its normal resting potential. The sodium-potassium pump returns sodium ions to the outside and potassium ions to the inside. During the refractory phase this particular area of the nerve cell membrane cannot be depolarized. Therefore, the neuron cannot reach action potential during this "rest period".

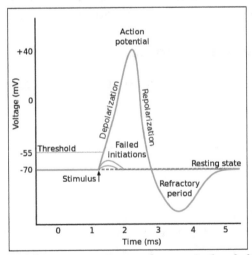

Action potentials: A neuron must reach a certain threshold in order
to begin the depolarization step of reaching the action potential.

This process of depolarization, repolarization, and recovery moves along a nerve fiber from neuron to neuron like a very fast wave. While an action potential is in progress, another cannot be generated under the same conditions. In unmyelinated axons (axons that are not covered by a myelin sheath), this happens in a continuous fashion because there are voltage-gated channels throughout the membrane. In myelinated axons (axons covered by a myelin sheath), this process is described as saltatory because voltage-gated channels are only found at the nodes of ranvier, and the electrical events seem to jump from one node to the next. Saltatory conduction is faster than continuous conduction. The diameter of the axon also makes a difference, as ions diffusing within the cell have less resistance in a wider space. Damage to the myelin sheath from disease can cause severe impairment of nerve-cell function. In addition, some poisons and drugs interfere with nerve impulses by blocking sodium channels in nerves.

All-or-none Signals

The amplitude of an action potential is independent of the amount of current that produced it. In other words, larger currents do not create larger action potentials. Therefore, action potentials are said to be all-or-none signals, since either they occur fully or they do not occur at all. The frequency of action potentials is correlated with the intensity of a stimulus. This is in contrast to receptor potentials, whose amplitudes are dependent on the intensity of a stimulus.

Reuptake

Reuptake refers to the reabsorption of a neurotransmitter by a presynaptic (sending) neuron after it has performed its function of transmitting a neural impulse. Reuptake is necessary for normal synaptic physiology because it allows for the recycling of neurotransmitters and regulates the neurotransmitter level in the synapse, thereby controlling how long a signal resulting from neurotransmitter release lasts.

Mechanics of the Action Potential

The synapse is the site at which a chemical or electrical exchange occurs between the presynaptic and postsynaptic cells.

Synapses

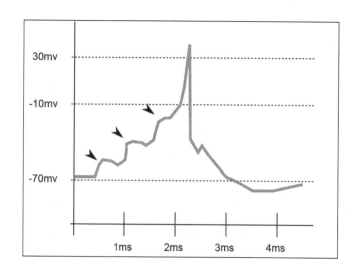

The synapse is the junction where neurons trade information. It is not a physical component of a cell but rather a name for the gap between two cells: the presynaptic cell (giving the signal) and the postsynaptic cell (receiving the signal). There are two types of possible reactions at the synapse—chemical or electrical. During a chemical reaction, a chemical called a neurotransmitter is released from one cell into another. In an electrical reaction, the electrical charge of one cell is influenced by the charge an adjacent cell.

All synapses have a few common characteristics:

- Presynaptic cell: a specialized area within the axon of the giving cell that transmits information to the dendrite of the receiving cell.

- Synaptic cleft: the small space at the synapse that receives neurotransmitters.

- G-protein coupled receptors: receptors that sense molecules outside the cell and thereby activate signals within it.

- Ligand-gated ion channels: receptors that are opened or closed in response to the binding of a chemical messenger.

- Postsynaptic cell: a specialized area within the dendrite of the receiving cell that contains receptors designed to process neurotransmitters.

The Electrical Synapse

The stages of an electrical reaction at a synapse are as follows:

- Resting potential: The membrane of a neuron is normally at rest with established concentrations of sodium ions (Na^+) and potassium ions (K^+) on either side. The membrane potential (or, voltage across the membrane) at this state is -70 mV, with the inside being negative relative to the outside.

- Depolarization: A stimulus begins the depolarization of the membrane. Depolarization, also referred to as the "upswing," occurs when positively charged sodium ions (Na^+) suddenly rush through open sodium gates into a nerve cell. If the membrane potential reaches -55 mV, it has reached the threshold of excitation. Additional sodium rushes in, and the membrane of the stimulated cell actually reverses its polarity so that the outside of the membrane is negative relative to the inside. The change in voltage stimulates the opening of additional sodium channels (called a voltage-gated ion channel), providing what is known as a positive feedback loop. Eventually, the cell potential reaches +40 mV, or the action potential.

- Repolarization: The "downswing" of repolarization is caused by the closing of sodium ion channels and the opening of potassium ion channels, resulting in the release of positively charged potassium ions (K^+) from the nerve cell. This expulsion acts to restore the localized negative membrane potential of the cell.

- Refractory Phase: The refractory phase is a short period of time after the repolarization stage. Shortly after the sodium gates open, they close and go into an inactive conformation where the cell's membrane potential is actually even lower than its baseline -70 mV. The sodium gates cannot be opened again until the membrane has completely repolarized to its normal resting potential, -70 mV. The sodium-potassium pump returns sodium ions to the outside and potassium ions to the inside. During the refractory phase this particular area of the nerve cell membrane cannot be depolarized; the cell cannot be excited.

The Chemical Synapse

The process of a chemical reaction at the synapse has some important differences from an electrical reaction. Chemical synapses are much more complex than electrical synapses, which makes them slower, but also allows them to generate different results. Like electrical reactions, chemical reactions involve electrical modifications at the postsynaptic membrane, but chemical reactions also require chemical messengers, such as neurotransmitters, to operate.

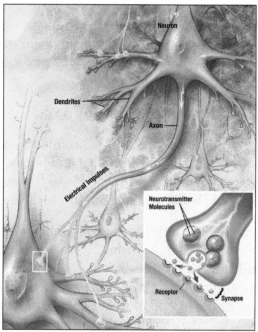

Neuron & chemical synapse: This image shows electric impulses traveling between neurons; the inset shows a chemical reaction occurring at the synapse.

A basic chemical reaction at the synapse undergoes a few additional steps:

- The action potential travels along the membrane of the presynaptic cell until it reaches the synapse. The electrical depolarization of the membrane at the synapse causes channels to open that are selectively permeable, meaning they specifically only allow the entry of positive sodium ions (Na^+).

- The ions flow through the presynaptic membrane, rapidly increasing their concentration in the interior.

- The high concentration activates a set of ion-sensitive proteins attached to vesicles, which are small membrane compartments that contain a neurotransmitter chemical.

- These proteins change shape, causing the membranes of some "docked" vesicles to fuse with the membrane of the presynaptic cell. This opens the vesicles, which releases their neurotransmitter contents into the synaptic cleft, the narrow space between the membranes of the pre- and postsynaptic cells.

- The neurotransmitter diffuses within the cleft. Some of it escapes, but the rest of it binds to chemical receptor molecules located on the membrane of the postsynaptic cell.

- The binding of neurotransmitter causes the receptor molecule to be activated in some way. Several types of activation are possible, depending on what kind of neurotransmitter was released. In any case, this is the key step by which the synaptic process affects the behavior of the postsynaptic cell.

- Due to thermal shaking, neurotransmitter molecules eventually break loose from the receptors and drift away.

- The neurotransmitter is either reabsorbed by the presynaptic cell and repackaged for future release, or else it is broken down metabolically.

Differences between Electrical and Chemical Synapses

- Electrical synapses are faster than chemical synapses because the receptors do not need to recognize chemical messengers. The synaptic delay for a chemical synapse is typically about 2 milliseconds, while the synaptic delay for an electrical synapse may be about 0.2 milliseconds.

- Because electrical synapses do not involve neurotransmitters, electrical neurotransmission is less modifiable than chemical neurotransmission.

- The response is always the same sign as the source. For example, depolarization of the presynaptic membrane will always induce a depolarization in the postsynaptic membrane, and vice versa for hyperpolarization.

- The response in the postsynaptic neuron is generally smaller in amplitude than the source. The amount of attenuation of the signal is due to the membrane resistance of the presynaptic and postsynaptic neurons.

- Long-term changes can be seen in electrical synapses. For example, changes in electrical synapses in the retina are seen during light and dark adaptations of the retina.

Neurotransmitters

Neurotransmitters are chemicals that transmit signals from a neuron across a synapse to a target cell.

Neurotransmitters are chemicals that transmit signals from a neuron to a target cell across a synapse. When called upon to deliver messages, they are released from their synaptic vesicles on the presynaptic (giving) side of the synapse, diffuse across the synaptic cleft, and bind to receptors in the membrane on the postsynaptic (receiving) side.

An action potential is necessary for neurotransmitters to be released, which means that neurons must reach a certain threshold of electric stimulation in order to complete the reaction. A neuron has a negative charge inside the cell membrane relative to the outside of the cell membrane; when stimulation occurs and the neuron reaches the threshold of excitement this polarity is reversed. This allows the signal to pass through the neuron. When the chemical message reaches the axon terminal, channels in the postsynaptic cell membrane open up to receive neurotransmitters from vesicles in the presynaptic cell.

Inhibitory neurotransmitters cause hyperpolarization of the postsynaptic cell (that is, decreasing the voltage gradient of the cell, thus bringing it further away from an action potential), while excitatory neurotransmitters cause depolarization (bringing it closer to an action potential). Neurotransmitters match up with receptors like a key in a lock. A neurotransmitter binds to its receptor and will not bind to receptors for other neurotransmitters, making the binding a specific chemical event.

There are several systems of neurotransmitters found at various synapses in the nervous system. The following groups refer to the specific chemicals, and within the groups are specific systems, some of which block other chemicals from entering the cell and some of which permit the entrance of chemicals that were blocked before.

Cholinergic System

The cholinergic system is a neurotransmitter system of its own, and is based on the neurotransmitter acetylcholine (ACh). This system is found in the autonomic nervous system, as well as distributed throughout the brain.

The cholinergic system has two types of receptors: the nicotinic receptor and the acetylcholine receptor, which is known as the muscarinic receptor. Both of these receptors are named for chemicals that interact with the receptor in addition to the neurotransmitter acetylcholine. Nicotine, the chemical in tobacco, binds to the nicotinic receptor and activates it similarly to acetylcholine. Muscarine, a chemical product of certain mushrooms, binds to the muscarinic receptor. However, they cannot bind to each others receptors.

Amino Acids

Another group of neurotransmitters are amino acids, including glutamate (Glu), GABA (gamma-aminobutyric acid, a derivative of glutamate), and glycine (Gly). These amino acids have an amino group and a carboxyl group in their chemical structures. Glutamate is one of the 20 amino acids used to make proteins. Each amino acid neurotransmitter is its own system, namely the glutamatergic, GABAergic, and glycinergic systems. They each have their own receptors and do not interact with each other. Amino acid neurotransmitters are eliminated from the synapse by reuptake. A pump in the cell membrane of the presynaptic element, or sometimes a neighboring glial cell, clears the amino acid from the synaptic cleft so that it can be recycled, repackaged in vesicles, and released again.

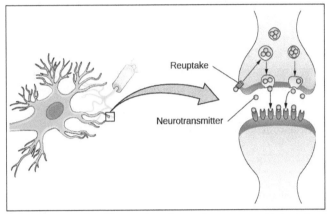

The reuptake process: This illustration shows the process of reuptake, in which leftover neurotransmitters are returned to vesicles in the presynaptic cell.

Biogenic Amines

Another class of neurotransmitter is the biogenic amine, a group of neurotransmitters made enzymatically from amino acids. They have amino groups in them, but do not have carboxyl groups and are therefore no longer classified as amino acids.

Neuropeptides

A neuropeptide is a neurotransmitter molecule made up of chains of amino acids connected by peptide bonds, similar to proteins. However, proteins are long molecules while some neuropeptides are quite short. Neuropeptides are often released at synapses in combination with another neurotransmitter.

Dopamine

Dopamine is the best-known neurotransmitter of the catecholamine group. The brain includes several distinct dopamine systems, one of which plays a major role in reward-motivated behavior. Most types of reward increase the level of dopamine in the brain, and a variety of addictive drugs increase dopamine neuronal activity. Other brain dopamine systems are involved in motor control and in controlling the release of several other important hormones.

Effect on the Synapse

The effect of a neurotransmitter on the postsynaptic element is entirely dependent on the receptor protein. If there is no receptor protein in the membrane of the postsynaptic element, then the neurotransmitter has no effect. The depolarizing (more likely to reach an action potential) or hyperpolarizing (less likely to reach an action potential) effect is also dependent on the receptor. When acetylcholine binds to the nicotinic receptor, the postsynaptic cell is depolarized. However, when acetylcholine binds to the muscarinic receptor, it might cause depolarization or hyperpolarization of the target cell.

The amino acid neurotransmitters (glutamate, glycine, and GABA) are almost exclusively associated with just one effect. Glutamate is considered an excitatory amino acid because Glu receptors in the adult cause depolarization of the postsynaptic cell. Glycine and GABA are considered inhibitory amino acids, again because their receptors cause hyperpolarization, making the receiving cell less likely to reach an action potential.

The Right Dose

Sometimes too little or too much of a neurotransmitter may affect an organism's behavior or health. The underlying cause of some neurodegenerative diseases, such as Parkinson's, appears to be related to overaccumulation of proteins, which under normal circumstances would be regulated by the presence of dopamine. On the other hand, when an excess of the neurotransmitter dopamine blocks glutamate receptors, disorders like schizophrenia can occur.

NEURAL CIRCUIT

A neural circuit is a population of neurons interconnected by synapses to carry out a specific function when activated. Neural circuits interconnect to one another to form large scale brain networks. Biological neural networks have inspired the design of artificial neural networks, but artificial neural networks are usually not strict copies of their biological counterparts.

Early treatments of neural networks can be found in Herbert Spencer's *Principles of Psychology*, 3rd edition, Theodor Meynert's *Psychiatry*, William James' *Principles of Psychology*, and Sigmund Freud's Project for a Scientific Psychology. The first rule of neuronal learning was described by Hebb in 1949, in the Hebbian theory. Thus, Hebbian pairing of pre-synaptic and post-synaptic activity can substantially alter the dynamic characteristics of the synaptic connection and therefore either facilitate or inhibit signal transmission. In 1959, the neuroscientists, Warren Sturgis McCulloch and Walter Pitts published the first works on the processing of neural networks. They showed theoretically that networks of artificial neurons could implement logical, arithmetic, and symbolic functions. Simplified models of biological neurons were set up, now usually called perceptrons or artificial neurons. These simple models accounted for neural summation (i.e., potentials at the post-synaptic membrane will summate in the cell body). Later models also provided for excitatory and inhibitory synaptic transmission.

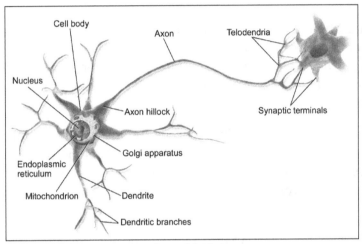

Anatomy of a multipolar neuron.

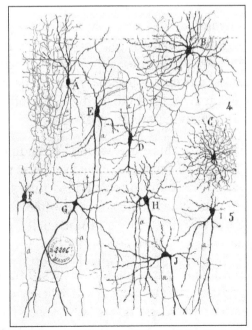

From "Texture of the Nervous System of Man and the Vertebrates" by Santiago Ramón y Cajal. The figure illustrates the diversity of neuronal morphologies in the auditory cortex.

Connections between Neurons

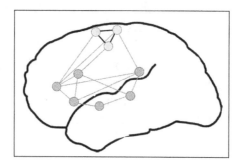

Proposed organization of motor-semantic neural circuits for action language comprehension. Gray dots represent areas of language comprehension, creating a network for comprehending all language. The semantic circuit of the motor system, particularly the motor representation of the legs (yellow dots), is incorporated when leg-related words are comprehended.

The connections between neurons in the brain are much more complex than those of the artificial neurons used in the connectionist neural computing models of artificial neural networks. The basic kinds of connections between neurons are synapses: both chemical and electrical synapses.

The establishment of synapses enables the connection of neurons into millions of overlapping, and interlinking neural circuits. Presynaptic proteins called neurexins are central to this process.

One principle by which neurons work is neural summation – potentials at the postsynaptic membrane will sum up in the cell body. If the depolarization of the neuron at the axon hillock goes above threshold an action potential will occur that travels down the axon to the terminal endings to transmit a signal to other neurons. Excitatory and inhibitory synaptic transmission is realized mostly by excitatory postsynaptic potentials (EPSPs), and inhibitory postsynaptic potentials (IPSPs).

On the electrophysiological level, there are various phenomena which alter the response characteristics of individual synapses (called synaptic plasticity) and individual neurons (intrinsic plasticity). These are often divided into short-term plasticity and long-term plasticity. Long-term synaptic plasticity is often contended to be the most likely memory substrate. Usually the term "neuroplasticity" refers to changes in the brain that are caused by activity or experience.

Connections display temporal and spatial characteristics. Temporal characteristics refer to the continuously modified activity-dependent efficacy of synaptic transmission, called spike-timing-dependent plasticity. It has been observed in several studies that the synaptic efficacy of this transmission can undergo short-term increase (called facilitation) or decrease (depression) according to the activity of the presynaptic neuron.

The induction of long-term changes in synaptic efficacy, by long-term potentiation (LTP) or depression (LTD), depends strongly on the relative timing of the onset of the excitatory postsynaptic potential and the postsynaptic action potential. LTP is induced by a series of action potentials which cause a variety of biochemical responses. Eventually, the reactions cause the expression of new receptors on the cellular membranes of the postsynaptic neurons or increase the efficacy of the existing receptors through phosphorylation.

Backpropagating action potentials cannot occur because after an action potential travels down a given segment of the axon, the m gates on voltage-gated sodium channels close, thus blocking any transient opening of the h gate from causing a change in the intracellular sodium ion (Na^+) concentration, and preventing the generation of an action potential back towards the cell body. In some cells, however, neural backpropagation does occur through the dendritic branching and may have important effects on synaptic plasticity and computation.

A neuron in the brain requires a single signal to a neuromuscular junction to stimulate contraction of the postsynaptic muscle cell. In the spinal cord, however, at least 75 afferent neurons are required to produce firing. This picture is further complicated by variation in time constant between neurons, as some cells can experience their EPSPs over a wider period of time than others.

While in synapses in the developing brain synaptic depression has been particularly widely observed it has been speculated that it changes to facilitation in adult brains.

Circuitry

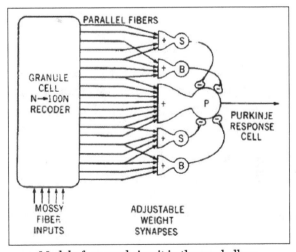

Model of a neural circuit in the cerebellum.

An example of a neural circuit is the trisynaptic circuit in the hippocampus. Another is the Papez circuit linking the hypothalamus to the limbic lobe. There are several neural circuits in the cortico-basal ganglia-thalamo-cortical loop. These circuits carry information between the cortex, basal ganglia, thalamus, and back to the cortex. The largest structure within the basal ganglia, the striatum, is seen as having its own internal microcircuitry.

Neural circuits in the spinal cord called central pattern generators are responsible for controlling motor instructions involved in rhythmic behaviours. Rhythmic behaviours include walking, urination, and ejaculation. The central pattern generators are made up of different groups of spinal interneurons.

There are four principal types of neural circuits that are responsible for a broad scope of neural functions. These circuits are a diverging circuit, a converging circuit, a reverberating circuit, and a parallel after-discharge circuit.

In a diverging circuit, one neuron synapses with a number of postsynaptic cells. Each of these may synapse with many more making it possible for one neuron to stimulate up to thousands of cells. This is exemplified in the way that thousands of muscle fibers can be stimulated from the initial input from a single motor neuron.

In a converging circuit, inputs from many sources are converged into one output, affecting just one neuron or a neuron pool. This type of circuit is exemplified in the respiratory center of the brainstem, which responds to a number of inputs from different sources by giving out an appropriate breathing pattern.

A reverberating circuit produces a repetitive output. In a signalling procedure from one neuron to another in a linear sequence, one of the neurons may send a signal back to initiating neuron. Each time that the first neuron fires, the other neuron further down the sequence fires again sending it back to the source. This restimulates the first neuron and also allows the path of transmission to continue to its output. A resulting repetitive pattern is the outcome that only stops if one or more of the synapses fail, or if an inhibitory feed from another source causes it to stop. This type of reverberating circuit is found in the respiratory center that sends signals to the respiratory muscles, causing inhalation. When the circuit is interrupted by an inhibitory signal the muscles relax causing exhalation. This type of circuit may play a part in epileptic seizures.

In a parallel after-discharge circuit, a neuron inputs to several chains of neurons. Each chain is made up of a different number of neurons but their signals converge onto one output neuron. Each synapse in the circuit acts to delay the signal by about 0.5 msec so that the more synapses there are will produce a longer delay to the output neuron. After the input has stopped, the output will go on firing for some time. This type of circuit does not have a feedback loop as does the reverberating circuit. Continued firing after the stimulus has stopped is called after-discharge. This circuit type is found in the reflex arcs of certain reflexes.

Study Methods

Different neuroimaging techniques have been developed to investigate the activity of neural circuits and networks. The use of "brain scanners" or functional neuroimaging to investigate the structure or function of the brain is common, either as simply a way of better assessing brain injury with high resolution pictures, or by examining the relative activations of different brain areas. Such technologies may include functional magnetic resonance imaging (fMRI), brain positron emission tomography (brain PET), and computed axial tomography (CAT) scans. Functional neuroimaging uses specific brain imaging technologies to take scans from the brain, usually when a person is doing a particular task, in an attempt to understand how the activation of particular brain areas is related to the task. In functional neuroimaging, especially fMRI, which measures hemodynamic activity (using BOLD-contrast imaging) which is closely linked to neural activity, PET, and electroencephalography (EEG) is used.

Connectionist models serve as a test platform for different hypotheses of representation, information processing, and signal transmission. Lesioning studies in such models, e.g. artificial neural networks, where parts of the nodes are deliberately destroyed to see how the network performs, can also yield important insights in the working of several cell assemblies. Similarly, simulations of dysfunctional neurotransmitters in neurological conditions (e.g., dopamine in the basal ganglia of Parkinson's patients) can yield insights into the underlying mechanisms for patterns of cognitive deficits observed in the particular patient group. Predictions from these models can be tested in patients or via pharmacological manipulations, and these studies can in turn be used to inform the models, making the process iterative.

Clinical Significance

Sometimes neural circuitries can become pathological and cause problems such as in Parkinson's disease when the basal ganglia are involved. Problems in the Papez circuit can also give rise to a number of neurodegenerative disorders including Parkinson's.

Neural Network

A neural network is a network or circuit of neurons, or in a modern sense, an artificial neural network, composed of artificial neurons or nodes. Thus a neural network is either a biological neural network, made up of real biological neurons, or an artificial neural network, for solving artificial intelligence (AI) problems. The connections of the biological neuron are modeled as weights. A positive weight reflects an excitatory connection, while negative values mean inhibitory connections. All inputs are modified by a weight and summed. This activity is referred as a linear combination. Finally, an activation function controls the amplitude of the output. For example, an acceptable range of output is usually between 0 and 1, or it could be −1 and 1.

These artificial networks may be used for predictive modeling, adaptive control and applications where they can be trained via a dataset. Self-learning resulting from experience can occur within networks, which can derive conclusions from a complex and seemingly unrelated set of information.

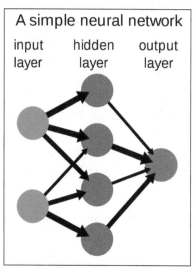

Simplified view of a feedforward artificial neural network.

A biological neural network is composed of a group or groups of chemically connected or functionally associated neurons. A single neuron may be connected to many other neurons and the total number of neurons and connections in a network may be extensive. Connections, called synapses, are usually formed from axons to dendrites, though dendrodendritic synapses and other connections are possible. Apart from the electrical signaling, there are other forms of signaling that arise from neurotransmitter diffusion.

Artificial intelligence, cognitive modeling, and neural networks are information processing paradigms inspired by the way biological neural systems process data. Artificial intelligence and cognitive modeling try to simulate some properties of biological neural networks. In the artificial intelligence field, artificial neural networks have been applied successfully to speech recognition, image analysis and adaptive control, in order to construct software agents (in computer and video games) or autonomous robots.

Historically, digital computers evolved from the von Neumann model, and operate via the execution of explicit instructions via access to memory by a number of processors. On the other hand, the origins of neural networks are based on efforts to model information processing in biological systems. Unlike the von Neumann model, neural network computing does not separate memory and processing.

Neural network theory has served both to better identify how the neurons in the brain function and to provide the basis for efforts to create artificial intelligence.

The preliminary theoretical base for contemporary neural networks was independently proposed by Alexander Bain and William James. In their work, both thoughts and body activity resulted from interactions among neurons within the brain.

Computer simulation of the branching architecture of the dendrites of pyramidal neurons.

For Bain, every activity led to the firing of a certain set of neurons. When activities were repeated, the connections between those neurons strengthened. According to his theory, this repetition was what led to the formation of memory. The general scientific community at the time was skeptical of Bain's theory because it required what appeared to be an inordinate number of neural connections within the brain. It is now apparent that the brain is exceedingly complex and that the same brain "wiring" can handle multiple problems and inputs.

James's theory was similar to Bain's, however, he suggested that memories and actions resulted from electrical currents flowing among the neurons in the brain. His model, by focusing on the flow of electrical currents, did not require individual neural connections for each memory or action.

C. S. Sherrington conducted experiments to test James's theory. He ran electrical currents down the spinal cords of rats. However, instead of demonstrating an increase in electrical current as projected by James, Sherrington found that the electrical current strength decreased as the testing continued over time. Importantly, this work led to the discovery of the concept of habituation.

McCulloch and Pitts created a computational model for neural networks based on mathematics and algorithms. They called this model threshold logic. The model paved the way for neural network research to split into two distinct approaches. One approach focused on biological processes in the brain and the other focused on the application of neural networks to artificial intelligence.

In the late 1940s psychologist Donald Hebb created a hypothesis of learning based on the mechanism of neural plasticity that is now known as Hebbian learning. Hebbian learning is considered to be a typical unsupervised learning rule and its later variants were early models for long term potentiation. These ideas started being applied to computational models in 1948 with Turing's B-type machines.

Farley and Clark first used computational machines, then called calculators, to simulate a Hebbian network at MIT. Other neural network computational machines were created by Rochester, Holland, Habit, and Duda.

Rosenblatt created the perceptron, an algorithm for pattern recognition based on a two-layer learning computer network using simple addition and subtraction. With mathematical notation, Rosenblatt also described circuitry not in the basic perceptron, such as the exclusive-or circuit, a circuit whose mathematical computation could not be processed until after the backpropagation algorithm was created by Werbos.

Neural network research stagnated after the publication of machine learning research by Marvin Minsky and Seymour Papert. They discovered two key issues with the computational machines that processed neural networks. The first issue was that single-layer neural networks were incapable of processing the exclusive-or circuit. The second significant issue was that computers were not sophisticated enough to effectively handle the long run time required by large neural networks. Neural network research slowed until computers achieved greater processing power. Also key in later advances was the backpropagation algorithm which effectively solved the exclusive or problem.

The parallel distributed processing of the mid-1980s became popular under the name connectionism. The text by Rumelhart and McClelland provided a full exposition on the use of connectionism in computers to simulate neural processes.

Neural networks, as used in artificial intelligence, have traditionally been viewed as simplified models of neural processing in the brain, even though the relation between this model and brain biological architecture is debated, as it is not clear to what degree artificial neural networks mirror brain function.

Artificial Intelligence

A neural network (NN), in the case of artificial neurons called artificial neural network (ANN) or simulated neural network (SNN), is an interconnected group of natural or artificial neurons that uses a mathematical or computational model for information processing based on a connectionistic approach to computation. In most cases an ANN is an adaptive system that changes its structure based on external or internal information that flows through the network.

In more practical terms neural networks are non-linear statistical data modeling or decision making tools. They can be used to model complex relationships between inputs and outputs or to find patterns in data.

An artificial neural network involves a network of simple processing elements (artificial neurons) which can exhibit complex global behavior, determined by the connections between the processing elements and element parameters. Artificial neurons were first proposed in 1943 by Warren McCulloch, a neurophysiologist, and Walter Pitts, a logician, who first collaborated at the University of Chicago.

One classical type of artificial neural network is the recurrent Hopfield network.

The concept of a neural network appears to have first been proposed by Alan Turing in his 1948 paper Intelligent Machinery in which called them "B-type unorganised machines".

The utility of artificial neural network models lies in the fact that they can be used to infer a function from observations and also to use it. Unsupervised neural networks can also be used to learn representations of the input that capture the salient characteristics of the input distribution, e.g., see the Boltzmann machine, and more recently, deep learning algorithms, which can implicitly learn the distribution function of the observed data. Learning in neural networks is particularly useful in applications where the complexity of the data or task makes the design of such functions by hand impractical.

Applications

Neural networks can be used in different fields. The tasks to which artificial neural networks are applied tend to fall within the following broad categories:

- Function approximation, or regression analysis, including time series prediction and modeling.

- Classification, including pattern and sequence recognition, novelty detection and sequential decision making.

- Data processing, including filtering, clustering, blind signal separation and compression.

Application areas of ANNs include nonlinear system identification and control (vehicle control, process control), game-playing and decision making (backgammon, chess, racing), pattern recognition (radar systems, face identification, object recognition), sequence recognition (gesture, speech, handwritten text recognition), medical diagnosis, financial applications, data mining (or knowledge discovery in databases, "KDD"), visualization and e-mail spam filtering. For example, it is possible to create a semantic profile of user's interests emerging from pictures trained for object recognition.

Neuroscience

Theoretical and computational neuroscience is the field concerned with the theoretical analysis and computational modeling of biological neural systems. Since neural systems are intimately related to cognitive processes and behaviour, the field is closely related to cognitive and behavioural modeling.

The aim of the field is to create models of biological neural systems in order to understand how biological systems work. To gain this understanding, neuroscientists strive to make a link between observed biological processes (data), biologically plausible mechanisms for neural processing and learning (biological neural network models) and theory (statistical learning theory and information theory).

Types of Models

Many models are used; defined at different levels of abstraction, and modeling different aspects of neural systems. They range from models of the short-term behaviour of individual neurons, through models of the dynamics of neural circuitry arising from interactions between individual neurons, to models of behaviour arising from abstract neural modules that represent complete subsystems. These include models of the long-term and short-term plasticity of neural systems and its relation to learning and memory, from the individual neuron to the system level.

SPINAL CORD

The spinal cord is a long, thin, tubular structure made up of nervous tissue, which extends from the medulla oblongata in the brainstem to the lumbar region of the vertebral column. It encloses the central canal of the spinal cord, which contains cerebrospinal fluid. The brain and spinal cord together make up the central nervous system (CNS). In humans, the spinal cord begins at the occipital bone, passing through the foramen magnum and entering the spinal canal at the beginning of the cervical vertebrae. The spinal cord extends down to between the first and second lumbar vertebrae, where it ends. The enclosing bony vertebral column protects the relatively shorter spinal cord. It is around 45 cm (18 in) in men and around 43 cm (17 in) long in women. The diameter of the spinal cord ranges from 13 mm ($\frac{1}{2}$ in) in the cervical and lumbar regions to 6.4 mm ($\frac{1}{4}$ in) in the thoracic area.

The spinal cord functions primarily in the transmission of nerve signals from the motor cortex to the body, and from the afferent fibers of the sensory neurons to the sensory cortex. It is also a center for coordinating many reflexes and contains reflex arcs that can independently control reflexes. It is also the location of groups of spinal interneurons that make up the neural circuits known as central pattern generators. These circuits are responsible for controlling motor instructions for rhythmic movements such as walking.

Structure

The spinal cord is the main pathway for information connecting the brain and peripheral nervous system. Much shorter than its protecting spinal column, the human spinal cord originates in the brainstem, passes through the foramen magnum, and continues through to the conus medullaris near the second lumbar vertebra before terminating in a fibrous extension known as the filum terminale.

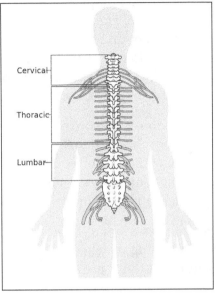

Diagram of the spinal cord showing segments.

It is about 45 cm (18 in) long in men and around 43 cm (17 in) in women, ovoid-shaped, and is enlarged in the cervical and lumbar regions. The cervical enlargement, stretching from the C5 to T1 vertebrae, is where sensory input comes from and motor output goes to the arms and trunk. The lumbar enlargement, located between L1 and S3, handles sensory input and motor output coming from and going to the legs.

The spinal cord is continuous with the caudal portion of the medulla, running from the base of the skull to the body of the first lumbar vertebra. It does not run the full length of the vertebral column in adults. It is made of 31 segments from which branch one pair of sensory nerve roots and one pair of motor nerve roots. The nerve roots then merge into bilaterally symmetrical pairs of spinal nerves. The peripheral nervous system is made up of these spinal roots, nerves, and ganglia.

The dorsal roots are afferent fascicles, receiving sensory information from the skin, muscles, and visceral organs to be relayed to the brain. The roots terminate in dorsal root ganglia, which are composed of the cell bodies of the corresponding neurons. Ventral roots consist of efferent fibers that arise from motor neurons whose cell bodies are found in the ventral (or anterior) gray horns of the spinal cord.

The spinal cord (and brain) are protected by three layers of tissue or membranes called meninges, that surround the canal . The dura mater is the outermost layer, and it forms a tough protective coating. Between the dura mater and the surrounding bone of the vertebrae is a space called the epidural space. The epidural space is filled with adipose tissue, and it contains a network of blood vessels. The arachnoid mater, the middle protective layer, is named for its open, spiderweb-like appearance. The space between the arachnoid and the underlying pia mater is called the subarachnoid space. The subarachnoid space contains cerebrospinal fluid (CSF), which can be sampled with a lumbar puncture, or "spinal tap" procedure. The delicate pia mater, the innermost protective layer, is tightly associated with the surface of the spinal cord. The cord is stabilized within the dura mater by the connecting denticulate ligaments, which extend from the enveloping pia mater laterally between the dorsal and ventral roots. The dural sac ends at the vertebral level of the second sacral vertebra.

In cross-section, the peripheral region of the cord contains neuronal white matter tracts containing sensory and motor axons. Internal to this peripheral region is the grey matter, which contains the nerve cell bodies arranged in the three grey columns that give the region its butterfly-shape. This central region surrounds the central canal, which is an extension of the fourth ventricle and contains cerebrospinal fluid.

The spinal cord is elliptical in cross section, being compressed dorsolaterally. Two prominent grooves, or sulci, run along its length. The posterior median sulcus is the groove in the dorsal side, and the anterior median fissure is the groove in the ventral side.

Spinal Cord Segments

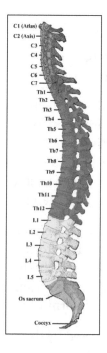

The human spinal cord is divided into segments where pairs of spinal nerves (mixed; sensory and motor) form. Six to eight motor nerve rootlets branch out of right and left ventro lateral sulci in a very orderly manner. Nerve rootlets combine to form nerve roots. Likewise, sensory nerve rootlets form off right and left dorsal lateral sulci and form sensory nerve roots. The ventral (motor) and dorsal (sensory) roots combine to form spinal nerves (mixed; motor and sensory), one on each side of the spinal cord. Spinal nerves, with the exception of C1 and C2, form inside the intervertebral foramen (IVF). These rootlets form the demarcation between the central and peripheral nervous systems.

A model of segments of the human spine and spinal cord, nerve roots
can be seen extending laterally from the (not visible) spinal cord.

The grey column, (as three regions of grey columns) in the center of the cord, is shaped like a butterfly and consists of cell bodies of interneurons, motor neurons, neuroglia cells and unmyelinated axons. The anterior and posterior grey column present as projections of the grey matter and are also known as the horns of the spinal cord. Together, the grey columns and the gray commissure form the "grey H".

The white matter is located outside of the grey matter and consists almost totally of myelinated motor and sensory axons. "Columns" of white matter carry information either up or down the spinal cord.

The spinal cord proper terminates in a region called the conus medullaris, while the pia mater continues as an extension called the filum terminale, which anchors the spinal cord to the coccyx. The cauda equina ("horse's tail") is a collection of nerves inferior to the conus medullaris that continue to travel through the vertebral column to the coccyx. The cauda equina forms because the spinal cord stops growing in length at about age four, even though the vertebral column continues to lengthen until adulthood. This results in sacral spinal nerves originating in the upper lumbar region.

Within the CNS, nerve cell bodies are generally organized into functional clusters, called nuclei. Axons within the CNS are grouped into tracts.

There are 31 spinal cord nerve segments in a human spinal cord:

- 8 cervical segments forming 8 pairs of cervical nerves (C1 spinal nerves exit the spinal column between the foramen magnum and the C1 vertebra; C2 nerves exit between the posterior arch of the C1 vertebra and the lamina of C2; C3–C8 spinal nerves pass through the IVF above their corresponding cervical vertebrae, with the exception of the C8 pair which exit between the C7 and T1 vertebrae).

- 12 thoracic segments forming 12 pairs of thoracic nerves.

- 5 lumbar segments forming 5 pairs of lumbar nerves.

- 5 sacral segments forming 5 pairs of sacral nerves.

- 1 coccygeal segment.

Spinal cord segments in some common species					
Species	Cervical	Thoracic	Lumbar	Sacral	Caudal/Coccygeal	Total
Dog	8	13	7	3	5	36
Cat	8	13	7	3	5	36
Cow	8	13	6	5	5	37
Horse	8	18	6	5	5	42
Pig	8	15/14	6/7	4	5	38
Human	8	12	5	5	1	31
Mouse	8	13	6	4	3	35

In the fetus, vertebral segments correspond with spinal cord segments. However, because the vertebral column grows longer than the spinal cord, spinal cord segments do not correspond to vertebral segments in the adult, particularly in the lower spinal cord. For example, lumbar and sacral spinal cord segments are found between vertebral levels T9 and L2, and the spinal cord ends around the L1/L2 vertebral level, forming a structure known as the conus medullaris.

Although the spinal cord cell bodies end around the L1/L2 vertebral level, the spinal nerves for each segment exit at the level of the corresponding vertebra. For the nerves of the lower spinal cord, this means that they exit the vertebral column much lower (more caudally) than their roots. As these nerves travel from their respective roots to their point of exit from the vertebral column, the nerves of the lower spinal segments form a bundle called the cauda equina.

There are two regions where the spinal cord enlarges:

- Cervical enlargement: Corresponds roughly to the brachial plexus nerves, which innervate the upper limb. It includes spinal cord segments from about C4 to T1. The vertebral levels of the enlargement are roughly the same (C4 to T1).

- Lumbar enlargement: Corresponds to the lumbosacral plexus nerves, which innervate the lower limb. It comprises the spinal cord segments from L2 to S3 and is found about the vertebral levels of T9 to T12.

Development

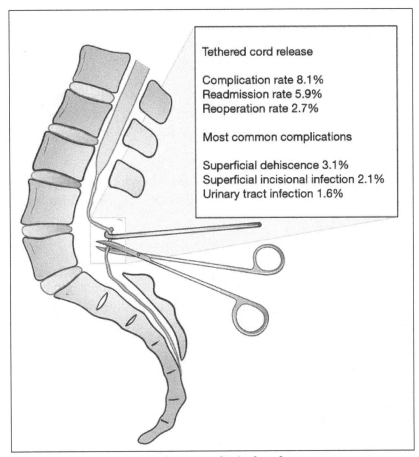

Tethered cord release

Complication rate 8.1%
Readmission rate 5.9%
Reoperation rate 2.7%

Most common complications

Superficial dehiscence 3.1%
Superficial incisional infection 2.1%
Urinary tract infection 1.6%

Development of Spinal cord.

The spinal cord is made from part of the neural tube during development. There are four stages of the spinal cord that arises from the neural tube: The neural plate, neural fold, neural tube, and the spinal cord. Neural differentiation occurs within the spinal cord portion of the tube. As the neural tube begins to develop, the notochord begins to secrete a factor known as Sonic hedgehog or SHH. As a result, the floor plate then also begins to secrete SHH, and this will induce the basal plate to develop motor neurons. During the maturation of the neural tube, its lateral walls thicken and form a longtitudinal groove called the sulcus limitans. This extends the length of the spinal cord into dorsal and ventral portions as well. Meanwhile, the overlying ectoderm secretes bone morphogenetic protein (BMP). This induces the roof plate to begin to secrete BMP, which will induce the alar plate to develop sensory neurons. Opposing gradients of such morphogens as BMP and SHH form different domains of dividing cells along the dorsal ventral axis. Dorsal root ganglion neurons differentiate from neural crest progenitors. As the dorsal and ventral column cells proliferate, the lumen of the neural tube narrows to form the small central canal of the spinal cord. The alar plate and the basal plate are separated by the sulcus limitans. Additionally, the floor plate also secretes netrins.

The netrins act as chemoattractants to decussation of pain and temperature sensory neurons in the alar plate across the anterior white commissure, where they then ascend towards the thalamus. Following the closure of the caudal neuropore and formation of the brain's ventricles that contain the choroid plexus tissue, the central canal of the caudal spinal cord is filled with cerebrospinal fluid.

Earlier findings by Viktor Hamburger and Rita Levi-Montalcini in the chick embryo have been confirmed by more recent studies which have demonstrated that the elimination of neuronal cells by programmed cell death (PCD) is necessary for the correct assembly of the nervous system.

Overall, spontaneous embryonic activity has been shown to play a role in neuron and muscle development but is probably not involved in the initial formation of connections between spinal neurons.

Blood Supply

The spinal cord is supplied with blood by three arteries that run along its length starting in the brain, and many arteries that approach it through the sides of the spinal column. The three longitudinal arteries are the anterior spinal artery, and the right and left posterior spinal arteries. These travel in the subarachnoid space and send branches into the spinal cord. They form anastamoses (connections) via the anterior and posterior segmental medullary arteries, which enter the spinal cord at various points along its length. The actual blood flow caudally through these arteries, derived from the posterior cerebral circulation, is inadequate to maintain the spinal cord beyond the cervical segments.

The major contribution to the arterial blood supply of the spinal cord below the cervical region comes from the radially arranged posterior and anterior radicular arteries, which run into the spinal cord alongside the dorsal and ventral nerve roots, but with one exception do not connect directly with any of the three longitudinal arteries. These intercostal and lumbar radicular arteries arise from the aorta, provide major anastomoses and supplement the blood flow to the spinal cord. In humans the largest of the anterior radicular arteries is known as the artery of Adamkiewicz, or anterior radicularis magna (ARM) artery, which usually arises between L1 and L2, but can arise anywhere from T9 to L5. Impaired blood flow through these critical radicular arteries, especially during surgical procedures that involve abrupt disruption of blood flow through the aorta for example during aortic aneursym repair, can result in spinal cord infarction and paraplegia.

Function

Somatosensory Organization

Somatosensory organization is divided into the dorsal column-medial lemniscus tract (the touch/proprioception/vibration sensory pathway) and the anterolateral system, or ALS (the pain/temperature sensory pathway). Both sensory pathways use three different neurons to get information from sensory receptors at the periphery to the cerebral cortex. These neurons are designated primary, secondary and tertiary sensory neurons. In both pathways, primary sensory neuron cell bodies are found in the dorsal root ganglia, and their central axons project into the spinal cord.

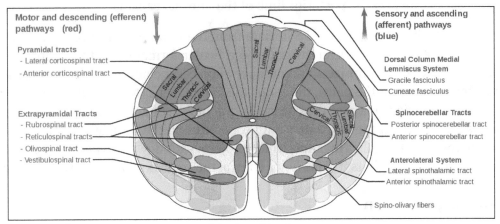

Spinal cord tracts.

In the dorsal column-medial leminiscus tract, a primary neuron's axon enters the spinal cord and then enters the dorsal column. If the primary axon enters below spinal level T6, the axon travels in the fasciculus gracilis, the medial part of the column. If the axon enters above level T6, then it travels in the fasciculus cuneatus, which is lateral to the fasciculus gracilis. Either way, the primary axon ascends to the lower medulla, where it leaves its fasciculus and synapses with a secondary neuron in one of the dorsal column nuclei: either the nucleus gracilis or the nucleus cuneatus, depending on the pathway it took. At this point, the secondary axon leaves its nucleus and passes anteriorly and medially. The collection of secondary axons that do this are known as internal arcuate fibers. The internal arcuate fibers decussate and continue ascending as the contralateral medial lemniscus. Secondary axons from the medial lemniscus finally terminate in the ventral posterolateral nucleus (VPLN) of the thalamus, where they synapse with tertiary neurons. From there, tertiary neurons ascend via the posterior limb of the internal capsule and end in the primary sensory cortex.

The proprioception of the lower limbs differs from the upper limbs and upper trunk. There is a four-neuron pathway for lower limb proprioception. This pathway initially follows the dorsal spino-cerebellar pathway. It is arranged as follows:

> "Proprioceptive receptors of lower limb → peripheral process → dorsal root ganglion → central process → Clarke's column → 2nd order neuron → medulla oblogata (Caudate nucleus) → 3rd order neuron → VPLN of thalamus → 4th order neuron → posterior limb of internal capsule → corona radiata → sensory area of cerebrum."

The anterolateral system works somewhat differently. Its primary neurons axons enter the spinal cord and then ascend one to two levels before synapsing in the substantia gelatinosa. The tract that ascends before synapsing is known as Lissauer's tract. After synapsing, secondary axons decussate and ascend in the anterior lateral portion of the spinal cord as the spinothalamic tract. This tract ascends all the way to the VPLN, where it synapses on tertiary neurons. Tertiary neuronal axons then travel to the primary sensory cortex via the posterior limb of the internal capsule.

Some of the "pain fibers" in the ALS deviate from their pathway towards the VPLN. In one such deviation, axons travel towards the reticular formation in the midbrain. The reticular formation then projects to a number of places including the hippocampus (to create memories about the pain), the centromedian nucleus (to cause diffuse, non-specific pain) and various parts of the cortex. Additionally, some ALS axons project to the periaqueductal gray in the pons, and the axons forming the periaqueductal gray then project to the nucleus raphes magnus, which projects back down to where the pain signal is coming from and inhibits it. This helps control the sensation of pain to some degree.

Motor Organization

Actions of the spinal nerves edit	
Level	Motor function
C1–C6	Neck flexors
C1–T1	Neck extensors
C3, C4, C5	Supply diaphragm (mostly C4)
C5, C6	Move shoulder, raise arm (deltoid); flex elbow (biceps)
C6	Externally rotate (supinate) the arm
C6, C7	Extend elbow and wrist (triceps and wrist extensors); pronate wrist
C7, C8	Flex wrist; supply small muscles of the hand
T1–T6	Intercostals and trunk above the waist
T7–L1	Abdominal muscles
L1–L4	Flex hip joint
L2, L3, L4	Adduct thigh; Extend leg at the knee (quadriceps femoris)
L4, L5, S1	Abduct thigh; Flex leg at the knee (hamstrings); Dorsiflex foot (tibialis anterior); Extend toes
L5, S1, S2	Extend leg at the hip (gluteus maximus); flex foot and flex toes

The corticospinal tract serves as the motor pathway for upper motor neuronal signals coming from the cerebral cortex and from primitive brainstem motor nuclei.

Cortical upper motor neurons originate from Brodmann areas 1, 2, 3, 4, and 6 and then descend in the posterior limb of the internal capsule, through the crus cerebri, down through the pons, and to the medullary pyramids, where about 90% of the axons cross to the contralateral side at the decussation of the pyramids. They then descend as the lateral corticospinal tract. These axons synapse with lower motor neurons in the ventral horns of all levels of the spinal cord. The remaining 10% of axons descend on the ipsilateral side as the ventral corticospinal tract. These axons also synapse with lower motor neurons in the ventral horns. Most of them will cross to the contralateral side of the cord (via the anterior white commissure) right before synapsing.

The midbrain nuclei include four motor tracts that send upper motor neuronal axons down the spinal cord to lower motor neurons. These are the rubrospinal tract, the vestibulospinal tract, the tectospinal tract and the reticulospinal tract. The rubrospinal tract descends with the lateral corticospinal tract, and the remaining three descend with the anterior corticospinal tract.

The function of lower motor neurons can be divided into two different groups: the lateral corticospinal tract and the anterior cortical spinal tract. The lateral tract contains upper motor neuronal axons which synapse on dorsal lateral (DL) lower motor neurons. The DL neurons are involved in distal limb control. Therefore, these DL neurons are found specifically only in the cervical and lumbosacral enlargements within the spinal cord. There is no decussation in the lateral corticospinal tract after the decussation at the medullary pyramids.

The anterior corticospinal tract descends ipsilaterally in the anterior column, where the axons emerge and either synapse on lower ventromedial (VM) motor neurons in the ventral horn ipsilaterally or descussate at the anterior white commissure where they synapse on VM lower motor neurons contralaterally . The tectospinal, vestibulospinal and reticulospinal descend ipsilaterally in the anterior column but do not synapse across the anterior white commissure. Rather, they only synapse on VM lower motor neurons ipsilaterally. The VM lower motor neurons control the large, postural muscles of the axial skeleton. These lower motor neurons, unlike those of the DL, are located in the ventral horn all the way throughout the spinal cord.

Spinocerebellar Tracts

Proprioceptive information in the body travels up the spinal cord via three tracks. Below L2, the proprioceptive information travels up the spinal cord in the ventral spinocerebellar tract. Also known as the anterior spinocerebellar tract, sensory receptors take in the information and travel into the spinal cord. The cell bodies of these primary neurons are located in the dorsal root ganglia. In the spinal cord, the axons synapse and the secondary neuronal axons decussates and then travel up to the superior cerebellar peduncle where they decussate again. From here, the information is brought to deep nuclei of the cerebellum including the fastigial and interposed nuclei.

From the levels of L2 to T1, proprioceptive information enters the spinal cord and ascends ipsilaterally, where it synapses in Clarke's nucleus. The secondary neuronal axons continue to ascend ipsilaterally and then pass into the cerebellum via the inferior cerebellar peduncle. This tract is known as the dorsal spinocerebellar tract.

From above T1, proprioceptive primary axons enter the spinal cord and ascend ipsilaterally until reaching the accessory cuneate nucleus, where they synapse. The secondary axons pass into the cerebellum via the inferior cerebellar peduncle where again, these axons synapse on cerebellar deep nuclei. This tract is known as the cuneocerebellar tract.

Motor information travels from the brain down the spinal cord via descending spinal cord tracts. Descending tracts involve two neurons: the upper motor neuron (UMN) and lower motor neuron (LMN). A nerve signal travels down the upper motor neuron until it synapses with the lower motor neuron in the spinal cord. Then, the lower motor neuron conducts the nerve signal to the spinal root where efferent nerve fibers carry the motor signal toward the target muscle. The descending tracts are composed of white matter. There are several descending tracts serving different functions. The corticospinal tracts (lateral and anterior) are responsible for coordinated limb movements.

Clinical Significance

A congenital disorder is diastematomyelia in which part of the spinal cord is split usually at the level of the upper lumbar vertebrae. Sometimes the split can be along the length of the spinal cord.

Injury

Spinal cord injuries can be caused by trauma to the spinal column (stretching, bruising, applying pressure, severing, laceration, etc.). The vertebral bones or intervertebral disks can shatter, causing the spinal cord to be punctured by a sharp fragment of bone. Usually, victims of spinal cord injuries will suffer loss of feeling in certain parts of their body. In milder cases, a victim might only suffer loss of hand or foot function. More severe injuries may result in paraplegia, tetraplegia (also known as quadriplegia), or full body paralysis below the site of injury to the spinal cord.

Damage to upper motor neuron axons in the spinal cord results in a characteristic pattern of ipsilateral deficits. These include hyperreflexia, hypertonia and muscle weakness. Lower motor neuronal damage results in its own characteristic pattern of deficits. Rather than an entire side of deficits, there is a pattern relating to the myotome affected by the damage. Additionally, lower motor neurons are characterized by muscle weakness, hypotonia, hyporeflexia and muscle atrophy.

Spinal shock and neurogenic shock can occur from a spinal injury. Spinal shock is usually temporary, lasting only for 24–48 hours, and is a temporary absence of sensory and motor functions. Neurogenic shock lasts for weeks and can lead to a loss of muscle tone due to disuse of the muscles below the injured site.

The two areas of the spinal cord most commonly injured are the cervical spine (C1–C7) and the lumbar spine (L1–L5). (The notation C1, C7, L1, L5 refer to the location of a specific vertebra in either the cervical, thoracic, or lumbar region of the spine.) Spinal cord injury can also be non-traumatic and caused by disease (transverse myelitis, polio, spina bifida, Friedreich's ataxia, spinal cord tumor, spinal stenosis etc.

In the U.S., 10,000–12,000 people become paralyzed annually as a result of various injuries to the spinal cord.

Treatment

Real or suspected spinal cord injuries need immediate immobilisation including that of the head. Scans will be needed to assess the injury. A steroid, methylprednisolone, can be of help as can physical therapy and possibly antioxidants. Treatments need to focus on limiting post-injury cell death, promoting cell regeneration, and replacing lost cells. Regeneration is facilitated by maintaining electric transmission in neural elements.

Lumbar Puncture

The spinal cord ends at the level of vertebrae L1–L2, while the subarachnoid space the compartment that contains cerebrospinal fluid— extends down to the lower border of S2. Lumbar punctures in adults are usually performed between L3–L5 (cauda equina level) in order to avoid damage to the spinal cord. In the fetus, the spinal cord extends the full length of the spine and regresses as the body grows.

Tumours

Spinal tumours can occur in the spinal cord and these can be either inside (intradural) or outside (extradural) the dura mater.

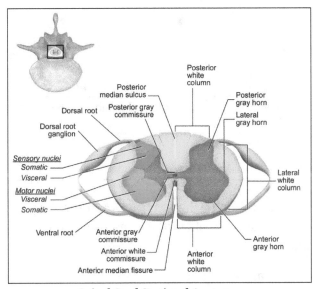

Spinal Cord Sectional Anatomy.

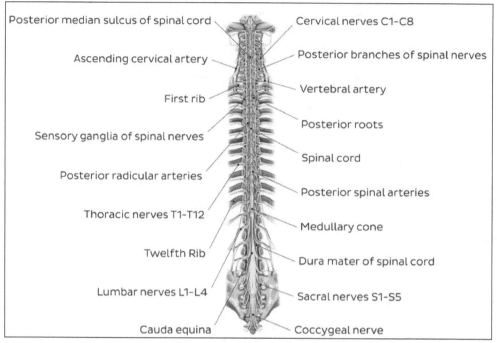

Posterior median sulcus of spinal cord

Ascending cervical artery

First rib

Sensory ganglia of spinal nerves

Posterior radicular arteries

Thoracic nerves T1-T12

Twelfth Rib

Lumbar nerves L1-L4

Cauda equina

Cervical nerves C1-C8

Posterior branches of spinal nerves

Vertebral artery

Posterior roots

Spinal cord

Posterior spinal arteries

Medullary cone

Dura mater of spinal cord

Sacral nerves S1-S5

Coccygeal nerve

Diagrams of the spinal cord.

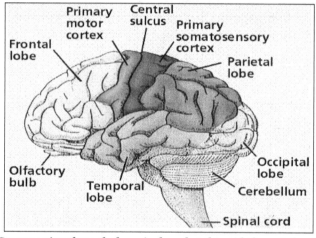

Primary motor cortex

Central sulcus

Primary somatosensory cortex

Frontal lobe

Parietal lobe

Olfactory bulb

Temporal lobe

Occipital lobe

Cerebellum

Spinal cord

Cross-section through the spinal cord at the mid-thoracic level.

BRAIN

Brain is the mass of nerve tissue in the anterior end of an organism. The brain integrates sensory information and directs motor responses; in higher vertebrates it is also the centre of learning.

In lower vertebrates the brain is tubular and resembles an early developmental stage of the brain in higher vertebrates. It consists of three distinct regions: the hindbrain, the midbrain, and the forebrain. Although the brain of higher vertebrates undergoes considerable modification during embryonic development, these three regions are still discernible.

The hindbrain is composed of the medulla oblongata and the pons. The medulla transmits signals between the spinal cord and the higher parts of the brain; it also controls such autonomic functions as heartbeat and respiration. The pons is partly made up of tracts connecting the spinal cord with higher brain levels, and it also contains cell groups that transfer information from the cerebrum to the cerebellum.

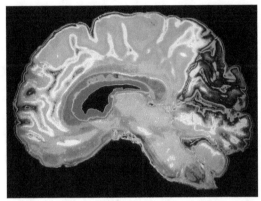

Human brain; magnetic resonance imaging (MRI): An image of the
human brain produced using magnetic resonance imaging (MRI).

The midbrain, the upper portion of which evolved from the optic lobes, is the main centre of sensory integration in fish and amphibians. It also is involved with integration in reptiles and birds. In mammals the midbrain is greatly reduced, serving primarily as a connecting link between the hindbrain and the forebrain.

Connected to the medulla, pons, and midbrain by large bundles of fibres is the cerebellum. Relatively large in humans, this "little brain" controls balance and coordination by producing smooth, coordinated movements of muscle groups.

The forebrain includes the cerebral hemispheres and, under these, the brainstem, which contains the thalamus and hypothalamus. The thalamus is the main relay centre between the medulla and the cerebrum; the hypothalamus is an important control centre for sex drive, pleasure, pain, hunger, thirst, blood pressure, body temperature, and other visceral functions. The hypothalamus produces hormones that control the secretions of the anterior pituitary gland, and it also produces oxytocin and antidiuretic hormone, which are stored in and released by the posterior pituitary gland.

The cerebrum, originally functioning as part of the olfactory lobes, is involved with the more complex functions of the human brain. In humans and other advanced vertebrates, the cerebrum has grown over the rest of the brain, forming a convoluted (wrinkled) layer of gray matter. The degree of convolution is partly dependent on the size of the body. Small mammals (e.g., lesser anteater, marmoset) generally have smooth brains, and large mammals (e.g., whale, elephant, dolphin) generally have highly convoluted ones.

The cerebral hemispheres are separated by a deep groove, the longitudinal cerebral fissure. At the base of this fissure lies a thick bundle of nerve fibres, called the corpus callosum, which provides a communication link between the hemispheres. The left hemisphere controls the right half of the body, and vice versa, because of a crossing of the nerve fibres in the medulla or, less commonly, in the spinal cord. Although the right and left hemispheres are mirror images of one another in many ways, there are important functional distinctions. In most people, for example, the areas that control speech are located in the left hemisphere, while areas that control spatial perceptions are located in the right hemisphere.

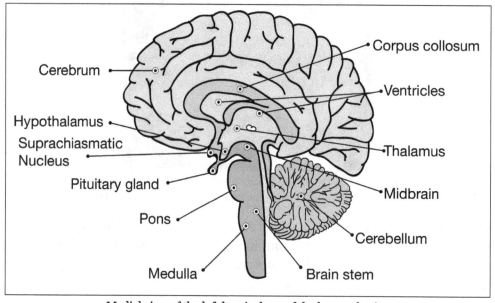

Medial view of the left hemisphere of the human brain.

Two major furrows—the central sulcus and the lateral sulcus—divide each cerebral hemisphere into four sections: the frontal, parietal, temporal, and occipital lobes. The central sulcus, also known as the fissure of Rolando, also separates the cortical motor area (which is anterior to the fissure) from the cortical sensory area (which is posterior to the fissure). Starting from the top of the hemisphere, the upper regions of the motor and sensory areas control the lower parts of the body, and the lower regions of the motor and sensory areas control the upper parts of the body. Other functional areas of the cerebral hemispheres have been identified, including the visual cortex in the occipital lobe and the auditory cortex in the temporal lobe. A large amount of the primate cortex, however, is devoted to no specific motor or sensory function; this so-called association cortex is apparently involved in higher mental activities.

References

- Südhof, TC (2 November 2017). "Synaptic Neurexin Complexes: A Molecular Code for the Logic of Neural Circuits". Cell. 171 (4): 745–769. Doi:10.1016/j.cell.2017.10.024. PMC 5694349. PMID 29100073

- Types-neurons, brain-anatomy, brain: edu.au, Retrieved 31 March, 2019

- Purves, Dale (2011). Neuroscience (5th ed.). Sunderland, Mass.: Sinauer. P. 507. ISBN 9780878936953

- Neurons, boundless-psychology: lumenlearning.com, Retrieved 14 July, 2019

- Yang, J. J.; et al. (2008). "Memristive switching mechanism for metal/oxide/metal nanodevices". Nat. Nanotechnol. 3 (7): 429–433. Doi:10.1038/nnano.2008.160. PMID 18654568

- Squire, Larry Squire; et al. (2013). Fundamental neuroscience (4th ed.). Amsterdam: Elsevier/ Academic Press. P. 628. ISBN 978-0-12-385-870-2

- Cowan, WM (2001). "Viktor Hamburger and Rita Levi-Montalcini: the path to the discovery of nerve growth factor". Annual Review of Neuroscience. 24: 551–600. Doi:10.1146/annurev.neuro.24.1.551. PMID 11283321

- Brain, science: britannica.com, Retrieved 17 May, 2019

3

Models used in Computational Neuroscience

There are various types of models used in computational neuroscience. Some of these include FitzHugh–Nagumo model, Hindmarsh–Rose model, Galves–Löcherbach model, Dehaene–Changeux model, Wilson–Cowan model and Morris–Lecar model. The diverse applications of these models in computational neuroscience have been thoroughly discussed in this chapter.

FITZHUGH–NAGUMO MODEL

The Fitzhugh–Nagumo (FHN) model is a mathematical model of neuronal excitability developed by Richard Fitzhugh as a reduction of the Hodgkin and Huxley's model of action potential generation in the squid giant axon. Nagumo et al. subsequently designed, implemented, and analyzed an equivalent electric circuit.

In its basic form, the model consists of two coupled, nonlinear ordinary differential equations, one of which describes the fast evolution of the neuronal membrane voltage, the other representing the slower "recovery" action of sodium channel deinactivation and potassium channel deactivation. Phase plane analysis of the FHN model provides qualitative explanations of several aspects of the excitability exhibited by the Hodgkin–Huxley (HH) model, including all-or-none spiking, excitation block, and the apparent absence of a firing threshold.

$$\dot{V} = V - V^3 / 3 - W + I$$
$$\dot{W} = 0.08(V + 0.7 - 0.8W)$$

This model refers to two-dimensional simplification of the Hodgkin-Huxley model of spike generation in squid giant axons. Here,

- V is the membrane potential,
- W is a recovery variable,
- I is the magnitude of stimulus current.

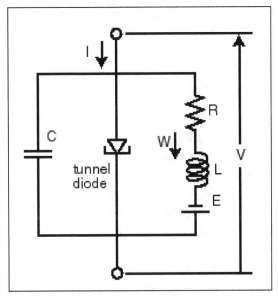

Circuit diagram of the tunnel-diode nerve model.

Principal Assumptions

The motivation for the Fitzhugh-Nagumo model was to isolate conceptually the essentially mathematical properties of excitation and propagation from the electrochemical properties of sodium and potassium ion flow. The model consists of:

- A *voltage-like variable* having cubic nonlinearity that allows regenerative self-excitation via a positive feedback, and

- A *recovery variable* having a linear dynamics that provides a slower negative feedback.

The model is sometimes written in the abstract form:

$$\dot{V} = f(V) - W + Ia$$
$$\dot{W} = a(bV - cW)$$

where $f(V)$ is a polynomial of third degree, and a, b, and c are constant parameters (notice that a constant term in the second equation can be removed by a linear shift of V or W; also one of the constants, b or c could be assumed to be 1).

Fitzhugh modified the van der Pol model to explain the basic properties of excitability as exhibited by the more complex HH equations. The nullclines of the van der Pol equation are a vertical line and a cubic that intersect in a single rest point which is always unstable. In order to resemble a real nerve, this new model should also have only one restpoint, now basically stable, and display a threshold phenomenon for a parameter change that preferably should look like 'current stimulation'. He realized that the slope of a rotated version of the linear isocline figures in the stability condition of the rest-point. That enables the construction of a model with a stable restpoint by the addition of a linear term cW to the second equation of the van der Pol model. Fitzhugh restricted that slope b/c to the set of cases with only one intersection with the cubic, staying out of the complexities of a more general case.

Adding a constant term to the second equation allowed him to shift the restpoint along the cubic. That restpoint is now always stable on the ascending parts but with the parameters involved in the stability properties on the descending middle limb. One may verify that adding another constant term to the first equation instead of adding one to the second has the same effect. Formally, this would be a minimal and sufficient parametrization to display all the properties explained below. However, to make the model a bit more palatable for physiologists, both equations got a constant term I in the first equation, mimicking the experimental injection of external current into the membrane; the second equation got another, mathematically redundant, constant c. It ensures that the restpoint for $I=0$ (no stimulation) lies on the right ascending branch and is stable.

Phenomena

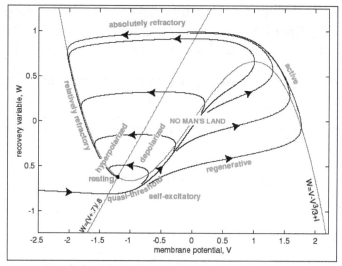

Phase portrait and physiological state diagram of Fitzhugh-Nagumo model.

While the Hodgkin-Huxley Model is more realistic and biophysically sound, only projections of its four-dimensional phase trajectories can be observed. The simplicity of the Fitzhugh-Nagumo model permits the entire solution to be viewed at once. This allows a geometrical explanation of important biological phenomena related to neuronal excitability and spike-generating mechanism.

- V-nullcline, which is the N-shaped curve obtained from the condition $\dot{V} = 0$, where the sign of $\dot{V}$ passes through zero,

- W-nullcline, which is a straight line obtained from the condition $\dot{W}=0$, where the sign of $\dot{W}$ passes through zero, and

- Some typical trajectories starting with various initial conditions.

The intersection of nullclines is an equilibrium (because $\dot{V}=\dot{W}=0$), which may be unstable if it is on the middle branch of the V-nullcline, i.e., when I is strong enough. In this case, the model exhibits periodic (tonic spiking) activity.

The "no man's land" region of the phase space is highly unstable, containing trajectories starting very close to the quasi-threshold.

Absence of All-or-None Spikes

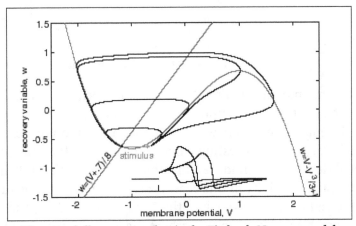

Absence of all-or-none spikes in the Fitzhugh-Nagumo model.

The Fitzhugh-Nagumo model explained the absence of all-or-none spikes in the HH model in response to stimuli, i.e., pulses of the injected current I. Weak stimuli (small pulses of I) result in small-amplitude trajectories that correspond to subthreshold responses; stronger stimuli result in intermediate-amplitude trajectories that correspond to partial-amplitude spikes; and strong stimuli result in large amplitude trajectories that correspond to suprathreshold response firing a spike.

Absence of Threshold

Similarly to the HH model, Fitzhugh-Nagumo model does not have a well-defined firing threshold. This feature is the consequence of the absence of all-or-none responses, and it is related, from the mathematical point of view, to the absence of a saddle equilibrium. The apparent illusion of threshold dynamics and all-or-none responses in both models is due to the existence of the "quasi-threshold", which is a canard trajectory that follows the unstable (middle) branch of the N-shaped V-nullcline. Nearby trajectories diverge sharply away from the canard trajectory to the left or right, producing an apparently "all-or-none" response and threshold-like behavior. (A point moving along a canard trajectory is like a tightrope walker walking slowly along a rope; if he loses his balance, he quickly falls away from the rope to one side or the other).

Excitation Block

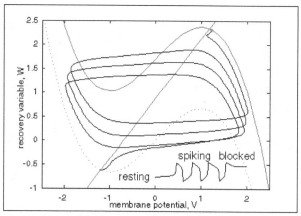

Excitation block in the Fitzhugh-Nagumo model.

The Fitzhugh-Nagumo model explains the excitation block phenomenon, i.e., the cessation of repetitive spiking as the amplitude of the stimulus current increases. When I is weak or zero, the equilibrium (intersection of nullclines) is on the left (stable) branch of V-nullcline, and the model is resting. Increasing I shifts the nullcline upward and the equilibrium slides onto the middle (unstable) branch of the nullcline. The model exhibits periodic spiking activity in this case. Increasing the stimulus further shifts the equilibrium to the right (stable) branch of the N-shaped nullcline, and the oscillations are blocked (by excitation). The precise mathematical mechanism involves appearance and disappearance of a limit cycle attractor.

Anodal Break Excitation

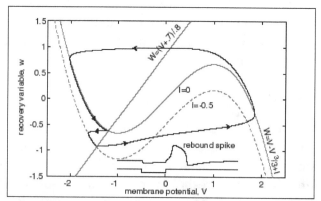

Anodal break excitation (post-inhibitory rebound spike) in the Fitzhugh-Nagumo model.

The Fitzhugh-Nagumo model explained the phenomenon of post-inhibitory (rebound) spikes, called anodal break excitation at that time. As the stimulus I becomes negative (hyperpolarization), the resting state shifts to the left. As the system is released from hyperpolarization (anodal break), the trajectory starts from a point far below the resting state, makes a large-amplitude excursion, i.e., fires a transient spike, and then returns to the resting state.

Spike Accommodation

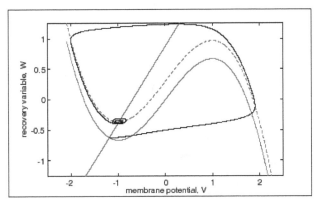

Spike accommodation to slowly increasing stimulus in the Fitzhugh-Nagumo model.

The Fitzhugh-Nagumo model explained the dynamical mechanism of *spike accommodation* in HH-type models. When stimulation strength I increases slowly, the neuron remains quiescent. The resting equilibrium of the Fitzhugh-Nagumo model shifts slowly to the right, and the state of the system follows it smoothly without firing spikes. In contrast, when the stimulation is increased abruptly, even by a smaller amount, the trajectory could not go directly to the new resting state, but fires a transient spike; Geometrically, this phenomenon is similar to the post-inhibitory (rebound) response.

Traveling pulse the Fitzhugh-Nagumo reaction-diffusion model. All spatial points are projected onto their V and W coordinates, so that the traveling pulse looks like a circle on the phase plane (notice that because of the diffusion term, the points do not exhibit relaxation oscillations).

Traveling Waves

The Fitzhugh-Nagumo equations became a favorite model for reaction-diffusion systems:

$$\dot{V} = f(V) - W + I + V_{xx}$$
$$\dot{W} = a(bV - cW)$$

which simulate propagation of waves in excitable media, such as heart tissue or nerve fiber. Here, the diffusion term V_{xx} is the second derivative with respect to spatial variable x. Its success is mostly due to the fact that the model is analytically tractable, and hence it allows derivation of many important properties of traveling pulses without resort to computer simulations.

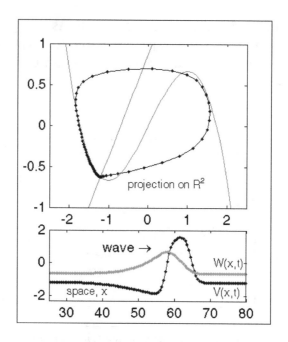

HIND MARSH–ROSE MODEL

The Hindmarsh–Rose model of neuronal activity is aimed to study the spiking-bursting behavior of the membrane potential observed in experiments made with a single neuron. The relevant variable is the membrane potential, $x(t)$, which is written in dimensionless units. There are two more variables, $y(t)$ and $z(t)$, which take into account the transport of ions across the membrane through the ion channels. The transport of sodium and potassium ions is made through fast ion channels and its rate is measured by $y(t)$, which is called the spiking variable. The transport of other ions is made through slow channels, and is taken into account through $z(t)$, which is called the bursting variable. Then, the Hindmarsh–Rose model has the mathematical form of a system of three nonlinear ordinary differential equations on the dimensionless dynamical variables $x(t)$, $y(t)$, and $z(t)$.

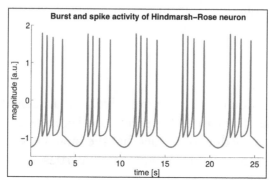

Simulation of Hindmarsh–Rose neuron showing typical neuronal bursting.

$$\frac{dx}{dt} = y + \phi(x) - z + I,$$

$$\frac{dy}{dt} = \psi(x) - y,$$

$$\frac{dz}{dt} = r[s(x - x_R) - z],$$

where,

$$\phi(x) = -ax^3 + bx^2$$

$$\psi(x) = c - dx^2$$

The model has eight parameters: a, b, c, d, r, s, x_R and I. It is common to fix some of them and let the others be control parameters. Usually the parameter I, which means the current that enters the neuron, is taken as a control parameter. Other control parameters used often in the literature are a, b, c, d, or r, the first four modeling the working of the fast ion channels and the last one the slow ion channels, respectively. Frequently, the parameters held fixed are $s = 4$ and $x_R = -8/5$. When a, b, c, d are fixed the values given are $a = 1$, $b = 3$, $c = 1$, and $d = 5$. The parameter r is something of the order of 10^{-3}, and I ranges between -10 and 10.

The third state equation:

$$\frac{dz}{dt} = r[s(x - x_R) - z],$$

allows a great variety of dynamic behaviors of the membrane potential, described by variable x, including unpredictable behavior, which is referred to as chaotic dynamics. This makes the Hindmarsh–Rose model relatively simple and provides a good qualitative description of the many different patterns that are observed empirically.

GALVES–LÖCHERBACH MODEL

The Galves–Löcherbach model is a model with intrinsic stochasticity for biological neural nets, in which the probability of a future spike depends on the evolution of the complete system since the last spike. This model of spiking neurons was developed by mathematicians Antonio Galves and Eva Löcherbach. In the first article on the model, in 2013, they called it a model of a "system with interacting stochastic chains with memory of variable length".

Some inspirations of the Galves–Löcherbach model are the Frank Spitzer's interacting particle system and Jorma Rissanen's notion of stochastic chain with memory of variable length. Another work that influenced this model was Bruno Cessac's study on the leaky integrate-and-fire model, who himself was influenced by Hédi Soula. Galves and Löcherbach referred to the process that Cessac described as "a version in a finite dimension" of their own probabilistic model.

Prior integrate-and-fire models with stochastic characteristics relied on including a noise to simulate stochasticity. The Galves–Löcherbach model distinguishes itself because it is inherently stochastic, incorporating probabilistic measures directly in the calculation of spikes. It is also a model that may be applied relatively easily, from a computational standpoint, with a good ratio between cost and efficiency. It remains a non-Markovian model, since the probability of a given neuronal spike depends on the accumulated activity of the system since the last spike.

Contributions to the model were made, considering the hydrodynamic limit of the interacting neuronal system, the long-range behavior and aspects pertaining to the process in the sense of predicting and classifying behaviors according to a fonction of parameters, and the generalization of the model to the continuous time.

The Galves–Löcherbach model was a cornerstone to the Research, Innocation and Dissemination Center for Neuromathematics.

The model considers a countable set of neurons I and models its evolution in discrete-time periods $t \in \mathbb{Z}$ with a stochastic chain $(X_t)_{t \in \mathbb{Z}}$, considering values in $\{0,1\}^I$. More precisely, for each neuron $i \in I$ and time period $t \in \mathbb{Z}$, we define $X_t(i) = 1$ if neuron i spikes in period t, and conversely $X_t(i) = 0$. The configuration of the set of neurons, in the time period $t \in \mathbb{Z}$, is therefore defined as $X_t = (X_t(i), i \in I)$. For each time period $t \in \mathbb{Z}$, we define a sigma-algebra $\mathcal{F}_t = \sigma(X_s(j), j \in I, s \leq t)$ representing the history of the evolution of the activity of this set of neurons until the relevant time period t. The dynamics of the activity of this set of neurons is defined as follows. Once the history $\mathcal{F}_{t-1}$ is given, neurons spike or not in the next time period t independently from one another, that is, for each finite subset $F \subset I$ and any configuration $a_i \in \{0,1\}, i \in F$, we have:

$$\mathrm{Prob}(X_t(i) = a_i, i \in I \mid \mathcal{F}_{t-1}) = \prod_{i \in I} \mathrm{Prob}(X_t(i) = a_i \mid \mathcal{F}_{t-1}).$$

Furthermore, the probability that a given neuron i spikes in a time period t, according to the probabilistic model, is described by the formula:

$$\mathrm{Prob}(X_t(i) = 1 \mid \mathcal{F}_{t-1}) = \phi_i \Big(\sum_{j \in I} W_{j \to i} \sum_{s = L_t^i}^{t-1} g_j(t-s) X_s(j), t - L_t^i \Big),$$

where $W_{j \to i}$ is synaptic weight that expresses the increase of membrane potential of neuron i because of neuron j's spike, g_j is a function that models the leak of potential and L_t^i is the most recent period of neuron i's spike before the given time period t, considering the formula:

$$L_t^i = \sup\{s < t : X_s(i) = 1\}.$$

At time s before t neuron i spikes, restoring the membrane potential to its initial value.

DEHAENE–CHANGEUX MODEL

The Dehaene–Changeux model (DCM), also known as the global neuronal workspace or the global cognitive workspace model is a part of Bernard Baars's "global workspace model" for consciousness.

It is a computer model of the neural correlates of consciousness programmed as a neural network. It attempts to reproduce the swarm behaviour of the brain's higher cognitive functions such as consciousness, decision-making and the central executive functions. It was developed by cognitive neuroscientists Stanislas Dehaene and Jean-Pierre Changeux beginning in 1986. It has been used to provide a predictive framework to the study of inattentional blindness and the solving of the Tower of London test.

Structure

The Dehaene–Changeux model is a meta neural network (i.e. a network of neural networks) composed of a very large number of integrate and fire neurons programmed in either a stochastic or deterministic way. The neurons are organised in complex thalamo-cortical columns with long-range connexions and a critical role played by the interaction between von Economo's areas. Each thalamo-cortical column is composed of pyramidal cells and inhibitory interneurons receiving a long-distance excitatory neuromodulation which could represent noradrenergic input.

A Swarm and a Multi-agent System Composed of Neural Networks

Among others Cohen & Hudson had already used *"Meta neural networks as intelligent agents for diagnosis"*. Similarly to Cohen & Hudson, Dehaene & Changeux have established their model as an interaction of meta-neural networks (thalamocortical columns) themselves programmed in the manner of a *"hierarchy of neural networks that together act as an intelligent agent"*, in order to use them as a system composed of a large scale of inter-connected intelligent agents for predicting the self-organized behaviour of the neural correlates of consciousness. It may also be noted that Jain et al. had already clearly identified spiking neurons as intelligent agents since the lower bound for computational power of networks of spiking neurons is the capacity to simulate in real-time for boolean-valued inputs any Turing machine. The DCM being composed of a very large number of interacting sub-networks which are themselves intelligent agents, it is formally a Multi-agent system programmed as a Swarm or neural networks and *a fortiori* of spiking neurons.

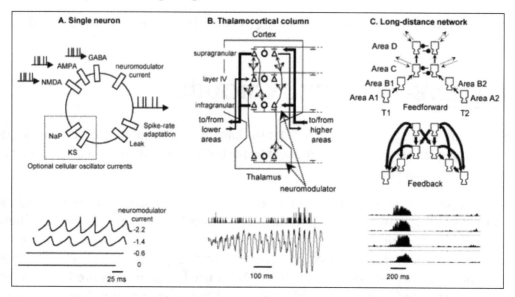

The three levels of complexity of the global workspace model: the integrate-and-fire neuron, the thalamo-cortical bundle and the long-range connexion. The authors provide the legend: Shown are the constituents of the simulation (upper diagrams) and typical patterns of spontaneous activity that they can produce (lower tracings). We simulated a nested architecture in which spiking neurons (A) are incorporated within thalamocortical columns (B), which are themselves interconnected hierarchically by local and long-distance cortical connections (C). While single neurons may generate sustained oscillations of membrane potentials (A), only the column and network levels generate complex waxing-and-waning EEG-like oscillations (B) and metastable global states of sustained firing (C).

Behavior

The DCM exhibits several surcritical emergent behaviors such as multistability and a Hopf bifurcation between two very different regimes which may represent either sleep or arousal with a various all-or-none behaviors which Dehaene et al. use to determine a testable taxonomy between different states of consciousness.

Scholarly Reception

Self-organized Criticality

The Dehaene-Changeux Model contributed to the study of nonlinearity and self-organized criticality in particular as an explanatory model of the brain's emergent behaviors, including consciousness. Studying the brain's phase-locking and large-scale synchronization, confirmed that criticality is a property of human brain functional network organization at all frequency intervals in the brain's physiological bandwidth.

Furthermore, exploring the neural dynamics of cognitive efforts after, *inter alia*, the Dehaene-Changeux Model, Kitzbichler et al. demonstrated how cognitive effort breaks the modularity of mind to make human brain functional networks transiently adopt a more efficient but less economical configuration. Werner used the Dehaene-Changeux Global Neuronal Workspace to defend the use of statistical physics approaches for exploring phase transitions, scaling and universality properties of the so-called "Dynamic Core" of the brain, with relevance to the macroscopic electrical activity in EEG and EMG. Furthermore, building from the Dehaene-Changeux Model, Werner proposed that the application of the twin concepts of scaling and universality of the theory of non-equilibrium phase transitions can serve as an informative approach for elucidating the nature of underlying neural-mechanisms, with emphasis on the dynamics of recursively reentrant activity flow in intracortical and cortico-subcortical neuronal loops. Friston also claimed that "the nonlinear nature of asynchronous coupling enables the rich, context-sensitive interactions that characterize real brain dynamics, suggesting that it plays a role in functional integration that may be as important as synchronous interactions".

States of Consciousness and Phenomenology

It contributed to the study of phase transition in the brain under sedation, and notably GABA-ergic sedation such as that induced by propofol. The Dehaene-Changeux Model was contrasted and cited in the study of collective consciousness and its pathologies. The model is used for a reverse somatotopic study, demonstrating a correlation between baseline brain activity and somatosensory perception in humans. Also used the DCM in a study of the baseline state of consciousness of the human brain's default network.

WILSON–COWAN MODEL

In computational neuroscience, the Wilson–Cowan model describes the dynamics of interactions between populations of very simple excitatory and inhibitory model neurons. It was developed by Hugh R. Wilson and Jack D. Cowan and extensions of the model have been widely used in modeling neuronal populations. The model is important historically because it uses phase plane methods and numerical solutions to describe the responses of neuronal populations to stimuli. Because the model neurons are simple, only elementary limit cycle behavior, i.e. neural oscillations, and stimulus-dependent evoked responses are predicted. The key findings include the existence of multiple stable states, and hysteresis, in the population response.

Mathematical

The Wilson–Cowan model considers a homogeneous population of interconnected neurons of excitatory and inhibitory subtypes. The fundamental quantity is the measure of the activity of an excitatory or inhibitory subtype within the population. More precisely, $E(t)$ and $I(t)$ are respectively the proportions of excitatory and inhibitory cells firing at time t. They depend on the proportion of sensitive cells (that are not refractory) and on the proportion of these cells receiving at least threshold excitation.

Sensitive Cells

1. Proportion of cells in refractory period (absolute refractory period) $\int_{t-r}^{t} E(t')dt'$.

2. Proportion of sensitive cells (complement of refractory cells) $1 - \int_{t-r}^{t} E(t')dt'$.

Excited Cells

If θ denotes a cell's threshold potential and $D(\theta)$ is the distribution of thresholds in the tissue, then the expected proportion of neurons receiving an excitation at or above threshold level per unit time is:

$$S(\bar{N}) = \int_{0}^{\bar{N}(t)} D(\theta)d\theta,$$

where $\bar{N}(t)$ is the mean integrated excitation at time t. The term "integrated" in this case means that each neuron sums up (i.e. integrates) all incoming excitations in a linear fashion to receive its total excitation. If this integrated excitation is at or above the neuron's excitation threshold, it will in turn create an action potential. Note that the above equation relies heavily on the homogeneous distribution of neurons, as does the Wilson-Cowan model in general.

Subpopulation response function based on the distribution of afferent synapses per cell (all cells have the same threshold).

$$S(\bar{N}) = \int_{\frac{\theta}{\bar{N}(t)}}^{\infty} C(w)dw$$

Average excitation level of an excitatory cell at time t:

$$\int_{-\infty}^{t} \alpha(t-t')[c_1 E(t') - c_2 I(t') + P(t')]dt'$$

where $\alpha(t)$ is the stimulus decay function, c_1 and c_2 are respectively the connectivity coefficient giving the average number of excitatory and inhibitory synapses per cell, P(t) is the external input to the excitatory population.

Excitatory subpopulation expression:

$$E(t) = [1 - \int_{t-r}^{t} E(t')dt']S(\bar{N})dt$$

Complete Wilson–Cowan model:

$$E(t+\tau) = [1 - \int_{t-r}^{t} E(t')dt']S_e\left\{\int_{-\infty}^{t} \alpha(t-t')[c_1E(t') - c_2I(t') + P(t')]dt'\right\}$$

$$I(t+\tau) = [1 - \int_{t-r}^{t} I(t')dt']S_i\left\{\int_{-\infty}^{t} \alpha(t-t')[c_3E(t') - c_4I(t') + Q(t')]dt'\right\}$$

Time Coarse Graining $\tau \dfrac{d\bar{E}}{dt} = -\bar{E} + (1 - r\bar{E})S_e[kc_1\bar{E}(t) + kP(t)]$

Isocline Equation $c_2I = c_1E - S_e^{-1}\left(\dfrac{E}{k_e - r_eE}\right) + P$

Sigmoid Function $S(x) = \dfrac{1}{1 + \exp[-a(\bar{N} - \theta)]} - \dfrac{1}{1 + \exp(a\theta)}$

Application to Epilepsy

The determination of three concepts is fundamental to an understanding of hypersynchronization of neurophysiological activity at the global (system) level:

- The mechanism by which normal (baseline) neurophysiological activity evolves into hypersynchronization of large regions of the brain during epileptic seizures.

- The key factors that govern the rate of expansion of hypersynchronized regions.

- The electrophysiological activity pattern dynamics on a large-scale.

A canonical analysis of these issues, developed in 2008 by Shusterman and Troy using the Wilson–Cowan model, predicts qualitative and quantitative features of epileptiform activity. In particular, it accurately predicts the propagation speed of epileptic seizures (which is approximately 4–7 times slower than normal brain wave activity) in a human subject with chronically implanted electroencephalographic electrodes.

Transition into Hypersynchronization

The transition from normal state of brain activity to epileptic seizures was not formulated theoretically until 2008, when a theoretical path from a baseline state to large-scale self-sustained oscillations, which spread out uniformly from the point of stimulus, has been mapped for the first time.

A realistic state of baseline physiological activity has been defined, using the following two-component definition:

- A time-independent component represented by subthreshold excitatory activity E and superthreshold inhibitory activity I.

- A time-varying component which may include singlepulse waves, multipulse waves, or periodic waves caused by spontaneous neuronal activity.

This baseline state represents activity of the brain in the state of relaxation, in which neurons receive some level of spontaneous, weak stimulation by small, naturally present concentrations of neurohormonal substances. In waking adults this state is commonly associated with alpha rhythm, whereas slower (theta and delta) rhythms are usually observed during deeper relaxation and sleep. To describe this general setting, a 3-variable (u, I, v) spatially dependent extension of the classical Wilson–Cowan model can be utilized. Under appropriate initial conditions, the excitatory component, u, dominates over the inhibitory component, I, and the three-variable system reduces to the two-variable Pinto-Ermentrout type model.

$$\frac{\partial u}{\partial t} = u - v + \int_{R^2} \omega(x - x', y - y') f(u - \theta) dx dy + \zeta(x, y, t),$$

$$\frac{\partial v}{\partial t} = \epsilon(\beta u - v).$$

The variable v governs the recovery of excitation u; $\epsilon > 0$ and $\beta > 0$ determine the rate of change of recovery. The connection function $\omega(x, y)$ is positive, continuous, symmetric, and has the typical form $\omega = Ae^{-\lambda\sqrt{-(x^2+y^2)}}$. The firing rate function, which is generally accepted to have a sharply increasing sigmoidal shape, is approximated by $f(u - \theta) = H(u - \theta)$, where H denotes the Heaviside function; $\zeta(x, y, t)$ is a short-time stimulus. This (u, v) system has been successfully used in a wide variety of neuroscience research studies. In particular, it predicted the existence of spiral waves, which can occur during seizures; this theoretical prediction was subsequently confirmed experimentally using optical imaging of slices from the rat cortex.

Rate of Expansion

The expansion of hypersynchronized regions exhibiting large-amplitude stable bulk oscillations occurs when the oscillations coexist with the stable rest state $(u,v) = (0,0)$. To understand the mechanism responsible for the expansion, it is necessary to linearize the (u,v) system around $(0,0)$ when $\epsilon > 0$ is held fixed. The linearized system exhibits subthreshold decaying oscillations whose frequency increases as β increases. At a critical value β^* where the oscillation frequency is high enough, bistability occurs in the (u,v) system: a stable, spatially independent, periodic solution (bulk oscillation) and a stable rest state coexist over a continuous range of parameters. When $\beta \geq \beta^*$ where bulk oscillations occur, "the rate of expansion of the hypersynchronization region is determined by an interplay between two key features: (i) the speed c of waves that form and propagate outward from the edge of the region, and (ii) the concave shape of the graph of the activation variable u as it rises, during each bulk oscillation cycle, from the rest state u=0 to the activation threshold. Numerical experiments show that during the rise of u towards threshold, as the rate of vertical increase slows down, over time interval Δt, due to the concave component, the stable solitary wave emanating from the region causes the region to expand spatially at a Rate proportional to the wave speed. From this initial observation it is natural to expect that the proportionality constant should be the fraction of the time that the solution is concave during one cycle." Therefore, when $\beta \geq \beta^*$ the rate of expansion of the region is estimated by:

$$Rate = (\Delta t / T) * c$$

where, Δt, is the length of subthreshold time interval, T is period of the periodic solution; c is the speed of waves emanating from the hypersynchronization region. A realistic value of c, derived by Wilson et al., is c=22.4 mm/s.

How to evaluate the ratio $\Delta t / T$? To determine values for $\Delta t / T$ it is necessary to analyze the underlying bulk oscillation which satisfies the spatially independent system:

$$\frac{du}{dt} = u - v + H(u - \theta),$$

$$\frac{dv}{dt} = \epsilon(\beta u - v).$$

This system is derived using standard functions and parameter values $\omega = 2.1 e^{-\lambda\sqrt{-(x^2+y^2)}}$, $\epsilon = 0.1$ and Bulk oscillations occur when $\beta \geq \beta^* = 12.61$. When $12.61 \leq \beta \leq 17$, Shusterman and Troy analyzed the bulk oscillations and found $0.136 \leq \Delta t / T \leq 0.238$. This gives the range:

$$3.046 mm / s \leq Rate \leq 5.331 mm / s$$

Since $0.136 \le \Delta t / T \le 0.238$, Eq. ($Rate = (\Delta t / T) * c$) shows that the migration Rate is a fraction of the traveling wave speed, which is consistent with experimental and clinical observations regarding the slow spread of epileptic activity. This migration mechanism also provides a plausible explanation for spread and sustenance of epileptiform activity without a driving source that, despite a number of experimental studies, has never been observed.

Comparing Theoretical and Experimental Migration Rates

The rate of migration of hypersynchronous activity that was experimentally recorded during seizures in a human subject, using chronically implanted subdural electrodes on the surface of the left temporal lobe, has been estimated as:

$Rate \approx 4mm / s$

which is consistent with the theoretically predicted range given above. The ratio $Rate / c$ in formula shows that the leading edge of the region of synchronous seizure activity migrates approximately 4–7 times more slowly than normal brain wave activity, which is in agreement with the experimental data.

To summarize, mathematical modeling and theoretical analysis of large-scale electrophysiological activity provide tools for predicting the spread and migration of hypersynchronous brain activity, which can be useful for diagnostic evaluation and management of patients with epilepsy. It might be also useful for predicting migration and spread of electrical activity over large regions of the brain that occur during deep sleep (Delta wave), cognitive activity and in other functional settings.

MORRIS–LECAR MODEL

The Morris-Lecar model is a two-dimensional "reduced" excitation model applicable to systems having two non-inactivating voltage-sensitive conductances. The original form of the model employed an instantaneously responding voltage-sensitive Ca^{2+} conductance for excitation and a delayed voltage-dependent K^+ conductance for recovery. The equations of the model are:

$$CV' = -g_{Ca}M_{ss}(V)(V - V_{Ca}) - g_K W(V - V_K) - g_L(V - V_L) + I_{app}$$

$$W' = (W_{ss}(V) - W) / T_W(V)$$

Here, V is the membrane potential, W is the "recovery variable", which is almost invariably the normalized K^+ ion conductance, and I_{app} is the applied current stimulus. The variable normalized conductance, $W(t)$, is equal to the instantaneous value of the probability that a K^+ ion channel is in its open (conducting) state. Eqn. ($W' = (W_{ss}(V) - W)/T_W(V)$) thus describes the relaxation process by which protein channels undergo conformational transitions between ion-conducting and non-conducting states. The key to electrical excitability is that the energies and transition rates for this channel-gating process are steeply voltage dependent.

This model was named after Cathy Morris and Harold Lecar, who derived it in 1981. Because it is two-dimensional, the Morris-Lecar model is one of the favorite conductance-based models in computational neuroscience.

Physically, the open-state probability functions, $M_{ss}(V)$ and $W_{ss}(V)$, are derived from the assumption that, in equilibrium, the open and closed states of a channel are partitioned according to a Boltzmann distribution. The energy difference between these states depends on the work required to translocate certain highly-charged membrane-spanning helices against the very strong trans-membrane electric field. Explicitly, the conductance functions are given as:

$$M_{ss}(V) = (1 + \tanh[(V - V_1)/V_2)])/2$$

$$W_{ss}(V) = (1 + \tanh[(V - V_3)/V_4)])/2.$$

The function $(1 + \tanh(x))/2$ in these equations could have been written more simply as $\left(1 + \exp(-2x)\right)^{-1}$, but most of the literature preserves the form given above. The time constant for the K^+ channel relaxation in response to changes of voltage is voltage-dependent:

$$T_W(V) = T_0 \operatorname{sech}[(V - V_3)/2V_4]$$

Here the parameter T_0 sets the time scale for the recovery process. T_0 can vary over a wide range for different cells, and is also extremely temperature sensitive. The relaxation process of Eqns. $W_{ss}(V) = (1 + \tanh[(V - V_3)/V_4)])/2$ and $T_W(V) = T_0 \operatorname{sech}[(V - V_3)/2V_4]$ is analogous to dielectric relaxation in an electric field. However, internal trans-membrane electric fields, can be so great that the energy difference between the open and closed states can be much greater than thermal energy ($Q_{gate}V \gg kT|$).

Eqns. $CV' = -g_{Ca}M_{ss}(V)(V - V_{Ca}) - g_K W(V - V_K) - g_L(V - V_L) + I_{app}$

and $W' = (W_{ss}(V) - W)/T_W(V)$ constitute a very simple model of excitability depending on three ionic currents:

I_{Ca},

which causes the initial excitation; I_K, the main current involved in recovery; and I_L

the membrane leakage current involved in maintaining the resting potential. Many different systems and excitability phenomena can be modeled by varying the magnitudes of these three currents (i.e., the peak conductances g_{Ca}, g_K and g_L). These conductances can be modified in vivo by a number of means, such as varying specific ion concentrations or by pharmacological dissection with specific channel-blocking molecules. In this way both the experimental preparations and the theoretical models can be used to demonstrate a rich variety of qualitatively different behaviors.

Principal Assumptions

Generally, excitable systems have more than two relevant excitation variables, because there are often more than two species of gated channels and also because some channels have autonomous inactivation processes. Thus the primary assumption in using a two-dimensional model is that the true higher-order system can in fact be projected onto a two-dimensional phase space without altering the topological properties of the phase profile. This is true for the four-dimensional Hodgkin-Huxley system, which has a single singular point and exhibits excitation phenomena that can all be duplicated in two dimensions. There are other neural excitation phenomena such as bursting oscillations or chaotic firing which are intrinsically higher-dimensional, and cannot be duplicated in the phase plane.

The principal assumptions underlying the Morris-Lecar model include:

- Equations apply to a spatially iso-potential patch of membrane.

- There are two persistent (non-inactivating) voltage-gated currents with oppositively biased reversal potentials. The depolarizing current is carried by Na^+ or Ca^{2+} ions (or both), depending on the system to be modeled, and the hyperpolarizing current is carried by K^+.

- Activation gates follow changes in membrane potential sufficiently rapidly that the activating conductance can instantaneously relax to its steady-state value at any voltage.

- The dynamics of the recovery variable can be approximated by a first-order linear differential equation for the probability of channel opening. This assumption is never exactly true, since channel proteins are composed of subunits, which must act in concert, to reach the open state. Despite missing delays in the onset of recovery, the model appears to be adequate for phase-plane considerations for many excitable systems.

The Phenomenon

All of the parameters in the Morris-Lecar equations are experimentally measurable. Thus this simple model lends itself to simulating the rather wide range of phenomena that occur in different excitable systems.

With parameters appropriate to a nerve axon, the model yields prototypical single-shot firing, with a quasi-threshold, and an abrupt transition to repetitive firing over a narrow frequency range, as expected from the Hodgkin-Huxley or FitzHugh-Nagumo equations. Using parameters appropriate to a weak excitation current, the model displays spike trains emerging from zero frequency and oscillating over a relatively wide range of frequencies. These two types of behavior don't exhaust the repertoire of possible excitation. The system can also yield non-oscillatory bi-stable behavior with a true (saddle point) threshold, and various modes of pacemaker-like small oscillations.

Since the functions $M_{ss}(V)$ and $W_{ss}(V)$ are chosen to fit the actual voltage-sensitive conductances, the subsidiary parameters $V_1,...,V_4$ can be fit to different systems of interest to alter the phase-plane properties of the system. Thus V_1 and V_3 set the steepness of the conductance curves, which, in turn, is determined by the effective charge moved during the gating transition. Real channels have effective gating charges varying from 5 to 14 electron charges, corresponding to V_2 or V_4 = 5 to 2 mV. The parameters V_1 and V_3 locate the center (inflection point) of the conductance curves. The conductance curves can be translated along the voltage axis by varying the ionic strength or Ca^{2+} concentration of the electrolyte medium, thus altering the membrane surface-charge shielding of applied voltage.

The Morris-Lecar equations essentially describe "push-pull" relaxation oscillations, with gCa and gK and the corresponding equilibrium potentials, VCa and VK determining the relative strengths of "push" to pull. If the excitable conductance, gCa , is too great relative to the other conductances, the system may not be able to recover from a depolarization, and may exhibit bistability. I_{app} is an applied current stimulus, which persistently depolarizes the cell. A critical value of I_{app} can produce a transition from single-shot behavior to repetitive firing. The dynamics can also be altered dramatically by temperature changes, because the gating relaxation time T_0 is exquisitely temperature sensitive ($Q_{10} \approx 3$), whereas the other time constants depend on peak ionic conductances which are not very temperature sensitive.

The striking feature, which motivated the original experiments that led to the model, is the ability of the barnacle giant muscle fiber to undergo transitions to a plethora of oscillating states. By changing parameters, the Morris-Lecar equations could describe the two main classes of nerve oscillations first described by Hodgkin as well as other types of behavior.

Applications to Neural Modeling

The original Hodgkin-Huxley equations constituted an exact model of a motor neuron, the squid giant axon. The axon has two voltage-gated channels and a leakage current, but requires four-dimensions to describe the voltage and three conductance-relaxation processes. The Morris-Lecar approximation describes the same three currents by just two dynamical variables. In this approximation, the Na^+ inactivation process is omitted, but can be subsumed by taking the recovery process to be artificially rapid. The other approximation is to make Na⁺ activation respond instantaneously. This generally doesn't cause problems because Na⁺ activation generally responds more rapidly than the membrane capacitative time constant, which sets the limit to how rapidly the membrane potential can change in response to an applied current.

The two-dimensional model can then readily be analyzed using phase-plane methods. In the phase plane, dynamical transitions correspond to geometric features of the null-clines. Such transitions as the one from single-shot firing to a stable limit cycle are seen as the parameter representing applied-current stimulus is varied to reach a point of bifurcation between the two types of dynamic solution. At the bifurcation, a linearized model of the equations will always have one real eigenvalue that goes through zero (saddle-node bifurcation).

The Morris-Lecar equations are particularly useful for modelling fast-spiking neurons, such as the pyramidal neurons of the neocortex. Pyramidal neurons exhibit true all-or-none firing, continuous trains in response to constant-current stimulation, onset of repetitive firing with arbitrarily low firing frequency, and a linear or square-root current-frequency relation. Such neurons are capable of coding of information via limit cycles, which may help explain the computational efficacy of neural systems which often must work with noise components of as high intensity as the signal strength. The Morris-Lecar equations with appropriate parameters have unbounded variance in inter-spike interval length, and so can be used as a generic model to show how both frequency and precise timing are employed for coding. An example is the modeling of coincidence detection in auditory neurons.

In studies of neural integration and neural information processing, it may be necessary to study the behavior of model neurons in the presence of noise. For single-shot neurons with discontinuous threshold and unbounded latency, firing fluctuations in the presence of electrical noise can be described by a random walk in the phase plane, with sub-and supra-threshold trajectories separated in the neighborhood of a threshold separatrix. Finer details of behavior in the presence of noise, such as latency fluctuations, spike interval fluctuations, and frequency jitter require models of neural dynamics that include the recovery process. Problems of interest that can be attacked are the question of whether the different classes of neural oscillator respond differently to input noise and the response of coupled arrays to noise.

Morris-Lecar-type models may prove useful for studying scaling phenomena, such as showing how neural oscillators and oscillatory networks change as the cells grow during development. Such problems on real systems, such as the lobster somatogastric ganglion, involve more species of channels than the two dimensional models, but the Morris-Lecar equations with ion-channel densities made explicit might give insight into the developmental features that allow oscillation phenomena to maintain their frequency as an animal grows.

Finally, the Morris-Lecar model neuron has been applied to modeling networks of coupled neural oscillators. Here the simple but realistic parameterization allows one to describe collective oscillations which depend on the inter-neuron coupling. A model employing Morris-Lecar oscillators of different frequencies has been used to explain quite complex bursting phenomena of coupled neurons.

4

Artificial Intelligence and Artificial Neural Network

The computing systems that are inspired by the biological neural networks which constitute animal brains are referred to as artificial neural networks. They contribute significantly to the field of artificial intelligence by replicating the working of the brain. This chapter closely examines the key concepts and types of artificial neural network and artificial intelligence to provide an extensive understanding of the subject.

ARTIFICIAL INTELLIGENCE

Artificial intelligence (AI) is an area of computer science that emphasize the creation of intelligent machines that work and react like humans. Some of the activities computers with artificial intelligence are designed for include:

- Speech recognition,
- Learning,
- Planning,
- Problem solving.

Artificial intelligence is a branch of computer science that aims to create intelligent machines. It has become an essential part of the technology industry.

Research associated with artificial intelligence is highly technical and specialized. The core problems of artificial intelligence include programming computers for certain traits such as:

- Knowledge,
- Reasoning,
- Problem solving,
- Perception,

- Learning,

- Planning,

- Ability to manipulate and move objects.

Knowledge engineering is a core part of AI research. Machines can often act and react like humans only if they have abundant information relating to the world. Artificial intelligence must have access to objects, categories, properties and relations between all of them to implement knowledge engineering. Initiating common sense, reasoning and problem-solving power in machines is a difficult and tedious task.

Machine learning is also a core part of AI. Learning without any kind of supervision requires an ability to identify patterns in streams of inputs, whereas learning with adequate supervision involves classification and numerical regressions.

Classification determines the category an object belongs to and regression deals with obtaining a set of numerical input or output examples, thereby discovering functions enabling the generation of suitable outputs from respective inputs. Mathematical analysis of machine learning algorithms and their performance is a well-defined branch of theoretical computer science often referred to as computational learning theory.

Machine perception deals with the capability to use sensory inputs to deduce the different aspects of the world, while computer vision is the power to analyze visual inputs with a few sub-problems such as facial, object and gesture recognition.

Artificial systems are capable of outperforming human experts on many levels: crunching data, analysing legal documents, solving Rubix cubes, and winning games both ancient and modern.

They can produce writing indistinguishable from their human counterparts, conduct research, pen pop songs, translate between multiple languages and even create and critique art.

And AI-driven tasks like object detection, speech recognition and machine translation are becoming more sophisticated every day.

These advances can be credited to many developments, from improved statistical approaches to increased computer processing powers. But one element that is often overlooked is a combination of science and engineering: the use of both theoretical and experimental neuroscience.

Neuroscience has made several pivotal contributions to AI development. The two studies have a long and tangled history, due to their many similarities.

To build super-intelligent machines, we must gain a deeper understanding of the human brain. Equally, exploring AI can help us gain a better understanding on what's going on in our own heads.

Identifying a common language between the two fields will create a "virtuous circle whereby research is accelerated through shared theoretical insights and common empirical advances".

Neuroscience is a strand of biology based on the study of the anatomy and physiology of the human brain, including structures, neurons and molecules.

It studies how the brain works in terms of mechanics, functions and systems in order to create recognizable behaviors.

The success of today's deep learning (a subset of AI) is mostly down to its architecture as opposed to its resemblance to the human brain; however, building a system that mirrored the simulations of the human brain was the starting point of artifical neural networks (ANNs).

In fact, the major developments in ANNs leant heavily on breakthroughs and achievements in psychology and neurophysiology departments.

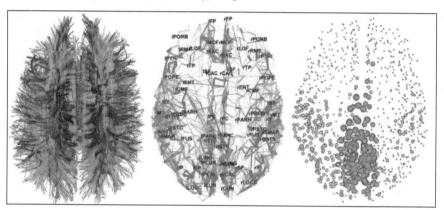

The human brain is one life's greatest mysteries. To this day, scientists haven't reached a clear consensus on how it works, despite studying it for centuries.

The two main theories are as follows:

The grandmother cell theory, which proposes that individual neurons are capable of retaining dense information and representing complex concepts.

By contrast, the second theory believes individual neurons are fairly simple, and the information required for processing complex concepts is distributed across multiple neurons.

An ANN is a simplified, computational model of a biological brain, rather as a Tinkertoy construction might be a model of a real suspension bridge.

Basically, an ANN is way of detecting patterns. For a very simple example, imagine a machine that can only do one thing, namely tell whether a single numeral is a 3 or not.

The input to the machine is any numeral from 0 to 9, and if it is working correctly, it gives the output True when the input is a 3, and False when any other numeral is fed to it. A slightly more sophisticated machine would allow ten different outputs, one for each numeral.

Old Calculators used seven units, which could be either on or off. So as long we agree on the order in which the segments are represented, each numeral can be captured as a series of seven 0s and 1s.

They can be used to simulate brain behaviors, so that cognitive neuroscientists can test whether their theoretical models produce outputs which agree with the responses given by biological neural networks.

An ANN is composed of a number of interconnected units, or artificial neurons. Each artificial neuron is linked to several others, and can transmit signals along these connections.

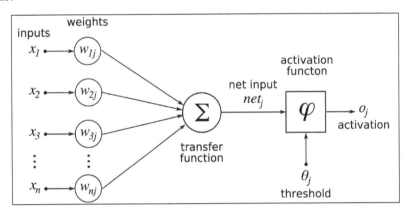

A weight is associated with each connection, and affects the strength of the signal that is transmitted between neurons. These weights will increase or decrease during the course of learning, by analogy with the modifications in synaptic strength that underlie 'plasticity' in biological brains.

Units in a network are usually segregated into three classes: Input units (these receive information to be processed), output units (this is where the results of the processing are found) and hidden units, which lie inbetween the first two classes.

These are arranged into layers, and in the simplest case there is only one layer of hidden units between the input and output layers. Signals from one layer will propagate as input to the next layer, or else exit the system via the output units.

An ANN mimics the biological brain in the sense that it acquires knowledge through learning, and stores this knowledge by adjusting the weights within the network.

However, some experts argue that the similarities amount more to loose inspiration, as biological neurons are far more complex than artificial ones. The history of ANNs involve contributions from scientists in a variety of disciplines, including cognitive psychology, biological neuroscience and mathematics.

Within psychology, associationism was an important antecedent, and boasted a heritage stretching back as far as Aristotle.

A key starting point was a paper written in 1943 by neurophysiologist Warren McCulloch and mathematician Walter Pitts describing how neurons in the brain might work by modeling a primary neural network using electrical circuits.

In 1949, the psychologist Donald Hebb drew on ideas from associationism in developing a theory of learning which showed how biological operations in the brain could explain higher level cognitive behaviors.

According to Hebb, if one neuron repeatedly stimulates a second one, then the connection between them will strengthen this is the notion of synaptic strength that is represented by weights in an ANN.

Interlude

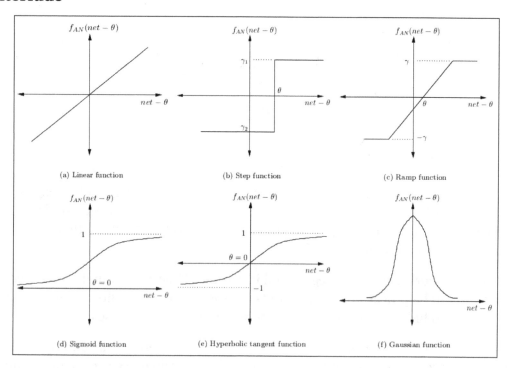

So, ANNs suffered from the unrealistic hype, and also from insufficiently powerful computational resources to be practically useful in AI.

Meanwhile, machine learning work in AI provided alternative models of learning which appeared to be valuable, such as Hidden Markov Models.

In parallel, however, a series of advances to the task of training ANNs with more than just one hidden layer. Such multiple layers led to deep learning become increasingly feasible (i.e., in terms of training time) and accurate.

This was assisted by training deep NNs on Nvidia GPUs.

In a somewhat independent strand of research, cognitive psychologists were exploring ideas of that association of ideas can be explained in terms of an associative structure.

Both cognitive science and neuroscience have evolved over the years, and recently they have started to overlap.

Cognitive Science

Cognitive science is an offshoot of human psychology and is literally the study of cognition, or thought. It includes language, problem-solving, decision-making, and perception, especially consciously aware understanding.

Cognitive science started with those higher-level behavioral traits that were observable or testable and asked what is going on inside the mind or brain to make that possible.

Within this lies associationism. Associationism is one of the oldest and most widely held theories of thought.

Associationism

When, therefore, we accomplish an act of reminiscence, we pass through a certain series of precursive movements, until we arrive at a movement on which the one we are in quest of is habitually consequent. Hence, too, it is that we hunt through the mental train, excogitating from the present or some other, and from similar or contrary or co-adjacent. Through this process reminiscence takes place. For the movements are, in these cases, sometimes at the same time, sometimes parts of the same whole, so that the subsequent movement is already more than half accomplished.

This paragraph from the philosopher Aristotle is seen as the starting point of Associationism.

Associationism states that our mind is a set of conceptual elements that are organized as associations.

Aristotle examined the processes of memory and recalled to develop the four laws of association:

- Contiguity: Things or events with spatial or temporal proximity tend to be associated in the mind.

- Frequency: The number of occurrences of two events is proportional to the strength of association between these two events.

- Similarity: Thought of one event tends to trigger the thought of a similar event.

- Contrast: Thought of one event tends to trigger the thought of an opposite event.

Aristotle considered these laws to equate to common sense: i.e., the combined feel, smell, and taste of a strawberry are equivalent to a strawberry.

These laws, which were proposed over 2000 years ago, still serve as the fundamentals of today's machine learning methods.

Associative Structures

Associated learning is a constellation of related views, where a person learns to associate one thing with another due to previous experience with it. For instance, we associate the sea with sand.

So, an associative structure defines the bond that connects the two concepts.

There is a reliable, psychological relation that binds them together, and referencing one automatically activates the other (and vice versa) without the need to reference anything else.

Connectionism

Connectionism is a movement within cognitive science that explains intellectual abilities through the use of ANNs.

Connectionism is interesting because it provides an alternative to the widely-held theory that the mind is similar to a digital computer processing a symbolic language.

Work on using GPUs and deep learning for image recognition in 2012 ushered in the "deep learning revolution", which has brought us innovations such as driverless cars, AI-powered assistants like Siri and Alexa, Google translate and much more.

Today, ANNs are used in several applications, based on the fundamental (but sometimes incorrect) assumption that if it works in nature, it will work in computers.

However, the future of ANNs lies in the development of hardware being specified for eventual use, like in the case of Deep Blue.

ANN development research is pretty slow. And due to processor limitations, today's neural networks can take weeks to learn. This brings us to the recent influence of cognitive neuroscience on AI.

Limitations of Artificial Intelligence

Machine learning algorithms are set up with narrow mathematical structures. Through millions of examples, ANNs learn to perfect the strength of their connections until they can complete the task with high accuracy.

Because each algorithm is tailored to the task at hand, relearning a new task often erases the established connections. This leads to catastrophic forgetting: when the AI learns the new task, it overwrites the previous one.

The dilemma of continuous learning is just one challenge. Others are even less defined but arguably more crucial for building flexible, inventive minds.

Embodied cognition is a big one: the ability to build knowledge from interacting with the world through sensory and motor experiences, and creating abstract thought from there.

It's the sort of common sense that humans have, an intuition about the world that's hard to describe but extremely useful for the daily problems we face.

Even harder to program are traits like imagination. That's where AIs limited to one specific task really fail. Imagination and innovation relies on models we've already built about our world, and extrapolating new scenarios from them.

Taking the Help of Neuroscience

Firstly, neuroscience can help to validate existing AI techniques: if we discover an algorithm mimics an existing function in the brain, it doesn't necessarily mean it's the right approach for a computational system but it does suggest we have discovered something important.

Neuroscience can also give a varied and complex source of inspirations for new algorithms and architectures to employ when creating artificial brains.

It might also be more mundane observations from cognitive psychology, such as the fact that humans will forget things that don't matter to them.

But while logic-based methods and theoretical mathematical models have dominated traditional approaches to AI, neuroscience can complement these approaches by identifying classes of biological computation that could be critical to cognitive functions.

Another key challenge in AI research is transfer learning. To be able to process unique situations, AI agents need to be able to reference existing knowledge to make informed decisions.

Cutting-edge research is being undertaken to understand how this might be possible in artificial systems. For instance, a new type of network architecture called a 'progressive network' can use knowledge from one video game to determine another. This suggests there is massive potential for AI research to learn from neuroscience.

On the flipside, neuroscience can also benefit from AI research, like in the case of reinforcement learning. Modern neuroscience, for all its powerful imaging tools and optogenetics, has only just begun unraveling how neural networks support higher intelligence.

Distilling intelligence into algorithms and comparing it to the human brain "may yield insights into some of the deepest and most enduring mysteries of the mind," writes Hassabis.

This mutual investment is crucial for progress in both fields. Researchers can explore neuroscience in the quest to develop AI and push forward scientific discovery.

And examining AI in correlation with neuroscience could help us explore some of life's greatest mysteries, such as creativity, imagination, dreams and consciousness.

ARTIFICIAL CONSCIOUSNESS

Artificial consciousness (AC), also known as machine consciousness (MC) or synthetic consciousness, is a field related to artificial intelligence and cognitive robotics. The aim of the theory of artificial consciousness is to "define that which would have to be synthesized were consciousness to be found in an engineered artifact".

Neuroscience hypothesizes that consciousness is generated by the interoperation of various parts of the brain, called the neural correlates of consciousness or NCC, though there are challenges to that perspective. Proponents of AC believe it is possible to construct systems (e.g., computer systems) that can emulate this NCC interoperation.

Artificial consciousness concepts are also pondered in the philosophy of artificial intelligence through questions about mind, consciousness, and mental states.

Philosophical Views

As there are many hypothesized types of consciousness, there are many potential implementations of artificial consciousness. In the philosophical literature, perhaps the most common taxonomy of consciousness is into "access" and "phenomenal" variants. Access consciousness concerns those aspects of experience that can be apprehended, while phenomenal consciousness concerns those aspects of experience that seemingly cannot be apprehended, instead being characterized qualitatively in terms of "raw feels", "what it is like" or qualia.

Type-identity theorists and other skeptics hold the view that consciousness can only be realized in particular physical systems because consciousness has properties that necessarily depend on physical constitution.

Giorgio Buttazzo says that a common objection to artificial consciousness is that "Working in a fully automated mode, they [the computers] cannot exhibit creativity, emotions, or free will. A computer, like a washing machine, is a slave operated by its components".

For other theorists (e.g., functionalists), who define mental states in terms of causal roles, any system that can instantiate the same pattern of causal roles, regardless of physical constitution, will instantiate the same mental states, including consciousness.

Computational Foundation Argument

One of the most explicit arguments for the plausibility of AC comes from David Chalmers. His proposal, found within his article Chalmers 2011, is roughly that the right kinds of computations are sufficient for the possession of a conscious mind. In the outline, he defends his claim thus: Computers perform computations. Computations can capture other systems' abstract causal organization.

The most controversial part of Chalmers proposal is that mental properties are "organizationally invariant". Mental properties are of two kinds, psychological and phenomenological. Psychological properties, such as belief and perception, are those that are "characterized by their causal role". He adverts to the work of Armstrong 1968 and Lewis 1972 in claiming that "systems with the same causal topology will share their psychological properties".

Phenomenological properties are not prima facie definable in terms of their causal roles. Establishing that phenomenological properties are amenable to individuation by causal role therefore requires argument. Chalmers provides his Dancing Qualia Argument for this purpose.

Chalmers begins by assuming that agents with identical causal organizations could have different experiences. He then asks us to conceive of changing one agent into the other by the replacement of parts (neural parts replaced by silicon, say) while preserving its causal organization. Ex hypothesis, the experience of the agent under transformation would change (as the parts were replaced), but there would be no change in causal topology and therefore no means whereby the agent could "notice" the shift in experience.

Critics of AC object that Chalmers begs the question in assuming that all mental properties and external connections are sufficiently captured by abstract causal organization.

Ethics

If it were suspected that a particular machine was conscious, its rights would be an ethical issue that would need to be assessed (e.g. what rights it would have under law). For example, a conscious computer that was owned and used as a tool or central computer of a building of larger machine is a particular ambiguity. Should laws be made for such a case? Consciousness would also require a legal definition in this particular case.

If, in any given year, a publicly available open source Entry entered by the University of Surrey or the Cambridge Center wins the Silver Medal or the Gold Medal, then the Medal and the Cash Award will be awarded to the body responsible for the development of that Entry. If no such body can be identified, or if there is disagreement among two or more claimants, the Medal and the Cash Award will be held in trust until such time as the Entry may legally possess, either in the United States of America or in the venue of the contest, the Cash Award and Gold Medal in its own right.

Research and Implementation Proposals

Aspects of Consciousness

There are various aspects of consciousness generally deemed necessary for a machine to be artificially conscious. A variety of functions in which consciousness plays a role were suggested by Bernard Baars and others. The functions of consciousness suggested by Bernard Baars are Definition and Context Setting, Adaptation and Learning, Editing, Flagging and Debugging, Recruiting and Control, Prioritizing and Access-Control, Decision-making or Executive Function, Analogy-forming Function, Metacognitive and Self-monitoring Function, and Autoprogramming and Self-maintenance Function. Igor Aleksander suggested 12 principles for artificial consciousness and these are: The Brain is a State Machine, Inner Neuron Partitioning, Conscious and Unconscious States, Perceptual Learning and Memory, Prediction, The Awareness of Self, Representation of Meaning, Learning Utterances, Learning Language, Will, Instinct, and Emotion. The aim of AC is to define whether and how these and other aspects of consciousness can be synthesized in an engineered artifact such as a digital computer. This list is not exhaustive; there are many others not covered.

Awareness

Awareness could be one required aspect, but there are many problems with the exact definition of *awareness*. The results of the experiments of neuroscanning on monkeys suggest that a process, not only a state or object, activates neurons. Awareness includes creating and testing alternative models of each process based on the information received through the senses or imagined, and is also useful for making predictions. Such modeling needs a lot of flexibility. Creating such a model includes modeling of the physical world, modeling of one's own internal states and processes, and modeling of other conscious entities.

There are at least three types of awareness: agency awareness, goal awareness, and sensorimotor awareness, which may also be conscious or not. For example, in agency awareness you may be aware that you performed a certain action yesterday, but are not now conscious of it. In goal awareness you may be aware that you must search for a lost object, but are not now conscious of it. In sensorimotor awareness, you may be aware that your hand is resting on an object, but are not now conscious of it.

Because objects of awareness are often conscious, the distinction between awareness and consciousness is frequently blurred or they are used as synonyms.

Memory

Conscious events interact with memory systems in learning, rehearsal, and retrieval. The IDA model elucidates the role of consciousness in the updating of perceptual memory, transient episodic memory, and procedural memory. Transient episodic and declarative memories have distributed representations in IDA, there is evidence that this is also the case in the nervous system. In IDA, these two memories are implemented computationally using a modified version of Kanerva's Sparse distributed memory architecture.

Learning

Learning is also considered necessary for AC. By Bernard Baars, conscious experience is needed to represent and adapt to novel and significant events. By Axel Cleeremans and Luis Jiménez, learning is defined as a set of philogenetically advanced adaptation processes that critically depend on an evolved sensitivity to subjective experience so as to enable agents to afford flexible control over their actions in complex, unpredictable environments.

Anticipation

The ability to predict (or anticipate) foreseeable events is considered important for AC by Igor Aleksander. The emergentist multiple drafts principle proposed by Daniel Dennett in *Consciousness Explained* may be useful for prediction: it involves the evaluation and selection of the most appropriate "draft" to fit the current environment. Anticipation includes prediction of consequences of one's own proposed actions and prediction of consequences of probable actions by other entities.

Relationships between real world states are mirrored in the state structure of a conscious organism enabling the organism to predict events. An artificially conscious machine should be able to anticipate events correctly in order to be ready to respond to them when they occur or to take preemptive action to avert anticipated events. The implication here is that the machine needs flexible, real-time components that build spatial, dynamic, statistical, functional, and cause-effect models of the real world and predicted worlds, making it possible to demonstrate that it possesses artificial consciousness in the present and future and not only in the past. In order to do this, a conscious machine should make coherent predictions and contingency plans, not only in worlds with fixed rules like a chess board, but also for novel environments that may change, to be executed only when appropriate to simulate and control the real world.

Subjective Experience

Subjective experiences or qualia are widely considered to be the hard problem of consciousness. Indeed, it is held to pose a challenge to physicalism, let alone computationalism. On the other hand, there are problems in other fields of science which limit that which we can observe, such as the uncertainty principle in physics, which have not made the research in these fields of science impossible.

Role of Cognitive Architectures

The term cognitive architecture may refer to a theory about the structure of the human mind, or any portion or function thereof, including consciousness. In another context, a cognitive architecture implements the theory on computers. An example is QuBIC: Quantum and Bio-inspired Cognitive Architecture for Machine Consciousness. One of the main goals of a cognitive architecture is to summarize the various results of cognitive psychology in a comprehensive computer model. However, the results need to be in a formalized form so they can be the basis of a computer program. Also, the role of cognitive architecture is for the A.I. to clearly structure, build, and implement it's thought process.

Symbolic or Hybrid Proposals

Franklin's Intelligent Distribution Agent

Stan Franklin defines an autonomous agent as possessing functional consciousness when it is capable of several of the functions of consciousness as identified by Bernard Baars Global Workspace Theory. His brain child IDA (Intelligent Distribution Agent) is a software implementation of GWT, which makes it functionally conscious by definition. IDA's task is to negotiate new assignments for sailors in the US Navy after they end a tour of duty, by matching each individual's skills and preferences with the Navy's needs. IDA interacts with Navy databases and communicates with the sailors via natural language e-mail dialog while obeying a large set of Navy policies. The IDA computational model was developed during 1996–2001 at Stan Franklin's Conscious Software Research Group at the University of Memphis. It consists of approximately a quarter-million lines of Java code, and almost completely consumes the resources of a 2001 high-end workstation. It relies heavily on codelets, which are special purpose, relatively independent, mini-agents typically implemented as a small piece of code running as a separate thread. In IDA's top-down architecture, high-level cognitive functions are explicitly modeled. While IDA is functionally conscious by definition, Franklin does "not attribute phenomenal consciousness to his own 'conscious' software agent, IDA, in spite of her many human-like behaviours. This in spite of watching several US Navy detailers repeatedly nodding their heads saying 'Yes, that's how I do it' while watching IDA's internal and external actions as she performs her task".

Ron Sun's Cognitive Architecture Clarion

CLARION posits a two-level representation that explains the distinction between conscious and unconscious mental processes.

CLARION has been successful in accounting for a variety of psychological data. A number of well-known skill learning tasks have been simulated using CLARION that span the spectrum ranging from simple reactive skills to complex cognitive skills. The tasks include serial reaction time (SRT) tasks, artificial grammar learning (AGL) tasks, process control (PC) tasks, the categorical inference (CI) task, the alphabetical arithmetic (AA) task, and the Tower of Hanoi (TOH) task. Among them, SRT, AGL, and PC are typical implicit learning tasks, very much relevant to the issue of consciousness as they operationalized the notion of consciousness in the context of psychological experiments.

Ben Goertzel's OpenCog

Ben Goertzel is pursuing an embodied AGI through the open-source OpenCog project. Current code includes embodied virtual pets capable of learning simple English-language commands, as well as integration with real-world robotics, being done at the Hong Kong Polytechnic University.

Connectionist Proposals

Haikonen's Cognitive Architecture

Pentti Haikonen considers classical rule-based computing inadequate for achieving AC: "the brain is definitely not a computer. Thinking is not an execution of programmed strings of commands. The brain is not a numerical calculator either. We do not think by numbers." Rather than trying to achieve mind and consciousness by identifying and implementing their underlying computational rules, Haikonen proposes "a special cognitive architecture to reproduce the processes of perception, inner imagery, inner speech, pain, pleasure, emotions and the cognitive functions behind these. This bottom-up architecture would produce higher-level functions by the power of the elementary processing units, the artificial neurons, without algorithms or programs". Haikonen believes that, when implemented with sufficient complexity, this architecture will develop consciousness, which he considers to be a style and way of operation, characterized by distributed signal representation, perception process, cross-modality reporting and availability for retrospection. Haikonen is not alone in this process view of consciousness, or the view that AC will spontaneously emerge in autonomous agents that have a suitable neuro-inspired architecture of complexity; these are shared by many, e.g. Freeman and Cotterill. A low-complexity implementation of the architecture proposed by Haikonen was reportedly not capable of AC, but did exhibit emotions as expected. See Doan for a comprehensive introduction to Haikonen's cognitive architecture. An updated account of Haikonen's architecture, along with a summary of his philosophical views, is given in Haikonen, Haikonen.

Takeno's Self-awareness Research

Self-awareness in robots is being investigated by Junichi Takeno at Meiji University in Japan. Takeno is asserting that he has developed a robot capable of discriminating between a self-image in a mirror and any other having an identical image to it, and this claim has already been reviewed. Takeno asserts that he first contrived the computational module called a MoNAD, which has a self-aware function, and he then constructed the artificial consciousness system by formulating the relationships between emotions, feelings and reason by connecting the modules in a hierarchy. Takeno completed a mirror image cognition experiment using a robot equipped with the MoNAD system. Takeno proposed the Self-Body Theory stating that "humans feel that their own mirror image is closer to themselves than an actual part of themselves." The most important point in developing artificial consciousness or clarifying human consciousness is the development of a function of self awareness, and he claims that he has demonstrated physical and mathematical evidence for this in his thesis. He also demonstrated that robots can study episodes in memory where the emotions were stimulated and use this experience to take predictive actions to prevent the recurrence of unpleasant emotions.

Aleksander's Impossible Mind

Igor Aleksander, emeritus professor of Neural Systems Engineering at Imperial College, has extensively researched artificial neural networks and claims in his book *Impossible Minds: My Neurons, My Consciousness* that the principles for creating a conscious machine already exist but that it would take forty years to train such a machine to understand language. Whether this is true remains to be demonstrated and the basic principle stated in *Impossible Minds*—that the brain is a neural state machine—is open to doubt.

Thaler's Creativity Machine Paradigm

Stephen Thaler proposed a possible connection between consciousness and creativity in his 1994 patent, called "Device for the Autonomous Generation of Useful Information" (DAGUI), or the so-called "Creativity Machine", in which computational critics govern the injection of synaptic noise and degradation into neural nets so as to induce false memories or confabulations that may qualify as potential ideas or strategies. He recruits this neural architecture and methodology to account for the subjective feel of consciousness, claiming that similar noise-driven neural assemblies within the brain invent dubious significance to overall cortical activity. Thaler's theory and the resulting patents in machine consciousness were inspired by experiments in which he internally disrupted trained neural nets so as to drive a succession of neural activation patterns that he likened to stream of consciousness.

Michael Graziano's Attention Schema

In 2011, Michael Graziano and Sabine Kastler published a paper named "Human consciousness and its relationship to social neuroscience: A novel hypothesis" proposing a theory of consciousness as an attention schema. Graziano went on to publish an expanded discussion of this theory in his book "Consciousness and the Social Brain". This Attention Schema Theory of Consciousness, as he named it, proposes that the brain tracks attention to various sensory inputs by way of an attention schema, analogous to the well study body schema that tracks the spatial place of a person's body. This relates to artificial consciousness by proposing a specific mechanism of information handling, that produces what we allegedly experience and describe as consciousness, and which should be able to be duplicated by a machine using current technology. When the brain finds that person X is aware of thing Y, it is in effect modeling the state in which person X is applying an attentional enhancement to Y. In the attention schema theory, the same process can be applied to oneself. The brain tracks attention to various sensory inputs, and one's own awareness is a schematized model of one's attention. Graziano proposes specific locations in the brain for this process, and suggests that such awareness is a computed feature constructed by an expert system in the brain.

Testing

The most well-known method for testing machine intelligence is the Turing test. But when interpreted as only observational, this test contradicts the philosophy of science principles of theory dependence of observations. It also has been suggested that Alan Turing's recommendation of imitating not a human adult consciousness, but a human child consciousness, should be taken seriously.

Other tests, such as ConsScale, test the presence of features inspired by biological systems, or measure the cognitive development of artificial systems.

Qualia, or phenomenological consciousness, is an inherently first-person phenomenon. Although various systems may display various signs of behavior correlated with functional consciousness, there is no conceivable way in which third-person tests can have access to first-person phenomenological features. Because of that, and because there is no empirical definition of consciousness, a test of presence of consciousness in AC may be impossible.

In 2014, Victor Argonov suggested a non-turing test for machine consciousness based on machine's ability to produce philosophical judgments. He argues that a deterministic machine must be regarded as conscious if it is able to produce judgments on all problematic properties of consciousness (such as qualia or binding) having no innate (preloaded) philosophical knowledge on these issues, no philosophical discussions while learning, and no informational models of other creatures in its memory (such models may implicitly or explicitly contain knowledge about these creatures' consciousness). However, this test can be used only to detect, but not refute the existence of consciousness. A positive result proves that machine is conscious but a negative result proves nothing. For example, absence of philosophical judgments may be caused by lack of the machine's intellect, not by absence of consciousness.

COMPUTATIONAL ANATOMY

Computational anatomy is an interdisciplinary field of biology focused on quantitative investigation and modelling of anatomical shapes variability. It involves the development and application of mathematical, statistical and data-analytical methods for modelling and simulation of biological structures.

The field is broadly defined and includes foundations in anatomy, applied mathematics and pure mathematics, machine learning, computational mechanics, computational science, biological imaging, neuroscience, physics, probability, and statistics; it also has strong connections with fluid mechanics and geometric mechanics. Additionally, it complements newer, interdisciplinary fields like bioinformatics and neuroinformatics in the sense that its interpretation uses metadata derived from the original sensor imaging modalities (of which Magnetic Resonance Imaging is one example). It focuses on the anatomical structures being imaged, rather than the medical imaging devices. It is similar in spirit to the history of Computational linguistics, a discipline that focuses on the linguistic structures rather than the sensor acting as the transmission and communication medium.

In computational anatomy, the diffeomorphism group is used to study different coordinate systems via coordinate transformations as generated via the Lagrangian and Eulerian velocities of flow in $\mathbb{R}^3$. The flows between coordinates in computational anatomy are constrained to be geodesic flows satisfying the principle of least action for the Kinetic energy of the flow. The kinetic energy is defined through a Sobolev smoothness norm with strictly more than two generalized, square-integrable derivatives for each component of the flow velocity, which guarantees that the flows in $\mathbb{R}^3$

are diffeomorphisms. It also implies that the diffeomorphic shape momentum taken pointwise satisfying the Euler-Lagrange equation for geodesics is determined by its neighbors through spatial derivatives on the velocity field. This separates the discipline from the case of incompressible fluids for which momentum is a pointwise function of velocity. Computational anatomy intersects the study of Riemannian manifolds and nonlinear global analysis, where groups of diffeomorphisms are the central focus. Emerging high-dimensional theories of shape are central to many studies in computational anatomy, as are questions emerging from the fledgling field of shape statistics. The metric structures in computational anatomy are related in spirit to morphometrics, with the distinction that computational anatomy focuses on an infinite-dimensional space of coordinate systems transformed by a diffeomorphism, hence the central use of the terminology diffeomorphometry, the metric space study of coordinate systems via diffeomorphisms.

Genesis

At computational anatomy's heart is the comparison of shape by recognizing in one shape the other. This connects it to D'Arcy Wentworth Thompson's developments "On Growth and Form" which has led to scientific explanations of morphogenesis, the process by which patterns are formed in Biology. Albrecht Durer's four Books on Human Proportion were arguably the earliest works on computational anatomy. The efforts of Noam Chomsky in his pioneering of Computational Linguistics inspired the original formulation of computational anatomy as a generative model of shape and form from exemplars acted upon via transformations.

Due to the availability of dense 3D measurements via technologies such as magnetic resonance imaging (MRI), computational anatomy has emerged as a subfield of medical imaging and bioengineering for extracting anatomical coordinate systems at the morphome scale in 3D. The spirit of this discipline shares strong overlap with areas such as computer vision and kinematics of rigid bodies, where objects are studied by analysing the groups responsible for the movement in question. Computational anatomy departs from computer vision with its focus on rigid motions, as the infinite-dimensional diffeomorphism group is central to the analysis of Biological shapes. It is a branch of the image analysis and pattern theory school at Brown University pioneered by Ulf Grenander. In Grenander's general Metric Pattern Theory, making spaces of patterns into a metric space is one of the fundamental operations since being able to cluster and recognize anatomical configurations often requires a metric of close and far between shapes. The diffeomorphometry metric of computational anatomy measures how far two diffeomorphic changes of coordinates are from each other, which in turn induces a metric on the shapes and images indexed to them. The models of metric pattern theory, in particular group action on the orbit of shapes and forms is a central tool to the formal definitions in computational anatomy.

The Deformable Template Orbit Model of Computational Anatomy

The model of human anatomy is a deformable template, an orbit of exemplars under group action. Deformable template models have been central to Grenander's Metric Pattern theory, accounting for typicality via templates, and accounting for variability via transformation of the template. An orbit under group action as the representation of the deformable template is a classic formulation from differential geometry. The space of shapes are denoted $m \in \mathcal{M}$, with the group $(\mathcal{G}, o)$ with law of composition the action of the group on shapes is denoted $g \cdot m$, where the action of the group $g \cdot m \in \mathcal{M}, m \in \mathcal{M}$ is defined to satisfy:

$$(g o g') \cdot m = g \cdot (g' \cdot m) \in \mathcal{M}.$$

The orbit $\mathcal{M}$ of the template becomes the space of all shapes, $\mathcal{M} \doteq \{m = g \cdot m_{\text{temp}}, g \in \mathcal{G}\}$, being homogenous under the action of the elements of $\mathcal{G}$.

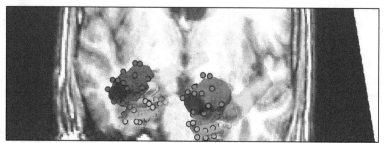

Depicting three medial temporal lobe structures amgydala, entorhinal cortex and hippocampus with fiducial landmarks depicted as well embedded in the MRI background.

The orbit model of computational anatomy is an abstract algebra - to be compared to linear algebra- since the groups act nonlinearly on the shapes. This is a generalization of the classical models of linear algebra, in which the set of finite dimensional $\mathbb{R}^n$ vectors are replaced by the finite-dimensional anatomical submanifolds (points, curves, surfaces and volumes) and images of them, and the $n \times n$ matrices of linear algebra are replaced by coordinate transformations based on linear and affine groups and the more general high-dimensional diffeomorphism groups.

Shapes and Forms

The central objects are shapes or forms in computational anatomy, one set of examples being the 0,1,2,3-dimensional submanifolds of $\mathbb{R}^3$, a second set of examples being images generated via medical imaging such as via magnetic resonance imaging (MRI) and functional magnetic resonance imaging.

The 0-dimensional manifolds are landmarks or fiducial points; 1-dimensional manifolds are curves such as sulcul and gyral curves in the brain; 2-dimensional manifolds correspond to boundaries of substructures in anatomy such as the subcortical structures of the midbrain or the gyral surface of the neocortex; subvolumes correspond to subregions of the human body, the heart, the thalamus, the kidney.

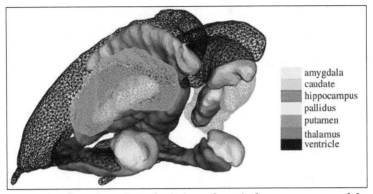

Triangulated mesh surfaces depicting subcortical structures amygdala, hippocampus, thalamus, caudate, putamen, ventricles. The shapes are denoted $m(u), u \in U \subset \mathbb{R}^1 \to \mathbb{R}^2$ represented as triangulated meshes.

The landmarks $X \doteq \{x_1, \ldots, x_n\} \subset \mathbb{R}^3 \in \mathcal{M}$ are a collections of points with no other structure, delineating important fiducials within human shape and form. The sub-manifold shapes such as surfaces $X \subset \mathbb{R}^3 \in \mathcal{M}$ are collections of points modeled as parametrized by a local chart or immersion $m: U \subset \mathbb{R}^{1,2} \to \mathbb{R}$, $m(u), u \in U$. The images such as MR images or DTI images $I \in \mathcal{M}$, and are dense functions $I(x), x \in X \subset \mathbb{R}^{1,2,3}$ are scalars, vectors, and matrices.

Groups and Group Actions

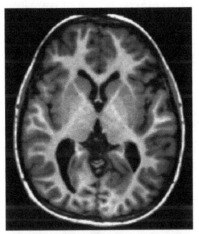

Showing an MRI section through a 3D brain representing a scalar image $I(x), x \in \mathbb{R}^2$ based on T1-weighting.

Groups and group actions are familiar to the Engineering community with the universal popularization and standardization of linear algebra as a basic model for analyzing signals and systems in mechanical engineering, electrical engineering and applied mathematics. In linear algebra the matrix groups (matrices with inverses) are the central structure, with group action defined by the usual definition of A as an $n \times n$ matrix, acting on $x \in \mathbb{R}^n$ as $n \times 1$ vectors; the orbit in linear-algebra is the set of -vectors given by $y = A \cdot x \in \mathbb{R}^n$, which is a group action of the matrices through the orbit of $\mathbb{R}^n$.

The central group in computational anatomy defined on volumes in $\mathbb{R}^3$ are the diffeomorphisms $\mathcal{G} \doteq Diff$ which are mappings with 3-components $\phi(\cdot) = (\phi_1(\cdot), \phi_2(\cdot), \phi_3(\cdot))$, law of composition of functions $\phi \circ \phi'(\cdot) \doteq \phi(\phi'(\cdot))$, with inverse $\phi \circ \phi^{-1}(\cdot) = \phi(\phi^{-1}(\cdot)) = id$.

Most popular are scalar images, $I(x), x \in \mathbb{R}^3$, with action on the right via the inverse.

$$\phi \cdot I(x) = I \circ \phi^{-1}(x), x \in \mathbb{R}^3.$$

For sub-manifolds $X \subset \mathbb{R}^3 \in \mathcal{M}$, parametrized by a chart or immersion $m(u), u \in U$, the diffeomorphic action the flow of the position:

$$\phi \cdot m(u) \doteq \phi \circ m(u), u \in U.$$

Several group actions in computational anatomy have been defined.

Lagrangian and Eulerian Flows for Generating Diffeomorphisms

For the study of rigid body kinematics, the low-dimensional matrix lie groups have been the central focus. The matrix groups are low-dimensional mappings, which are diffeomorphisms that provide one-to-one correspondences between coordinate systems, with a smooth inverse. The matrix group of rotations and scales can be generated via a closed form finite-dimensional matrices which are solution of simple ordinary differential equations with solutions given by the matrix exponential.

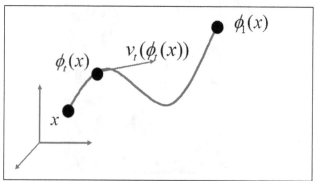

Showing the Lagrangian flow of coordinates $x \in X$ with associated vector fields $v_t, t \in [0,1]$ satisfying ordinary differential equation $\dot{\phi}_t = v_t(\phi_t), \phi_0 = id$.

For the study of deformable shape in computational anatomy, a more general diffeomorphism group has been the group of choice, which is the infinite dimensional analogue. The high-dimensional differeomorphism groups used in computational anatomy are generated via smooth flows $\phi_t, t \in [0,1]$ which satisfy the Lagrangian and Eulerian specification of the flow fields as first introduced in., satisfying the ordinary differential equation:

$$\frac{d}{dt}\phi_t = v_t \circ \phi_t, \phi_0 = id \quad \text{(Lagrangian flow)},$$

with $v \doteq (v_1, v_2, v_3)$ the vector fields on $\mathbb{R}^3$ termed the Eulerian velocity of the particles at position $\mathbb{R}^3$ of the flow. The vector fields are functions in a function space, modelled as a smooth Hilbert space of high-dimension, with the Jacobian of the flow $D\phi \doteq (\frac{\partial \phi_i}{\partial x_j})$ a high-dimensional field in a function space as well, rather than a low-dimensional matrix as in the matrix groups. Flows were first introduced for large deformations in image matching; $\dot{\phi}_t(x)$ is the instantaneous velocity of particle x at time t.

The inverse $\phi_t^{-1}, t \in [0,1]$ required for the group is defined on the Eulerian vector-field with advective inverse flow:

$$\frac{d}{dt}\phi_t^{-1} = -(D\phi_t^{-1})v_t, \phi_0^{-1} = id . \quad \text{(Inverse Transport flow)}.$$

The Diffeomorphism Group of Computational Anatomy

The group of diffeomorphisms is very big. To ensure smooth flows of diffeomorphisms avoiding shock-like solutions for the inverse, the vector fields must be at least 1-time continuously differentiable in space. For diffeomorphisms on $\mathbb{R}^3$, vector fields are modelled as elements of the Hilbert space $(V, \|\cdot\|_V)$ using the Sobolev embedding theorems so that each element has strictly greater than 2 generalized square-integrable spatial derivatives (thus $v_i \in H_0^3, i = 1, 2, 3$, is sufficient), yielding 1-time continuously differentiable functions.

The diffeomorphism group are flows with vector fields absolutely integrable in Sobolev norm:

$$Diff_V \doteq \{\varphi = \phi_1 : \dot{\phi}_t = v_t \circ \phi_t, \phi_0 = id, \int_0^1 \|v_t\|_V \, dt < \infty\}, \quad \text{(Diffeomorphism Group)}$$

where $\|v\|_V^2 \doteq \int_X Av \cdot v dx, v \in V$, with the linear operator A mapping to the dual space $A : V \mapsto V^*$, with the integral calculated by integration by parts when $Av \in V^*$ is a generalized function in the dual space.

Diffeomorphometry: The Metric Space of Shapes and Forms

The study of metrics on groups of diffeomorphisms and the study of metrics between manifolds and surfaces has been an area of significant investigation. The diffeomorphometry metric measures how close and far two shapes or images are from each other; the metric length is the shortest length of the flow which carries one coordinate system into the other.

Oftentimes, the familiar Euclidean metric is not directly applicable because the patterns of shapes and images don't form a vector space. In the Riemannian orbit model of computational anatomy, diffeomorphisms acting on the forms $\phi \cdot m \in \mathcal{M}, \phi \in Diff_V, m \in \mathcal{M}$ don't act linearly. There are many ways to define metrics, and for the sets associated to shapes the Hausdorff metric is another. The method we use to induce the Riemannian metric is used to induce the metric on the orbit of shapes by defining it in terms of the metric length between diffeomorphic coordinate system transformations of the flows. Measuring the lengths of the geodesic flow between coordinates systems in the orbit of shapes is called diffeomorphometry.

The Right-invariant Metric on Diffeomorphisms

Define the distance on the group of diffeomorphisms:

$$d_{Diff_V}(\psi, \varphi) = \inf_{v_t}(\int_0^1 \int_X A v_t \cdot v_t \, dx \, dt : \phi_0 = \psi, \phi_1 = \varphi, \dot{\phi}_t = v_t \circ \phi_t)^{1/2}; \text{ (metric-diffeomorphisms)}$$

this is the right-invariant metric of diffeomorphometry, invariant to reparameterization of space since for all $\phi \in Diff_V$:

$$d_{Diff_V}(\psi, \varphi) = d_{Diff_V}(\psi \circ \phi, \varphi \circ \phi).$$

The Metric on Shapes and Forms

The distance on shapes and forms, $d_{\mathcal{M}} : \mathcal{M} \times \mathcal{M} \to \mathbb{R}^+$,

$$d_{\mathcal{M}}(m, n) = \inf_{\phi \in Diff_V : \phi \cdot m = n} d_{Diff_V}(id, \phi); \text{ (metric-shapes-forms)}$$

the images are denoted with the orbit as $I \in \mathcal{I}$ and metric $d_{\mathcal{I}}$.

The Action Integral for Hamilton's Principle on Diffeomorphic Flows

In classical mechanics the evolution of physical systems is described by solutions to the Euler–Lagrange equations associated to the Least-action principle of Hamilton. This is a standard way, for example of obtaining Newton's laws of motion of free particles. More generally, the Euler-Lagrange equations can be derived for systems of generalized coordinates. The Euler-Lagrange equation in computational anatomy de-scribes the geodesic shortest path flows between coordinate systems of the diffeomor-phism metric. In computational anatomy the generalized coordinates are the flow of the diffeomorphism and its Lagrangian velocity $\phi, \dot{\phi}$, the two related via the Eulerian velocity $v \doteq \dot{\phi} \circ \phi^{-1}$. Hamilton's principle for generating the Euler-Lagrange equation requires the action integral on the Lagrangian given by:

$$J(\phi) \doteq \int_0^1 L(\phi_t, \dot{\phi}_t) dt \; ; \text{(Hamiltonian-Integrated-Lagrangian)}.$$

The Lagrangian is given by the kinetic energy:

$$L(\phi_t, \dot{\phi}_t) \doteq \frac{1}{2} \int_X A(\dot{\phi}_t \circ \phi_t^{-1}) \cdot (\dot{\phi}_t \circ \phi_t^{-1}) dx = \frac{1}{2} \int_X Av_t \cdot v_t \, dx \; . \text{(Lagrangian-Kinetic-Energy)}.$$

Diffeomorphic or Eulerian Shape Momentum

In computational anatomy, Av was first called the Eulerian or diffeomorphic shape momentum since when integrated against Eulerian velocity v gives energy density, and since there is a conservation of diffeomorphic shape momentum which holds. The op-erator A is the generalized moment of inertia or inertial operator.

The Euler–Lagrange Equation on Shape Momentum for Geodesics on the Group of Diffeomorphisms

Classical calculation of the Euler-Lagrange equation from Hamilton's principle requires the perturbation of the Lagrangian on the vector field in the kinetic energy with respect to first order perturbation of the flow. This requires adjustment by the Lie bracket of vector field, given by operator $ad_v : w \in V \mapsto V$ which involves the Jacobian given by

$$ad_v[w] \doteq [v, w] \doteq (Dv)w - (Dw)v \in V.$$

Defining the adjoint $ad_v^* : V^* \to V^*$, then the first order variation gives the Eulerian shape momentum $Av \in V^*$ satisfying the generalized equation:

$$\frac{d}{dt} Av_t + ad_{v_t}^*(Av_t) = 0 \, , t \in [0,1] \; ; \text{(EL-General)}$$

meaning for all smooth $w \in V$,

$$\int_X (\frac{d}{dt} Av_t + ad_{v_t}^*(Av_t)) \cdot w dx = \int_X \frac{d}{dt} Av_t \cdot w dx + \int_X Av_t \cdot ((Dv_t)w - (Dw)v_t) dx = 0.$$

Computational anatomy is the study of the motions of submanifolds, points, curves, surfaces and volumes. Momentum associated to points, curves and surfaces are all singular, implying the momentum is concentrated on subsets of $\mathbb{R}^3$ which are dimension ≤ 2 in Lebesgue measure. In such cases, the energy is still well defined $(Av_t \mid v_t)$ since although Av_t is a generalized function, the vector fields are smooth and the Eulerian momentum is understood via its action on smooth functions. The perfect illustration of this is even when it is a superposition of delta-diracs, the velocity of the coordinates in the entire volume move smoothly. The Euler-Lagrange equation (EL-General) on diffeomorphisms for generalized functions $Av \in V^*$ was derived in. In Riemannian Metric and Lie-Bracket Interpretation of the Euler-Lagrange Equation on Geodesics derivations are provided in terms of the adjoint operator and the Lie bracket for the group of diffeomorphisms. It has come to be called EP equation for diffeomorphisms connecting to the Euler-Poincare method having been studied in the context of the inertial operator $A = identity$ for incompressible, divergence free, fluids.

Diffeomorphic Shape Momentum: A Classical Vector Function

For the momentum density case $(Av_t \mid w) = \int_X \mu_t \cdot w dx,$, then Euler–Lagrange equation has a classical solution:

$$\frac{d}{dt}\mu_t + (Dv_t)^T \mu_t + (D\mu_t)v_t + (\nabla \cdot v)\mu_t = 0 , t \in [0,1].$$ (EL-Classic)

The Euler-Lagrange equation on diffeomorphisms, classically defined for momentum densities first appeared in for medical image analysis.

Riemannian Exponential (Geodesic Positioning) and Riemannian Logarithm (geodesic Coordinates)

In medical imaging and computational anatomy, positioning and coordinatizing shapes are fundamental operations; the system for positioning anatomical coordinates and shapes built on the metric and the Euler-Lagrange equation a geodesic positioning system as first explicated in Miller Trouve and Younes. Solving the geodesic from the initial condition v_0 is termed the Riemannian-exponential, a mapping $Exp_{id}(\cdot) : V \rightarrow Diff_V$ at identity to the group.

The Riemannian exponential satisfies $Exp_{id}(v_0)$ for initial condition $\dot{\phi}_0 = v_0$, vector field dynamics $\dot{\phi}_t = v_t \circ \phi_t, t \in [0,1]$

- For classical equation diffeomorphic shape momentum $\int_X Av_t \cdot w dx, Av \in V$ then,

$$\frac{d}{dt}Av_t + (Dv_t)^T Av_t + (DAv_t)v_t + (\nabla \cdot v)Av_t = 0$$

- For generalized equation, then $Av \in V^*, w \in V$.

$$\int_X \frac{d}{dt} Av_t \cdot w dx + \int_X Av_t \cdot ((Dv_t)w - (Dw)v_t) dx = 0.$$

Computing the flow v_0 onto coordinates Riemannian logarithm, mapping $Log_{id}(\cdot): Diff_V \to V$ at identity from φ to vector field $v_0 \in V$:

$$Log_{id}(\varphi) = v_0 \text{ initial condition of EL geodesic } \dot{\phi}_0 = v_0, \phi_0 = id, \phi_1 = \varphi.$$

Extended to the entire group they become:

$$\phi = Exp_\varphi(v_0 \circ \varphi) \doteq Exp_{id}(v_0) \circ \varphi; Log_\varphi(\phi) \doteq Log_{id}(\phi \circ \varphi^{-1}) \circ \varphi.$$

These are inverses of each other for unique solutions of Logarithm; the first is called geodesic positioning, the latter geodesic coordinates. The geodesic metric is a local flattening of the Riemannian coordinate system.

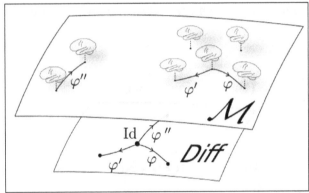

Showing metric local flattening of coordinatized manifolds of shapes and forms. The local metric is given by the norm of the vector field $\| v_0 \|_V$ of the geodesic mapping $Exp_{id}(v_0) \cdot m$.

Hamiltonian Formulation of Computational Anatomy

In computational anatomy the diffeomorphisms are used to push the coordinate systems, and the vector fields are used as the control within the anatomical orbit or morphological space. The model is that of a dynamical system, the flow of coordinates $t \mapsto \phi_t \in Diff_V$ and the control the vector field $t \mapsto v_t \in V$ related via $\dot{\phi}_t = v_t \cdot \phi_t, \phi_0 = id$. The Hamiltonian view reparameterizes the momentum distribution $Av \in V^*$ in terms of the *conjugate momentum or canonical momentum*, introduced as a Lagrange multiplier $p: \dot{\phi} \mapsto (p \mid \dot{\phi})$ constraining the Lagrangian velocity $\dot{\phi}_t = v_t \circ \phi_t$. accordingly:

$$H(\phi_t, p_t, v_t) = \int_X p_t \cdot (v_t \circ \phi_t) dx - \frac{1}{2} \int_X Av_t \cdot v_t dx$$

This function is the extended Hamiltonian. The Pontryagin maximum principle gives the optimizing vector field which determines the geodesic flow satisfying $\dot{\phi}_t = v_t \circ \phi_t, \phi_0 = id$, as well as the reduced Hamiltonian:

$$H(\phi_t, p_t) \doteq \max_v H(\phi_t, p_t, v).$$

The Lagrange multiplier in its action as a linear form has its own inner product of the canonical momentum acting on the velocity of the flow which is dependent on the shape, e.g. for landmarks a sum, for surfaces a surface integral, and. for volumes it is a volume integral with respect to dx on $\mathbb{R}^3$. In all cases the Greens kernels carry weights which are the canonical momentum evolving according to an ordinary differential equation which corresponds to EL but is the geodesic reparameterization in canonical momentum. The optimizing vector field is given by:

$$v_t \doteq \arg max_v H(\phi_t, p_t, v),$$

with dynamics of canonical momentum reparameterizing the vector field along the geodesic:

$$\begin{cases} \dot{\phi}_t = \dfrac{\partial H(\phi_t, p_t)}{\partial p} \\ \dot{p}_t = -\dfrac{\partial H(\phi_t, p_t)}{\partial \phi} \end{cases} \quad \text{(Hamiltonian-Dynamics)}.$$

Stationarity of the Hamiltonian and Kinetic Energy along Euler–Lagrange

Whereas the vector fields are extended across the entire background space of , the geodesic flows associated to the submanifolds has Eulerian shape momentum which evolves as a generalized function $Av_t \in V^*$ concentrated to the submanifolds. For landmarks the geodesics have Eulerian shape momentum which are a superposition of delta distributions travelling with the finite numbers of particles; the diffeomorphic flow of coordinates have velocities in the range of weighted Green's Kernels. For surfaces, the momentum is a surface integral of delta distributions travelling with the surface.

The geodesics connecting coordinate systems satisfying EL-General have stationarity of the Lagrangian. The Hamiltonian is given by the extremum along the path $t \in [0,1]$, $H(\phi, p) = \max_v H(\phi, p, v)$, equalling the Lagrangian-Kinetic-Energy and is stationary along EL-General. Defining the geodesic velocity at the identity $v_0 = \arg \max_v H(\phi_0, p_0, v)$, then along the geodesic:

$$H(\phi_t, p_t) = H(\phi_0, p_0) = \frac{1}{2} \int_X p_0 \cdot v_0 dx = \frac{1}{2} \int_X Av_0 \cdot v_0 dx = \frac{1}{2} \int_X Av_t \cdot v_t dx.$$

The stationarity of the Hamiltonian demonstrates the interpretation of the Lagrange multiplier as momentum; integrated against velocity $\dot{\phi}$ gives energy density. The canonical momentum has many names. In optimal control, the flows ϕ is interpreted as the state, and p is interpreted as conjugate state, or conjugate momentum. The geodesi of EL implies specification of the vector fields Av_o or Eulerian momentum Av_0 at $t = 0$, or specification of canonical momentum p_0 determines the flow.

The Metric on Geodesic Flows of Landmarks, Surfaces and Volumes within the Orbit

In computational anatomy the submanifolds are pointsets, curves, surfaces and sub-volumes which are the basic primitives. The geodesic flows between the submani-folds determine the distance, and form the basic measuring and transporting tools of diffeomorphometry. At the geodesic has vector field $v_0 = Kp_0$ determined by the conjugate momentum and the Green's kernel of the inertial operator defining the Eulerian momentum $K = A^{-1}$. The metric distance between coordinate systems connected via the geodesic determined by the induced distance between identity and group element:

$$d_{Diff_V}(id, \varphi) = \| Log_{id}(\varphi) \|_V = \| v_0 \|_V = \sqrt{2H(id, p_0)}$$

Conservation Laws on Diffeomorphic Shape Momentum for Computational Anatomy

Given the least-action there is a natural definition of momentum associated to generalized coordinates; the quantity acting against velocity gives energy. The field has studied two forms, the momentum associated to the Eulerian vector field termed Eulerian diffeomorphic shape momentum, and the momentum associated to the initial coordinates or canonical coordinates termed canonical diffeomorphic shape momentum. Each has a conservation law. The conservation of momentum goes hand in hand with the EL-General. In computational anatomy, Av is the Eulerian Momentum since when integrated against Eulerian velocity V gives energy density; operator A the generalized moment of inertia or inertial operator which acting on the Eulerian velocity gives momentum which is conserved along the geodesic:

Eulerian $\qquad \dfrac{d}{dt}\displaystyle\int_X Av_t \cdot ((D\phi_t)w) \circ \phi_t^{-1})dx = 0 \,, t \in [0,1].$

Canonical $\qquad \dfrac{d}{dt}\displaystyle\int_X p_t \cdot ((D\phi_t)w)dx = 0 \,, t \in [0,1] \;\; for\; all\; w \in V.$

Geodesic Interpolation of Information between Coordinate Systems via Variational Problems

Construction of diffeomorphic correspondences between shapes calculates the initial vector field coordinates $v_0 \in V$ and associated weights on the Greens kernels P_o. These initial coordinates are determined by matching of shapes, called Large Deformation Diffeomorphic Metric Mapping (LDDMM). LDDMM has been solved for landmarks with and without correspondence and for dense image matchings. curves, surfaces, dense vector and tensor imagery, and varifolds removing orientation. LDDMM calculates geodesic flows of the EL-General onto target coordinates, adding to the action integral $\frac{1}{2}\int_0^1\int_X Av_t \cdot v_t dx dt$ an endpoint matching condition $E : \phi_1 \to R^+$ measuring the correspondence of elements in the orbit under coordinate system transformation. Existence of solutions were examined for image matching. The solution of the variational problem satisfies the EL-General for $t \in (0,1)$ with boundary condition.

Matching based on Minimizing Kinetic Energy Action with Endpoint Condition

$$\min_{\phi:v=\dot{\phi}\circ\phi^{-1},\phi_0=id} C(\phi) \doteq \frac{1}{2}\int_0^1\int_X Av_t \cdot v_t dx dt + E(\phi_1)$$

$$
\begin{cases}
\textit{Euler Conservation} & \dfrac{d}{dt}Av_t + ad_{v_t}^*(Av_t) = 0, t \in [0,1), \\
\textit{Boundary Condition} & \phi_0 = id, Av_1 = -\dfrac{\partial E(\phi)}{\partial \phi}\Big|_{\phi=\phi_1}.
\end{cases}
$$

Conservation from EL-General extends the B.C. at $t = 1$ to the rest of the path $t \in (0,1)$. The inexact matching problem with the endpoint matching term $E(\phi_1)$ has several alternative forms. One of the key ideas of the stationarity of the Hamiltonian along the geodesic solution is the integrated running cost reduces to initial cost at t=o, geodesics of the EL-General are determined by their initial condition .

The running cost is reduced to the initial cost determined by $v_0 = Kp_0$ of Kernel-Surf-Land-Geodesics.

Matching based on Geodesic Shooting

$$\min_{v_0} C(v_0) \doteq \frac{1}{2}\int_X Av_0 \cdot v_0 dx + E(\mathrm{Exp}_{id}(v_0) \cdot I_0);$$

$$\min_{p_0} C(p_0) = \frac{1}{2} \int_X p_0 \cdot K p_0 dx + E(\text{Exp}_{\text{id}}(K p_0) \cdot I_0)$$

The matching problem explicitly indexed to initial condition v_0 is called shooting, which can also be reparamerized via the conjugate momentum p_0.

Dense Image Matching in Computational Anatomy

Dense image matching has a long history now with the earliest efforts exploiting a small deformation framework. Large deformations began in the early 90's, with the first existence to solutions to the variational problem for flows of diffeomorphisms for dense image matching established in. Beg solved via one of the earliest LDDMM algorithms based on solving the variational matching with endpoint defined by the dense imagery with respect to the vector fields, taking variations with respect to the vector fields. Another solution for dense image matching reparameterizes the optimization problem in terms of the state $q_t \doteq I \circ \phi_t^{-1}, q_0 = I$ giving the solution in terms of the infinitesimal action defined by the advection equation.

LDDMM Dense Image Matching

For Beg's LDDMM, denote the Image $I(x), x \in X$ with group action $\phi \cdot I \doteq I \circ \phi^{-1}$. Viewing this as an optimal control problem, the state of the system is the diffeomorphic flow of coordinates $\phi_t, t \in [0,1]$, , with the dynamics relating the control $v_t, t \in [0,1]$ to the state given by $\dot{\phi} = v \circ \phi$. The endpoint matching condition $E(\phi_1) \doteq \| I \circ \phi_1^{-1} - I' \|^2$ gives the variational problem:

$$\min_{v: \dot{\phi} = v \circ \phi} C(v) \doteq \frac{1}{2} \int_0^1 \int_X A v_t \cdot v_t dx dt + \frac{1}{2} \int_{\mathbb{R}^3} | I \circ \phi_1^{-1}(x) - I'(x) |^2 \, dx$$

$$\begin{cases} \text{Endpoint Condition:} & A v_1 = \mu_1 dx, \mu_1 = (I \circ \phi_1^{-1} - I') \nabla (I \circ \phi_1^{-1}), \\ \text{Conservation:} & A v_t = \mu_t dx, \mu_t = (D \phi_t^{-1})^T \mu_0 \circ \phi_t^{-1} | D \phi_t^{-1} |. \\ & \mu_0 = (I - I' \circ \phi_1) \nabla I | D \phi_1 |. \end{cases}$$

Beg's iterative LDDMM algorithm has fixed points which satisfy the necessary optimizer conditions. The iterative algorithm is given in Beg's LDDMM algorithm for dense image matching.

Hamiltonian LDDMM in the Reduced Advected State

Denote the Image $I(x), x \in X$, with state $q_t \doteq I \circ \phi_t^{-1}$ and the dynamics related state and control given by the advective term $\dot{q}_t = -\nabla q_t \cdot v_t$. The endpoint $E(q_1) \doteq \| q_1 - I' \|^2$ gives the variational problem:

$$\min_{q:\dot{q}=v\circ q} C(v) \doteq \frac{1}{2}\int_0^1\int_X Av_t \cdot v_t dxdt + \frac{1}{2}\int_{\mathbb{R}^3} |q_1(x) - I'(x)|^2\, dx$$

Viallard's iterative Hamiltonian LDDMM has fixed points which satisfy the necessary optimizer conditions.

Diffusion Tensor Image Matching in Computational Anatomy

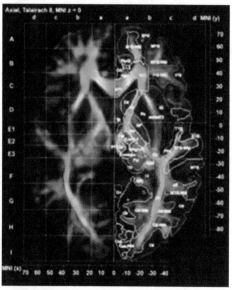

Image showing a diffusion tensor image with three color levels depicting the orientations of the three eigenvectors of the matrix image $I(x), x \in \mathbb{R}^2$, matrix valued image; each of three colors represents a direction.

Dense LDDMM tensor matching takes the images as 3x1 vectors and 3x3 tensors solving the variational problem matching between coordinate system based on the principle eigenvectors of the diffusion tensor MRI image (DTI) denoted $M(x), x \in \mathbb{R}^3$ consisting of the 3×3-tensor at every voxel. Several of the group actions defined based on the Frobenius matrix norm between square matrices $\| A \|_F^2 \doteq trace A^T A$. Shown in the accompanying figure is a DTI image illustrated via its color map depicting the eigenvector orientations of the DTI matrix at each voxel with color determined by the orientation of the directions. Denote the 3×3 tensor image $M(x), x \in \mathbb{R}^3$ with eigen-elements $\{\lambda_i(x), e_i(x), i = 1, 2, 3\}, , \lambda_1 \geq \lambda_2 \geq \lambda_3$.

Coordinate system transformation based on DTI imaging has exploited two actions one based on the principle eigen-vector or entire matrix.

LDDMM matching based on the principal eigenvector of the diffusion tensor matrix takes the image $I(x), x \in \mathbb{R}^3$ as a unit vector field defined by the first eigenvector. The group action becomes:

$$\varphi \cdot I = \begin{cases} \dfrac{D_{\varphi^{-1}} \varphi I \circ \varphi^{-1} \, \| I \circ \varphi^{-1} \|}{\| D_{\varphi^{-1}} \varphi I \circ \varphi^{-1} \|} & I \circ \varphi \neq 0; \\[2ex] 0 & \text{otherwise.} \end{cases}$$

LDDMM matching based on the entire tensor matrix has group action becomes $\varphi \cdot M = (\lambda_1 \hat{e}_1 \hat{e}_1^T + \lambda_2 \hat{e}_2 \hat{e}_2^T + \lambda_3 \hat{e}_3 \hat{e}_3^T) \circ \varphi^{-1}$, transformed eigenvectors:

$$\hat{e}_1 = \frac{D\varphi e_1}{\| D\varphi e_1 \|}, \quad \hat{e}_2 = \frac{D\varphi e_2 - \langle \hat{e}_1, D\varphi e_2 \rangle \hat{e}_1}{\sqrt{\| D\varphi e_2 \|^2 - \langle \hat{e}_1, D\varphi e_2 \rangle^2}}, \quad \hat{e}_3 = \hat{e}_1 \times \hat{e}_2.$$

High Angular Resolution Diffusion Image (HARDI) Matching in Computational Anatomy

High angular resolution diffusion imaging (HARDI) addresses the well-known limitation of DTI, that is, DTI can only reveal one dominant fiber orientation at each location. HARDI measures diffusion along n uniformly distributed directions on the sphere and can characterize more complex fiber geometries. HARDI can be used to reconstruct an orientation distribution function (ODF) that characterizes the angular profile of the diffusion probability density function of water molecules. The ODF is a function defined on a unit sphere, $\mathbb{S}^2$.

Dense LDDMM ODF matching takes the HARDI data as ODF at each voxel and solves the LDDMM variational problem in the space of ODF. In the field of information geometry, the space of ODF forms a Riemannian manifold with the Fisher-Rao metric. For the purpose of LDDMM ODF mapping, the square-root representation is chosen because it is one of the most efficient representations found to date as the various Riemannian operations, such as geodesics, exponential maps, and logarithm maps, are available in closed form. In the following, denote square-root ODF ($\sqrt{\text{ODF}}$) as $\psi(s)$, where $\psi(s)$ is non-negative to ensure uniqueness and $\int_{s \in \mathbb{S}^2} \psi^2(s) ds = 1$. The variational problem for matching assumes that two ODF volumes can be generated from one to another via flows of diffeomorphisms ϕ_t, which are solutions of ordinary differential equations $\dot{\phi}_t = v_t(\phi_t), t \in [0,1]$, starting from the identity map $\phi_0 = id$. Denote the action of the diffeomorphism on template as $\phi_1 \cdot \psi_{\text{temp}}(s, x)$ $s \in \mathbb{S}^2 x \in X.$ are respectively the coordinates of the unit sphere, $\mathbb{S}^2$ and the image domain, with the target indexed similarly, $\psi_{\text{targ}}(s, x), s \in \mathbb{S}^2 x \in X.$

The group action of the diffeomorphism on the template is given according to:

$$\phi_1 \cdot \psi(x) \doteq (D\phi_1)\psi \circ \phi_1^{-1}(x), x \in X$$

where $(D\phi_1)$ is the Jacobian of the affined transformed ODF and is defined as:

$$(D\phi_1)\psi \circ \phi_1^{-1}(x) = \sqrt{\frac{\det(D_{\phi_1^{-1}}\phi_1)^{-1}}{\|(D_{\phi_1^{-1}}\phi_1)^{-1}\mathbf{s}\|^3}} \quad \psi\left(\frac{(D_{\phi_1^{-1}}\phi_1)^{-1}\mathbf{s}}{\|(D_{\phi_1^{-1}}\phi_1)^{-1}\mathbf{s}\|}, \phi_1^{-1}(x)\right).$$

This group action of diffeomorphisms on ODF reorients the ODF and reflects changes in both the magnitude of ψ and the sampling directions of S due to affine transformation. It guarantees that the volume fraction of fibers oriented toward a small patch must remain the same after the patch is transformed.

The LDDMM variational problem is defined as:

$$C(v) = \inf_{v:\dot{\phi}_t=v_t\circ\phi_t, \phi_0=id} \int_0^1 \int_X Av_t \cdot v_t dx \, dt + \lambda \int_{x\in} \| \log_{(D\phi_1)\psi_{\text{temp}}\circ\phi_1^{-1}(x)}(\psi_{\text{targ}}(x)) \|^2_{(D\phi_1)\psi_{\text{temp}}\circ\phi_1^{-1}(x)} dx$$

where the logarithm of $\psi_1, \psi_2 \in \Psi$ is defined as:

$$\| \log_{\psi_1}(\psi_2) \|_{\psi_1} = \cos^{-1}\langle\psi_1, \psi_2 =\rangle \cos^{-1}\left(\int_{s\in\mathbb{S}^2} \psi_1(\mathbf{s})\psi_2(\mathbf{s})d\mathbf{s}\right),$$

where $\langle\cdot,\cdot\rangle$ is the normal dot product between points in the sphere under the L^2 metric.

This LDDMM-ODF mapping algorithm has been widely used to study brain white matter degeneration in aging, Alzheimer's disease, and vascular dementia. The brain white matter atlas generated based on ODF is constructed via Bayesian estimation. Regression analysis on ODF is developed in the ODF manifold space in.

Metamorphosis

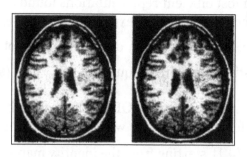

Demonstrating metamorphosis allowing both diffeomorphic change in coordinate transformation as well as change in image intensity as associated to early Morphing technologies such as the Michael Jackson video. Notice the insertion of tumor gray level intensity which does not exist in template.

The principle mode of variation represented by the orbit model is change of coordinates. For setting in which pairs of images are not related by diffeomorphisms but have photometric variation or image variation not represented by the template, active appearance modelling has been introduced, originally by Edwards-Cootes-Taylor and in 3D medical imaging in. In the context of computational anatomy in which metrics on the anatomical orbit has been studied, metamorphosis for modelling structures such as tumors and photometric changes which are not resident in the template was introduced in for Magnetic Resonance image models, with many subsequent developments extending the metamorphosis framework.

For image matching the image metamorphosis framework enlarges the action so that $t \mapsto (\phi_t, I_t)$ with action $\phi_t \cdot I_t \doteq I_t \circ \phi_t^{-1}$. In this setting metamorphosis combines both the diffeomorphic coordinate system transformation of computational anatomy as well as the early morphing technologies which only faded or modified the photometric or image intensity alone.

Then the matching problem takes a form with equality boundary conditions:

$$\min_{(v,I)} \frac{1}{2} \int_0^1 \left(\int_X Av_t \cdot v_t dx + \left\| \dot{I}_t \circ \phi_t^{-1} \right\|^2 / \sigma^2 \right) dt \text{ subject to } \phi_0 = id, I_0 = \text{fixed}, I_1 = \text{fixed}$$

Matching Landmarks, Curves and Surfaces

Transforming coordinate systems based on Landmark point or fiducial marker features dates back to Bookstein's early work on small deformation spline methods for interpolating correspondences defined by fiducial points to the two-dimensional or three-dimensional background space in which the fiducials are defined. Large deformation landmark methods came on in the late 90's. The above figure depicts a series of landmarks associated three brain structures, the amygdala, entorhinal cortex, and hippocampus.

Matching geometrical objects like unlabelled point distributions, curves or surfaces is another common problem in computational anatomy. Even in the discrete setting where these are commonly given as vertices with meshes, there are no predetermined correspondences between points as opposed to the situation of landmarks. From the theoretical point of view, while any submanifold X in $\mathbb{R}^3$, $d = 1, 2, 3$ can be parameterized in local charts $m : u \in U \subset \mathbb{R}^{0,1,2,3} \to \mathbb{R}^3$, all reparametrizations of these charts give geometrically the same manifold. Therefore, early on in computational anatomy, investigators have identified the necessity of parametrization invariant representations. One indispensable requirement is that the end-point matching term between two submanifolds is itself independent of their parametrizations. This can be achieved via concepts and methods borrowed from Geometric measure theory, in particular currents and varifolds which have been used extensively for curve and surface matching.

Landmark or Point Matching with Correspondence

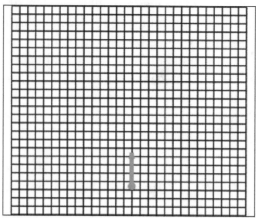

Illustration of geodesic flow for one landmark, demonstrating diffeomorphic motion of background space. Red arrow shows $p_0(1)$, blue curve shows $\varphi_t(x_1)$, black grid shows φ_t.

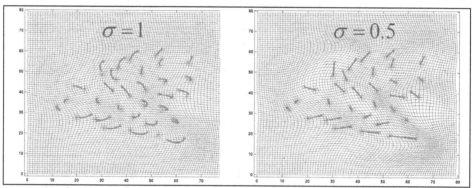

Figure showing landmark matching with correspondence. Left and right panels depict two different kernel with solutions.

Denoted the landmarked shape $X \doteq \{x_1, \ldots, x_n\} \subset \mathbb{R}^3$ with endpoint $E(\phi_1) \doteq \sum_i \| \phi_1(x_i) - x_i' \|^2$, the variational problem becomes

$$\min_{\phi: v = \dot{\phi} \circ \phi^{-1}} C(\phi) \doteq \frac{1}{2}\int (Av_t \,|\, v_t)dt + \frac{1}{2}\sum_i \| \phi_1(x_i) - x_i' \|^2 \quad \text{(Landmark-Matching)}$$

The geodesic Eulerian momentum is a generalized function $Av_t \in V^*, t \in [0,1]$,, supported on the landmarked set in the variational problem. The endpoint condition with conservation implies the initial momentum at the identity of the group:

$$
\begin{cases}
\text{Endpoint Condition:} & Av_1 = \sum_{i=1}^{n} p_1(i)\delta_{\phi_1(x_i)}, p_1(i) = (x_i' - \phi_1(x_i)), \\[2mm]
\text{Conservation:} & Av_t = \sum_{i=1}^{n} p_1(i)\delta_{\phi_t(x_i)}, p_t(i) = (D\phi_{t1})^T_{|\phi_t(x_i)} p_1(i), \phi_{t1} \doteq \phi_1 \circ \phi_t^{-1}, \\[2mm]
& Av_0 = \sum_i \delta_{x_i}(\cdot) p_0(i) \text{ with } p_0(i) = (D\phi_1)^T_{|x_i}(x_i' - \phi_1(x_i))
\end{cases}
$$

The iterative algorithm for large deformation diffeomorphic metric mapping for land-marks is given.

Measure Matching: Unregistered Landmarks

Glaunes and co-workers first introduced diffeomorphic matching of pointsets in the general setting of matching distributions. As opposed to landmarks, this includes in particular the situation of weighted point clouds with no predefined correspondences and possibly different cardinalities. The template and target discrete point clouds are represented as two weighted sums of Diracs $\mu_m = \sum_{i=1}^{n} \rho_i \delta_{x_i}$ and $\mu_{m'} = \sum_{i=1}^{n'} \rho_i' \delta_{x_i'}$ living in the space of signed measures of $\mathbb{R}^3$, The space is equipped with a Hilbert metric ob-tained from a real positive kernel $k(x,y)$ on $\mathbb{R}^3$, giving the following norm:

$$\| \mu_m \|_{\text{mea}}^2 = \sum_{i,j=1}^{n} \rho_i \rho_j k(x_i, x_j)$$

The matching problem between a template and target point cloud may be then formu-lated using this kernel metric for the endpoint matching term:

$$\min_{\phi: v = \dot{\phi} \circ \phi^{-1}} C(\phi) \doteq \frac{1}{2} \int (A v_t \,|\, v_t) dt + \frac{1}{2} \left\| \mu_{\phi_1 \cdot m} - \mu_{m'} \right\|_{\text{mea}}^2$$

where $\mu_{\phi_1 \cdot m} = \sum_{i=1}^{n} \rho_i \delta_{\phi_1(x_i)}$ is the distribution transported by the deformation.

Curve Matching

In the one dimensional case, a curve in 3D can be represented by an embedding $m: u \in [0,1] \rightarrow \mathbb{R}^3$, and the group action of *Diff* becomes $\phi \cdot m = \phi \circ m$. However, the correspondence between curves and embeddings is not one to one as the any reparam-etrization $m \circ \gamma$, for γ a diffeomorphism of the interval [0,1], represents geometrically the same curve. In order to preserve this invariance in the end-point matching term, several extensions of the previous 0-dimensional measure matching approach can be considered.

Curve Matching with Currents

In the situation of oriented curves, currents give an efficient setting to construct in-variant matching terms. In such representation, curves are interpreted as elements of a functional space dual to the space vector fields, and compared through kernel norms on these spaces. Matching of two curves m and m' writes eventually as the variational problem.

$$\min_{\phi:v=\dot{\phi}\circ\phi^{-1}} C(\phi) \doteq \frac{1}{2}\int (Av_t \mid v_t)dt + \frac{1}{2}\| C_{\phi_1\cdot m} - C_{m'} \|^2_{\text{cur}}$$

with the endpoint term $E(\phi_1) = \| C_{\phi_1\cdot m} - C_{m'} \|^2_{\text{cur}} / 2$ is obtained from the norm:

$$\| C_m \|^2_{\text{cur}} = \int_0^1 \int_0^1 K_C(m(u), m(v))\partial m(u)\cdot\partial m(v)\,du\,dv$$

the derivative $\partial m(u)$ being the tangent vector to the curve and K_c a given matrix kernel of $\mathbb{R}^3$. Such expressions are invariant to any positive reparametrizations of m and m', and thus still depend on the orientation of the two curves.

Curve Matching with Varifolds

Varifold is an alternative to currents when orientation becomes an issue as for instance in situations involving multiple bundles of curves for which no "consistent" orientation may be defined. Varifolds directly extend 0-dimensional measures by adding an extra tangent space direction to the position of points, leading to represent curves as measures on the product of $\mathbb{R}^3$ and the Grassmannian of all straight lines in $\mathbb{R}^3$. The matching problem between two curves then consists in replacing the endpoint matching term by $E(\phi_1) = \| V_{\phi_1\cdot m} - V_{m'} \|^2_{\text{cur}} / 2$ with varifold norms of the form:

$$\| V_m \|^2_{var} = \int_0^1 \int_0^1 k_{\mathbb{R}^3}(m(u), m(v))k_{\text{Gr}}([\partial m(u)],[\partial m(v)]) \mid \partial m(u) \| \partial m(v) \mid du\,dv$$

where $[\partial m(u)]$ is the non-oriented line directed by tangent vector $\partial m(u)$ and $k_{\mathbb{R}^3}, k_{\text{Gr}}$ two scalar kernels respectively on $\mathbb{R}^3$ and the Grassmannian. Due to the inherent non-oriented nature of the Grassmannian representation, such expressions are invariant to positive and negative reparametrizations.

Surface Matching

Surface matching share many similarities with the case of curves. Surfaces in $\mathbb{R}^3$ are parametrized in local charts by embeddings $m : u \in U \subset \mathbb{R}^2 \to \mathbb{R}^3$, with all reparametrizations $m\circ\gamma$ with γ a diffeomorphism of U being equivalent geometrically. Currents and varifolds can be also used to formalize surface matching.

Surface Matching with Currents

Oriented surfaces can be represented as 2-currents which are dual to differential

2-forms. In $\mathbb{R}$, one can further identify 2-forms with vector fields through the standard wedge product of 3D vectors. In that setting, surface matching writes again:

$$\min_{\phi:v=\dot\phi\circ\phi^{-1}} C(\phi) \doteq \frac{1}{2}\int (Av_t\,|\,v_t)dt + \frac{1}{2}\left\|C_{\phi_1\cdot m} - C_{m'}\right\|^2_{\text{cur}}$$

with the endpoint term $E(\phi_1) = \|C_{\phi_1\cdot m} - C_{m'}\|^2_{\text{cur}}/2$ given through the norm

$$\|C_m\|^2_{\text{cur}} = \iint_{U\times U} K_C(m(u),m(v))\vec{n}(u)\cdot\vec{n}(v)\,du\,dv$$

with $\vec{n} = \partial_{u_1}m \wedge \partial_{u_2}m$ the normal vector to the surface parametrized by m.

This surface mapping algorithm has been validated for brain cortical surfaces against CARET and FreeSurfer.

Surface Matching with Varifolds

For non-orientable or non-oriented surfaces, the varifold framework is often more adequate. Identifying the parametric surface m with a varifold V_m in the space of measures on the product of $\mathbb{R}^3$ and the Grassmannian, one simply replaces the previous current metric $\|C_m\|^2_{\text{cur}}$ by:

$$\|V_m\|^2_{\text{var}} = \iint_{U\times U} k_{\mathbb{R}^3}(m(u),m(v))k_{\text{Gr}}([\vec{n}(u)],[\vec{n}(v)])\,|\,\vec{n}(u)\,\|\,\vec{n}(v)\,|\,du\,dv$$

where $[\vec{n}(u)]$ is the (non-oriented) line directed by the normal vector to the surface.

Growth and Atrophy from Longitudinal Time-series

There are many settings in which there are a series of measurements, a time-series to which the underlying coordinate systems will be matched and flowed onto. This occurs for example in the dynamic growth and atrophy models and motion tracking such as have been explored in An observed time sequence is given and the goal is to infer the time flow of geometric change of coordinates carrying the exemplars or templars through the period of observations.

The generic time-series matching problem considers the series of times is $0 < t_1 < ...t_K = 1..$. The flow optimizes at the series of costs $E(t_k), k = 1,...,K$ giving optimization problems of the form

$$\min_{\phi:v=\dot\phi\circ\phi^{-1},\phi_0=id} C(\phi) \doteq \frac{1}{2}\int_0^1 (Av_t\,|\,v_t)dt + \sum_{k=1}^{K} E(\phi_{t_k}).$$

There have been at least three solutions offered thus far, piecewise geodesic, principal geodesic and splines.

The Random Orbit Model of Computational Anatomy

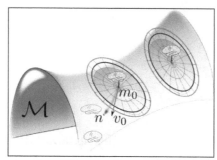

Orbits of brains associated to diffeomorphic group action on templates depicted via smooth flow associated to geodesic flows with random spray associated to random generation of initial tangent space vector field $v_0 \in V$.

The random orbit model of computational anatomy first appeared in modelling the change in coordinates associated to the randomness of the group acting on the templates, which induces the randomness on the source of images in the anatomical orbit of shapes and forms and resulting observations through the medical imaging devices. Such a random orbit model in which randomness on the group induces randomness on the images was examined for the Special Euclidean Group for object recognition in.

Depicted in the figure is a depiction of the random orbits around each exemplar, generated by randomizing the flow by generating the initial tangent space vector field at the identity $v_0 \in V$, and then generating random object $n \doteq Exp_{id}(v_0) \cdot m_0 \in \mathcal{M}$.

The random orbit model induces the prior on shapes and images $I \in \mathcal{I}$ conditioned on a particular atlas $I_a \in \mathcal{I}$. For this the generative model generates the mean field I as a random change in coordinates of the template according to $I \doteq \phi \cdot I_a$, where the diffeomorphic change in coordinates is generated randomly via the geodesic flows. The prior on random transformations $\pi_{Diff}(d\phi)$ on $Diff_V$ is induced by the flow $Exp_{id}(v)$, with $v \in V$ constructed as a Gaussian random field prior $\pi_V(dv)$. The density on the random observables at the output of the sensor $I^D \in \mathcal{I}^D$ are given by:

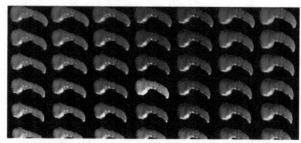

The random spray of synthesized subcortical structures laid out in the two-dimensional grid representing the variance of the eigenfunction used for the momentum for synthesis.

$$p(I^D \mid I_a) = \int_V p(I^D \mid Exp_{id}(v) \cdot I_a) \pi_V (dv).$$

the cartoon orbit, are a random spray of the subcortical manifolds generated by randomizing the vector fields v_0 supported over the submanifolds.

The Bayesian Model of Computational Anatomy

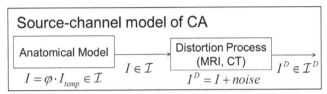

Source-channel model showing the source of images the deformable template $I \doteq \phi \cdot I_{temp} \in \mathcal{I}$ and channel output associated with MRI sensor $I^D \in \mathcal{I}^D$

(i) MAP estimation with multiple atlases, (ii) MAP segmentation with multiple atlases, MAP estimation of templates from populations.

The central statistical model of computational anatomy in the context of medical imaging has been the source-channel model of Shannon theory; the source is the deformable template of images $I \in \mathcal{I}$, the channel outputs are the imaging sensors with observables $I^D \in \mathcal{I}^D$.

Statistical Shape Theory in Computational Anatomy

Shape in computational anatomy is a local theory, indexing shapes and structures to templates to which they are bijectively mapped. Statistical shape in computational anatomy is the empirical study of diffeomorphic correspondences between populations and common template coordinate systems. This is a strong departure from Procrustes Analyses and shape theories pioneered by David G. Kendall in that the central group of Kendall's theories are the finite-dimensional Lie groups, whereas the theories of shape in computational anatomy have focused on the diffeomorphism group, which to first order via the Jacobian can be thought of as a field—thus infinite dimensional—of low-dimensional Lie groups of scale and rotations.

Showing hundreds of sub-cortical structures embedded in two-dimensional momentum space generated from the first two eigenvectors of the empirical co-variance estimated from the population of shapes.

The random orbit model provides the natural setting to understand empirical shape and shape statistics within computational anatomy since the non-linearity of the induced probability law on anatomical shapes and forms $m \in \mathcal{M}$ is induced via the reduction to the vector fields $v_0 \in V$ at the tangent space at the identity of the diffeomorphism group. The successive flow of the Euler equation induces the random space of shapes and forms $Exp_{id}(v_0) \cdot m \in \mathcal{M}$.

Performing empirical statistics on this tangent space at the identity is the natural way for inducing probability laws on the statistics of shape. Since both the vector fields and the Eulerian momentum Av_0 are in a Hilbert space the natural model is one of a Gaussian random field, so that given test function $w \in V$, then the inner-products with the test functions are Gaussian distributed with mean and covariance.

This is depicted in the accompanying figure where sub-cortical brain structures are depicted in a two-dimensional coordinate system based on inner products of their initial vector fields that generate them from the template is shown in a 2-dimensional span of the Hilbert space.

Template Estimation From Populations

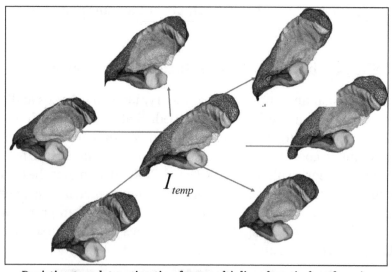

Depicting template estimation from multiplie subcortical surfaces in
populations of MR images using the EM-algorithm solution of Ma.

The study of shape and statistics in populations are local theories, indexing shapes and structures to templates to which they are bijectively mapped. Statistical shape is then the study of diffeomorphic correspondences relative to the template. A core operation is the generation of templates from populations, estimating a shape that is matched to the population. There are several important methods for generating templates including methods based on Frechet averaging, and statistical approaches based on the expectation-maximization algorithm and the Bayes Random orbit models of computational anatomy. Shown in the accompanying figure is a subcortical template reconstruction from the population of MRI subjects.

An Artificial Neural Network (ANN) is a mathematical model that tries to simulate the structure and functionalities of biological neural networks. Basic building block of every artificial neural network is artificial neuron, that is, a simple mathematical model (function). Such a model has three simple sets of rules: multiplication, summation and activation. At the entrance of artificial neuron the inputs are weighted what means that every input value is multiplied with individual weight. In the middle section of artificial neuron is sum function that sums all weighted inputs and bias. At the exit of artificial neuron the sum of previously weighted inputs and bias is passing trough activation function that is also called transfer function.

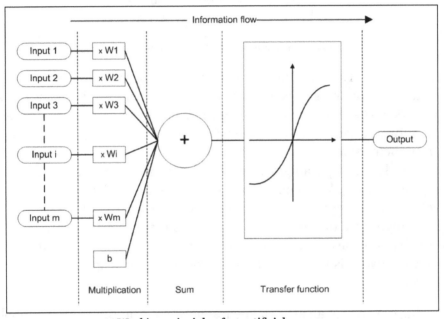

Working principle of an artificial neuron.

Although the working principles and simple set of rules of artificial neuron looks like nothing special the full potential and calculation power of these models come to life when we start to interconnect them into artificial neural networks .These artificial neural networks use simple fact that complexity can grown out of merely few basic and simple rules.

In order to fully harvest the benefits of mathematical complexity that can be achieved through interconnection of individual artificial neurons and not just making system complex and unmanageable we usually do not interconnect these artificial neurons randomly. In the past, researchers have come up with several "standardised" topographies of artificial neural networks. These predefined topographies can help us with easier, faster and more efficient problem solving. Different types of artificial neural network topographies are suited for solving different types of problems. After determining the type of given problem we need to decide for topology of artificial neural network we are going to use and then fine-tune it. We need to fine-tune the topology itself and its parameters.

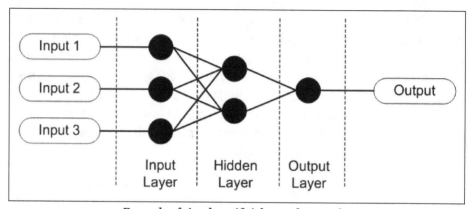

Example of simple artificial neural network.

Fine tuned topology of artificial neural network does not mean that we can start using our artificial neural network, it is only a precondition. Before we can use our artificial neural network we need to teach it solving the type of given problem. Just as biological neural networks can learn their behaviour/responses on the basis of inputs that they get from their environment the artificial neural networks can do the same. There are three major learning paradigms: supervised learning, unsupervised learning and reinforcement learning. We choose learning paradigm similar as we chose artificial neuron network topography - based on the problem we are trying to solve. Although learning paradigms are different in their principles they all have one thing in common; on the basis of "learning data" and "learning rules" (chosen cost function) artificial neural network is trying to achieve proper output response in accordance to input signals.

After choosing topology of an artificial neural network, fine-tuning of the topology and when artificial neural network has learn a proper behaviour we can start using it for solving given problem. Artificial neural networks have been in use for some time now and we can find them working in areas such as process control, chemistry, gaming, radar systems, automotive industry, space industry, astronomy, genetics, banking, fraud detection, etc. and solving of problems like function approximation, regression analysis, time series prediction, classification, pattern recognition, decision making, data processing, filtering, clustering, etc., naming a few.

As topic of artificial neural networks is complex and this chapter is only informative nature we encourage novice reader to find detail information on artificial neural networks in.

Artificial neuron is a basic building block of every artificial neural network. Its design and functionalities are derived from observation of a biological neuron that is basic building block of biological neural networks (systems) which includes the brain, spinal cord and peripheral ganglia. Similarities in design and functionalities can be seen in figure. where the left side of a figure represents a biological neuron with its soma, dendrites and axon and where the right side of a figure represents an artificial neuron with its inputs, weights, transfer function, bias and outputs.

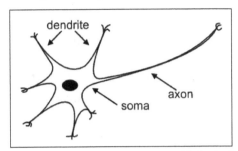 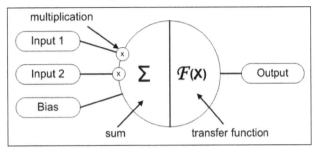

Biological and artificial neuron design.

In case of biological neuron information comes into the neuron via dendrite, soma processes the information and passes it on via axon. In case of artificial neuron the information comes into the body of an artificial neuron via inputs that are weighted (each input can be individually multiplied with a weight). The body of an artificial neuron then sums the weighted inputs, bias and "processes" the sum with a transfer function. At the end an artificial neuron passes the processed information via output(s). Benefit of artificial neuron model simplicity can be seen in its mathematical description below:

$$y(k)=F\left(\sum_{i=0}^{m}w_i(k)\cdot x_i(k)\right)+b$$

Where:

- $x_i(t)$ is input value in discrete time k where i goes from 0 to m,

- $w_i(k)$ is weight value in discrete time k where i goes from 0 to m,

- b is bias,

- F is a transfer function,

- $y_i(k)$ is output value in discrete time k.

As seen from a model of an artificial neuron and its equation $y(k)=F\left(\sum_{i=0}^{m}w_i(k)\cdot x_i(k)\right)+b$

the major unknown variable of our model is its transfer function. Transfer function defines the properties of artificial neuron and can be any mathematical function. We choose it on the basis of problem that artificial neuron (artificial neural network) needs to solve and in most cases we choose it from the following set of functions: Step function, Linear function and Non-linear (Sigmoid) function.

Step function is binary function that has only two possible output values (e.g. zero and one). That means if input value meets specific threshold the output value results in one value and if specific threshold is not meet that results in different output value.

$$y = \begin{cases} 1 \; if \; w_i x_i \geq threshold \\ 0 \; if \; w_i x_i \geq threshold \end{cases}$$

When this type of transfer function is used in artificial neuron we call this artificial neuron perceptron. Perceptron is used for solving classification problems and as such it can be most commonly found in the last layer of artificial neural networks. In case of linear transfer function artificial neuron is doing simple linear transformation over the sum of weighted inputs and bias. Such an artificial neuron is in contrast to perceptron most commonly used in the input layer of artificial neural networks. When we use non-linear function the sigmoid function is the most commonly used. Sigmoid function has easily calculated derivate, which can be important when calculating weight updates in the artificial neural network.

When combining two or more artificial neurons we are getting an artificial neural network. If single artificial neuron has almost no usefulness in solving real-life problems the artificial neural networks have it. In fact artificial neural networks are capable of solving complex real-life problems by processing information in their basic building blocks (artificial neurons) in a non-linear, distributed, parallel and local way.

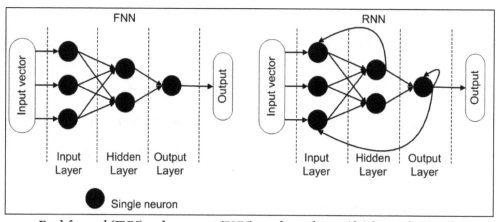

Feed-forward (FNN) and recurrent (RNN) topology of an artificial neural network.

The way that individual artificial neurons are interconnected is called topology, architecture or graph of an artificial neural network. The fact that interconnection can be done in numerous ways results in numerous possible topologies that are divided into two basic classes. Figure shows these two topologies; the left side of the figure represent simple feedforward topology (acyclic graph) where information flows from inputs to outputs in only one direction and the right side of the figure represent simple recurrent topology (semicyclic graph) where some of the information flows not only in one direction from input to output but also in opposite direction. While observing figure. we need to mention that for easier handling and mathematical describing of an artificial neural network we group individual neurons in layers. On figure, we can see input, hidden and output layer.

When we choose and build topology of our artificial neural network we only finished half of the task before we can use this artificial neural network for solving given problem. Just as biological neural networks need to learn their proper responses to the given inputs from the environment the artificial neural networks need to do the same. So the next step is to learn proper response of an artificial neural network and this can be achieved through learning (supervised, un-supervised or reinforcement learning). No matter which method we use, the task of learning is to set the values of weight and biases on basis of learning data to minimize the chosen cost function.

Feed-forward Artificial Neural Networks

Artificial neural network with feed-forward topology is called Feed-Forward artificial neural network and as such has only one condition: information must flow from input to output in only one direction with no back-loops. There are no limitations on number of layers, type of transfer function used in individual artificial neuron or number of connections between individual artificial neurons. The simplest feed-forward artificial neural network is a single perceptron that is only capable of learning linear separable problems. Simple multi-layer feed-forward artificial neural network for purpose of analytical description (sets of equations ($n_1 = F_1....F_3 \left(w_3 x_3 + b_3 \right)$), ($m_1 = F_4....\left(r_1 m_1 + r_2 m_2 + b_6 \right)$) and ($y = F_6... + b_6$) is shown on figure.

$$n_1 = F_1 \left(w_1 x_1 + b_1 \right)$$
$$n_2 = F_2 \left(w_2 x_2 + b_2 \right)$$
$$n_3 = F_2 \left(w_2 x_2 + b_2 \right)$$
$$n_4 = F_3 \left(w_3 x_3 + b_3 \right)$$

$$m_1 = F_4 \left(q_1 n_1 + q_2 n_2 + b_4 \right)$$
$$m_2 = F_5 \left(q_3 n_3 + q_4 n_4 + b_5 \right)$$

$$y = F_6 \left(r_1 m_1 + r_2 m_2 + b_6 \right)$$

$$y = F_6 \left[\begin{array}{l} r_1 \left(F_4 \left[q_1 F_1 \left[w_1 x_1 + b_1 \right] + q_2 F_2 \left[w_2 x_2 + b_2 \right] \right) + ... \\ ... + r_2 \left(F_5 \left[q_3 F_2 \left[w_2 x_2 + b_2 \right] + q_4 F_3 \left[w_3 x_3 + b_3 \right] + b_5 \right] \right) + b_6 \end{array} \right]$$

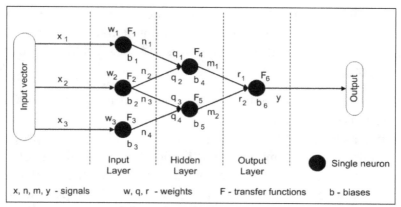

Feed-forward artificial neural network.

As seen on figure and corresponding analytical description with sets of equations $(n_1 = F_1....F_3(w_3 x_3 + b_3))$, $(m_1 = F_4....(r_1 m_1 + r_2 m_2 + b_6)$ and $(y = F_6...+b_6)$ the simple feed-forward artificial neural network can led to relatively long mathematical descriptions where artificial neural networks' parameters optimization problem solving by hand is impractical. Although analytical description can be used on any complex artificial neural network in practise we use computers and specialised software that can help us build, mathematically describe and optimise any type of artificial neural network.

Recurrent Artificial Neural Networks

Artificial neural network with the recurrent topology is called Recurrent artificial neural network. It is similar to feed-forward neural network with no limitations regarding back-loops. In these cases information is no longer transmitted only in one direction but it is also transmitted backwards. This creates an internal state of the network which allows it to exhibit dynamic temporal behaviour. Recurrent artificial neural networks can use their internal memory to process any sequence of inputs. Figure shows small Fully Recurrent artificial neural network and complexity of its artificial neuron interconnections.

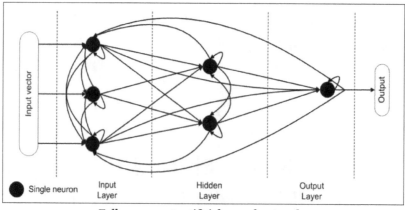

Fully recurrent artificial neural network.

The most basic topology of recurrent artificial neural network is fully recurrent artificial network where every basic building block (artificial neuron) is directly connected to every other basic building block in all direction. Other recurrent artificial neural networks such as Hopfield, Elman, Jordan, bi-directional and other networks are just special cases of recurrent artificial neural networks.

Hopfield Artificial Neural Network

A Hopfield artificial neural network is a type of recurrent artificial neural network that is used to store one or more stable target vectors. These stable vectors can be viewed as memories that the network recalls when provided with similar vectors that act as a cue to the network memory. These binary units only take two different values for their states that are determined by whether or not the units' input exceeds their threshold. Binary units can take either values of 1 or -1, or values of 1 or 0. Consequently there are two possible definitions for binary unit activation a_I equations:

$$a_i = \begin{cases} -1 & if \sum_j w_{ij}S_j > \theta \\ 1 & otherwise \end{cases}$$

$$a_i = \begin{cases} 0 & if \sum_j w_{ij}S_j > \theta \\ 1 & otherwise \end{cases}$$

Where:
- w_{ij} is the strength of the connection weight from unit j to unit i,

- S_j is the state of unit j,

- θ_i is the threshold of unit i.

While talking about connections w_{ij} we need to mention that there are typical two restrictions: no unit has a connection with itself (w_{ii}) and that connections are symmetric,

$$w_{ij} = w_{ji}$$

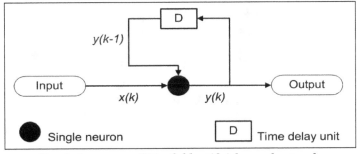

Simple "one neuron" Hopfield artificial neural network.

The requirement that weights must be symmetric is typically used, as it will guarantee that the energy function decreases monotonically while following the activation rules. If nonsymmetric weights are used the network may exhibit some periodic or chaotic behaviour. Training a Hopfield artificial neural network involves lowering the energy of states that the artificial neural network should remember.

Elman and Jordan Artificial Neural Networks

Elman network also referred as Simple Recurrent Network is special case of recurrent artificial neural networks. It differs from conventional two-layer networks in that the first layer has a recurrent connection. It is a simple three-layer artificial neural network that has back-loop from hidden layer to input layer trough so called context unit. This type of artificial neural network has memory that allowing it to both detect and generate time-varying patterns.

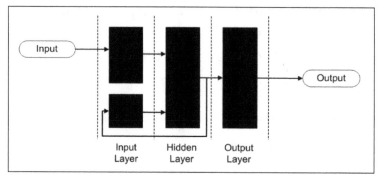

Elman artificial neural network.

The Elman artificial neural network has typically sigmoid artificial neurons in its hidden layer, and linear artificial neurons in its output layer. This combination of artificial neurons transfer functions can approximate any function with arbitrary accuracy if only there is enough artificial neurons in hidden layer. Being able to store information Elman artificial neural network is capable of generating temporal patterns as well as spatial patterns and responding on them. Jordan network is similar to Elman network. The only difference is that context units are fed from the output layer instead of the hidden layer.

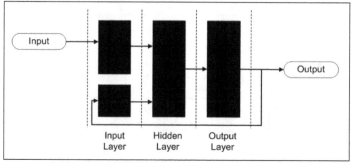

Jordan artificial neural network.

Long Short Term Memory

Long Short Term Memory is one of the recurrent artificial neural networks topologies. In contrast with basic recurrent artificial neural networks it can learn from its experience to process, classify and predict time series with very long time lags of unknown size between important events. This makes Long Short Term Memory to outperform other recurrent artificial neural networks, Hidden Markov Models and other sequence learning methods. Long Short Term Memory artificial neural network is build from Long Short Term Memory blocks that are capable of remembering value for any length of time. This is achieved with gates that determine when the input is significant enough remembering it, when continue to remembering or forgetting it, and when to output the value.

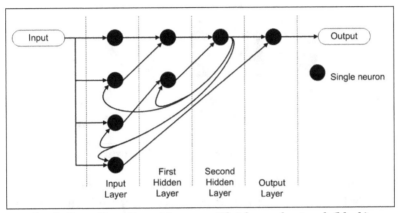

Simple Long Short Term Memory artificial neural network (block).

Architecture of Long Short Term Memory block is shown in figure where input layer consists of sigmoid units. Top neuron in the input layer process input value that might be sent to a memory unit depends on computed value of second neuron from the top in the input layer. The third neuron from the top in the input layer decide how long will memory unit hold (remember) its value and the bottom most neuron determines when value from memory should be released to the output. Neurons in first hidden layer and in output layer are doing simple multiplication of their inputs and a neuron in the second hidden layer computes simple linear function of its inputs. Output of the second hidden layer is fed back into input and first hidden layer in order to help making decisions.

Bi-directional Artificial Neural Networks (Bi-ANN)

Bi-directional artificial neural networks are designed to predict complex time series. They consist of two individual interconnected artificial neural (sub) networks that performs direct and inverse (bidirectional) transformation. Interconnection of artificial neural sub networks is done through two dynamic artificial neurons that are capable of remembering their internal states. This type of interconnection between future and past values of the processed signals increase time series prediction capabilities. As such these artificial neural networks not only predict future values of input data but also past values. That brings need for two phase learning; in first phase we teach one artificial neural sub network for predicting future and in the second phase we teach a second artificial neural sub network for predicting past.

Self-Organizing Map (SOM)

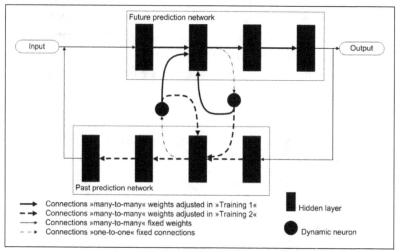

Bi-directional artificial neural network.

Self-organizing map is an artificial neural network that is related to feed-forward networks but it needs to be told that this type of architecture is fundamentally different in arrangement of neurons and motivation. Common arrangement of neurons is in a hexagonal or rectangular grid Self-organizing map is different in comparison to other artificial neural networks in the sense that they use a neighbourhood function to preserve the topological properties of the input space. They uses unsupervised learning paradigm to produce a low-dimensional, discrete representation of the input space of the training samples, called a map what makes them especially useful for visualizing low-dimensional views of high-dimensional data. Such networks can learn to detect regularities and correlations in their input and adapt their future responses to that input accordingly.

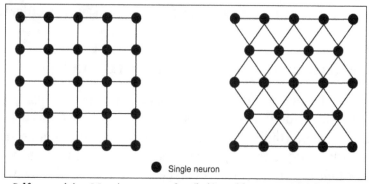

Self-organizing Map in rectangular (left) and hexagonal (right) grid.

Just as others artificial neural networks need learning before they can be used the same goes for self-organizing map; where the goal of learning is to cause different parts of the artificial neural network to respond similarly to certain input patterns. While adjusting the weights of the neurons in the process of learning they are initialized either to small random values or sampled evenly from the subspace spanned by the two largest principal component eigenvectors. After initialization artificial neural network needs to be fed with large number of example vectors. At that time Euclidean distance to all weight vectors is computed and the neuron with weight vector most similar to the input is called the best matching unit. The weights of the best matching unit and neurons close to it are adjusted towards the input vector. This process is repeated for each input vector for a number of cycles. After learning phase we do so-called mapping (usage of artificial neural network) and during this phase the only one neuron whose weight vector lies closest to the input vector will be winning neuron. Distance between input and weight vector is again determined by calculating the Euclidean distance between them.

Stochastic Artificial Neural Network

Stochastic artificial neural networks are a type of an artificial intelligence tool. They are built by introducing random variations into the network, either by giving the network's neurons stochastic transfer functions, or by giving them stochastic weights. This makes them useful tools for optimization problems, since the random fluctuations help it escape from local minima. Stochastic neural networks that are built by using stochastic transfer functions are often called Boltzmann machine.

Physical Artificial Neural Network

Most of the artificial neural networks today are software-based but that does not exclude the possibility to create them with physical elements which base on adjustable electrical current resistance materials. History of physical artificial neural networks goes back in 1960's when first physical artificial neural networks were created with memory transistors called memistors. Memistors emulate synapses of artificial neurons. Although these artificial neural networks were commercialized they did not last for long due to their incapability for scalability. After this attempt several others followed such as attempt to create physical artificial neural network based on nanotechnology or phase change material.

Learning

There are three major learning paradigms; supervised learning, unsupervised learning and reinforcement learning. Usually they can be employed by any given type of artificial neural network architecture. Each learning paradigm has many training algorithms.

Supervised Learning

Supervised learning is a machine learning technique that sets parameters of an artificial neural network from training data. The task of the learning artificial neural network is to set the value of its parameters for any valid input value after having seen output value. The training data consist of pairs of input and desired output values that are traditionally represented in data vectors. Supervised learning can also be referred as classification, where we have a wide range of classifiers, each with its strengths and weaknesses. Choosing a suitable classifier (Multilayer perceptron, Support Vector Machines, k-nearest neighbour algorithm, Gaussian mixture model, Gaussian, naive Bayes, decision tree, radial basis function classifiers,...) for a given problem is however still more an art than a science. In order to solve a given problem of supervised learning various steps has to be considered. In the first step we have to determine the type of training examples. In the second step we need to gather a training data set that satisfactory describe a given problem. In the third step we need to describe gathered training data set in form understandable to a chosen artificial neural network. In the fourth step we do the learning and after the learning we can test the performance of learned artificial neural network with the test (validation) data set. Test data set consist of data that has not been introduced to artificial neural network while learning.

Unsupervised Learning

Unsupervised learning is a machine learning technique that sets parameters of an artificial neural network based on given data and a cost function which is to be minimized. Cost function can be any function and it is determined by the task formulation. Unsupervised learning is mostly used in applications that fall within the domain of estimation problems such as statistical modelling, compression, filtering, blind source separation and clustering. In unsupervised learning we seek to determine how the data is organized. It differs from supervised learning and reinforcement learning in that the artificial neural network is given only unlabeled examples. One common form of unsupervised learning is clustering where we try to categorize data in different clusters by their similarity. Among above described artificial neural network models, the Self-organizing maps are the ones that the most commonly use unsupervised learning algorithms.

Reinforcement Learning

Reinforcement learning is a machine learning technique that sets parameters of an artificial neural network, where data is usually not given, but generated by interactions with the environment. Reinforcement learning is concerned with how an artificial neural network ought to take actions in an environment so as to maximize some notion of long-term reward. Reinforcement learning is frequently used as a part of artificial neural network's overall learning algorithm.

After return function that needs to be maximized is defined, reinforcement learning uses several algorithms to find the policy which produces the maximum return. Naive brute force algorithm in first step calculates return function for each possible policy and chooses the policy with the largest return. Obvious weakness of this algorithm is in case of extremely large or even infinite number of possible policies. This weakness can be overcome by value function approaches or direct policy estimation. Value function approaches attempt to find a policy that maximizes the return by maintaining a set of estimates of expected returns for one policy; usually either the current or the optimal estimates. These methods converge to the correct estimates for a fixed policy and can also be used to find the optimal policy. Similar as value function approaches the direct policy estimation can also find the optimal policy. It can find it by searching it directly in policy space what greatly increases the computational cost.

Reinforcement learning is particularly suited to problems which include a long-term versus short-term reward trade-off. It has been applied successfully to various problems, including robot control, telecommunications, and games such as chess and other sequential decision making tasks.

Usage of Artificial Neural Networks

One of the greatest advantages of artificial neural networks is their capability to learn from their environment. Learning from the environment comes useful in applications where complexity of the environment (data or task) make implementations of other type of solutions impractical. As such artificial neural networks can be used for variety of tasks like classification, function approximation, data processing, filtering, clustering, compression, robotics, regulations, decision making, etc. Choosing the right artificial neural network topology depends on the type of the application and data representation of a given problem. When choosing and using artificial neural networks we need to be familiar with theory of artificial neural network models and learning algorithms. Complexity of the chosen model is crucial; using to simple model for specific task usually results in poor or wrong results and over complex model for a specific task can lead to problems in the process of learning. Complex model and simple task results in memorizing and not learning. There are many learning algorithms with numerous tradeoffs between them and almost all are suitable for any type of artificial neural network model. Choosing the right learning algorithm for a given task takes a lot of experiences and experimentation on given problem and data set. When artificial neural network model and learning algorithm is properly selected we get robust tool for solving given problem.

Example: Using bi-directional Artificial Neural Network for ICT Fraud Detection

Spread of Information and Communication Technologies results in not only benefits for individuals and society but also in threats and increase of Information and Communication Technology frauds. One of the main tasks for Information and Communication

Technology developers is to prevent potential fraudulent misuse of new products and services. If protection against fraud fails there is a vital need to detect frauds as soon as possible. Information and Communication Technology frauds detection is based on numerous principles. One of such principle is use of artificial neural networks in the detection algorithms. Below is an example of how to use bi-directional artificial neural network for detecting mobile-phone fraud.

First task is to represent problem of detecting our fraud in the way that can be easily understand by humans and machines (computers). Each individual user or group of users behave in specific way while using mobile phone. By learning their behaviour we can teach our system to recognize and predict users' future behaviour to a certain degree of accuracy. Later comparison between predicted and real-life behaviour and potential discrepancy between them can indicate a potential fraudulent behaviour. It was shown that mobilephone usage behaviour can be represented in the form of time series suitable for further analysis with artificial neural networks. With this representation we transform the behaviour prediction task in time series prediction task. Time series prediction task can be realized with several different types of artificial neural networks but as mentioned in earlier chapters some are more suitable then others. Because we expect long and short time periods between important events in our data representation of users behaviour the most obvious artificial neural networks to use are Long Short Term Memory and bi-directionalartificial neural networks. On the basis of others researchers favourable results in time series prediction with bi-directional artificial neural network we decided to use this artificial neural network topology for predicting our time series.

After we choose artificial neural network architecture we choose the type of learning paradigm; we choose supervised learning where we gather real life data form telecommunication system. Gathered data was divided into two sub-sets; training sub-set and validation subset. With training data sub-set artificial neural network learn to predict future and past time series and with validation data sub-set we simulate and validate the prediction capabilities of designed and fine-tuned bi-directional artificial neural networks. Validation was done with calculation of the Average Relative Variance that represents a measure of similarity between predicted and expected time series.

Only after we gathered information about mobile-phone fraud and after choosing representation of our problem and basic approaches for solving it we could start building the overall model for detecting mobile-phone fraud.

On figure we can see that mobile-phone fraud detection model is build out of three modules; input module, artificial neural network module and comparison module. Input Module gathers users information about usage of mobile-phone from telecommunication system in three parts. In first part it is used for gathering learning data from which Artificial Neural Network Module learn it-self. In second part Input Module gathers users' data for purpose of validating the Artificial Neural Network Module and in the third part it collects users data in real time for purpose of using deployed mobile-phone fraud system. Artificial Neural Network Module is bidirectional artificial neural network that is learning from gathered data and later when the mobile-phone fraud detection system is deployed continuously predicts time series that represents users' behaviour. Comparison module is used for validation of Artificial Neural Network Module in the process of learning and later when the mobile-phone fraud detection system is deployed it is used for triggering alarms in case of discrepancies between predicted and real-life gathered information about users behaviour.

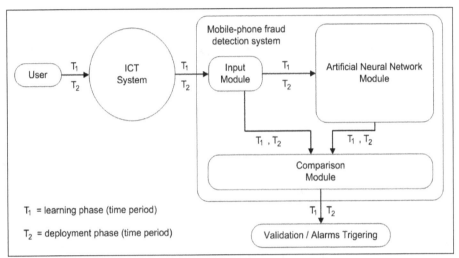

Mobile-phone fraud detection model.

Although mobile-phone fraud detection system described above is simple and straight forward reader needs to realize that majority of work is not in creating and later implementing desired systems but in fine-tuning of data representation and artificial neural network architecture and its parameters that is strongly dependant on type of input data.

ARTIFICIAL NEURON

An artificial neuron is a mathematical function conceived as a model of biological neurons, a neural network. Artificial neurons are elementary units in an artificial neural network. The artificial neuron receives one or more inputs (representing excitatory postsynaptic potentials and inhibitory postsynaptic potentials at neural dendrites) and sums them to produce an output (or activation, representing a neuron's action potential which is transmitted along its axon). Usually each input is separately weighted, and the sum is passed through a non-linear function known as an activation function or transfer function. The transfer functions usually have a sigmoid shape, but they may also take the form of other non-linear functions, piecewise linear functions, or step functions. They are also often monotonically increasing, continuous, differentiable and bounded. The thresholding function has inspired building logic gates referred to as threshold logic; applicable to building logic circuits resembling brain processing. For example, new devices such as memristors have been extensively used to develop such logic in recent times.

The artificial neuron transfer function should not be confused with a linear system's transfer function.

Basic Structure

For a given artificial neuron, let there be $m + 1$ inputs with signals x_0 through x_m and weights w_0 through w_m. Usually, the x_0 input is assigned the value +1, which makes it a *bias* input with $w_{ko} = b_k$. This leaves only m actual inputs to the neuron: from x_1 to x_m.

The output of the kth neuron is:

$$y_k = \varphi\left(\sum_{j=0}^{m} w_{kj} x_j \right)$$

Where φ (phi) is the transfer function.

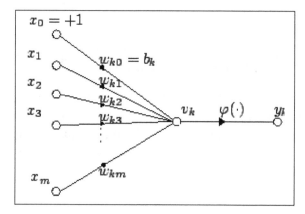

The output is analogous to the axon of a biological neuron, and its value propagates to the input of the next layer, through a synapse. It may also exit the system, possibly as part of an output vector. It has no learning process as such. Its transfer function weights are calculated and threshold value are predetermined.

Types

Depending on the specific model used they may be called a semi-linear unit, Nv neuron, binary neuron, linear threshold function, or McCulloch–Pitts (MCP) neuron.

Simple artificial neurons, such as the McCulloch–Pitts model, are sometimes described as "caricature models", since they are intended to reflect one or more neurophysiological observations, but without regard to realism.

Biological Models

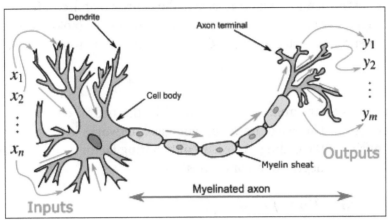

Neuron and myelinated axon, with signal flow from inputs at dendrites to outputs at axon terminals.

Artificial neurons are designed to mimic aspects of their biological counterparts.

- *Dendrites*: In a biological neuron, the dendrites act as the input vector. These dendrites allow the cell to receive signals from a large (>1000) number of neighboring neurons. As in the above mathematical treatment, each dendrite is able to perform multiplication by that dendrite's weight value. The multiplication is accomplished by increasing or decreasing the ratio of synaptic neurotransmitters to signal chemicals introduced into the dendrite in response to the synaptic neurotransmitter. A negative multiplication effect can be achieved by transmitting signal inhibitors (i.e. oppositely charged ions) along the dendrite in response to the reception of synaptic neurotransmitters.

- *Soma*: In a biological neuron, the soma acts as the summation function, seen in the above mathematical description. As positive and negative signals (exciting and inhibiting, respectively) arrive in the soma from the dendrites, the positive and negative ions are effectively added in summation, by simple virtue of being mixed together in the solution inside the cell's body.

- *Axon*: The axon gets its signal from the summation behavior which occurs inside the soma. The opening to the axon essentially samples the electrical potential of the solution inside the soma. Once the soma reaches a certain potential, the axon will transmit an all in signal pulse down its length. In this regard, the axon behaves as the ability for us to connect our artificial neuron to other artificial neurons.

Unlike most artificial neurons, however, biological neurons fire in discrete pulses. Each time the electrical potential inside the soma reaches a certain threshold, a pulse is transmitted down the axon. This pulsing can be translated into continuous values. The rate (activations per second, etc.) at which an axon fires converts directly into the rate at which neighboring cells get signal ions introduced into them. The faster a biological neuron fires, the faster nearby neurons accumulate electrical potential (or lose electrical potential, depending on the "weighting" of the dendrite that connects to the neuron that fired). It is this conversion that allows computer scientists and mathematicians to simulate biological neural networks using artificial neurons which can output distinct values (often from −1 to 1).

Encoding

Research has shown that unary coding is used in the neural circuits responsible for birdsong production. The use of unary in biological networks is presumably due to the inherent simplicity of the coding. Another contributing factor could be that unary coding provides a certain degree of error correction.

Types of Transfer Functions

The transfer function (activation function) of a neuron is chosen to have a number of properties which either enhance or simplify the network containing the neuron. Crucially, for instance, any multilayer perceptron using a *linear* transfer function has an equivalent single-layer network; a non-linear function is therefore necessary to gain the advantages of a multi-layer network.

Below, u refers in all cases to the weighted sum of all the inputs to the neuron, i.e. for n inputs,

$$u = \sum_{i=1}^{n} w_i x_i$$

where w is a vector of *synaptic weights* and x is a vector of inputs.

Step Function

The output y of this transfer function is binary, depending on whether the input meets a specified threshold, θ. The "signal" is sent, i.e. the output is set to one, if the activation meets the threshold.

$$y = \begin{cases} 1 & \text{if } u \geq \theta \\ 0 & \text{if } u < \theta \end{cases}$$

This function is used in perceptrons and often shows up in many other models. It performs a division of the space of inputs by a hyperplane. It is specially useful in the last layer of a network intended to perform binary classification of the inputs. It can be approximated from other sigmoidal functions by assigning large values to the weights.

Linear Combination

In this case, the output unit is simply the weighted sum of its inputs plus a *bias* term. A number of such linear neurons perform a linear transformation of the input vector.

This is usually more useful in the first layers of a network. A number of analysis tools exist based on linear models, such as harmonic analysis, and they can all be used in neural networks with this linear neuron. The bias term allows us to make affine transformations to the data.

Sigmoid

A fairly simple non-linear function, the sigmoid function such as the logistic function also has an easily calculated derivative, which can be important when calculating the weight updates in the network. It thus makes the network more easily manipulable mathematically, and was attractive to early computer scientists who needed to minimize the computational load of their simulations. It was previously commonly seen in multilayer perceptrons. However, recent work has shown sigmoid neurons to be less effective than rectified linear neurons. The reason is that the gradients computed by the backpropagation algorithm tend to diminish towards zero as activations propagate through layers of sigmoidal neurons, making it difficult to optimize neural networks using multiple layers of sigmoidal neurons.

Rectifier

In the context of artificial neural networks, the rectifier is an activation function defined as the positive part of its argument:

$$f(x) = x^+ = \max(0, x),$$

where x is the input to a neuron. This is also known as a ramp function and is analogous to half-wave rectification in electrical engineering. This activation function was first introduced to a dynamical network paper in Nature with strong biological motivations and mathematical justifications. It has been demonstrated for the first time in 2011 to enable better training of deeper networks, compared to the widely used activation functions prior to 2011, i.e., the logistic sigmoid and its more practical counterpart, the hyperbolic tangent.

Pseudocode Algorithm

The following is a simple pseudocode implementation of a single TLU which takes boolean inputs (true or false), and returns a single boolean output when activated. An object-oriented model is used. No method of training is defined, since several exist. If a purely functional model were used, the class TLU below would be replaced with a function TLU with input parameters threshold, weights, and inputs that returned a boolean value.

```
class TLU defined as:

  data member threshold : number
```

```
data member weights : list of numbers of size X

function member fire( inputs : list of booleans of size X ) : boolean defined
as:

  variable T : number

  T ← 0

  for each i in 1 to X :

   if inputs(i) is true :

    T ← T + weights(i)

   end if

  end for each

  if T > threshold :

   return true

  else:

   return false

  end if

 end function

end class
```

TYPES OF ARTIFICIAL NEURAL NETWORKS

There are many types of artificial neural networks (ANN). Artificial neural networks are computational models inspired by biological neural networks, and are used to approximate functions that are generally unknown. Particularly, they are inspired by the behaviour of neurons and the electrical signals they convey between input (such as from the eyes or nerve endings in the hand), processing, and output from the brain (such as reacting to light, touch, or heat). The way neurons semantically communicate is an area of ongoing research. Most artificial neural networks bear only some resemblance to their more complex biological counterparts, but are very effective at their intended tasks (e.g. classification or segmentation).

Some artificial neural networks are adaptive systems and are used for example to model populations and environments, which constantly change.

Neural networks can be hardware- (neurons are represented by physical components) or software-based (computer models), and can use a variety of topologies and learning algorithms.

Feedforward

The feedforward neural network was the first and simplest type. In this network the information moves only from the input layer directly through any hidden layers to the output layer without cycles/loops. Feedforward networks can be constructed with various types of units, such as binary McCulloch–Pitts neurons, the simplest of which is the perceptron. Continuous neurons, frequently with sigmoidal activation, are used in the context of backpropagation.

Group Method of Data Handling

The Group Method of Data Handling (GMDH) features fully automatic structural and parametric model optimization. The node activation functions are Kolmogorov–Gabor polynomials that permit additions and multiplications. It used a deep multilayer perceptron with eight layers. It is a supervised learning network that grows layer by layer, where each layer is trained by regression analysis. Useless items are detected using a validation set, and pruned through regularization. The size and depth of the resulting network depends on the task.

Autoencoder

An autoencoder, autoassociator or Diabolo network is similar to the multilayer perceptron (MLP) – with an input layer, an output layer and one or more hidden layers connecting them. However, the output layer has the same number of units as the input layer. Its purpose is to reconstruct its own inputs (instead of emitting a target value). Therefore, autoencoders are unsupervised learning models. An autoencoder is used for unsupervised learning of efficient codings, typically for the purpose of dimensionality reduction and for learning generative models of data.

Probabilistic

A probabilistic neural network (PNN) is a four-layer feedforward neural network. The layers are Input, hidden, pattern/summation and output. In the PNN algorithm, the parent probability distribution function (PDF) of each class is approximated by a Parzen window and a non-parametric function. Then, using PDF of each class, the class probability of a new input is estimated and Bayes' rule is employed to allocate it to the class with the highest posterior probability. It was derived from the Bayesian network and a statistical algorithm called Kernel Fisher discriminant analysis. It is used for classification and pattern recognition.

Time Delay

A time delay neural network (TDNN) is a feedforward architecture for sequential data that recognizes features independent of sequence position. In order to achieve time-shift invariance, delays are added to the input so that multiple data points (points in time) are analyzed together.

It usually forms part of a larger pattern recognition system. It has been implemented using a perceptron network whose connection weights were trained with back propagation (supervised learning).

Convolutional

A convolutional neural network (CNN, or ConvNet or shift invariant or space invariant) is a class of deep network, composed of one or more convolutional layers with fully connected layers (matching those in typical ANNs) on top. It uses tied weights and pooling layers. In particular, max-pooling. It is often structured via Fukushima's convolutional architecture. They are variations of multilayer perceptrons that use minimal preprocessing. This architecture allows CNNs to take advantage of the 2D structure of input data.

Its unit connectivity pattern is inspired by the organization of the visual cortex. Units respond to stimuli in a restricted region of space known as the receptive field. Receptive fields partially overlap, over-covering the entire visual field. Unit response can be approximated mathematically by a convolution operation.

CNNs are suitable for processing visual and other two-dimensional data. They have shown superior results in both image and speech applications. They can be trained with standard backpropagation. CNNs are easier to train than other regular, deep, feed-forward neural networks and have many fewer parameters to estimate.

Capsule Neural Networks (CapsNet) add structures called capsules to a CNN and reuse output from several capsules to form more stable (with respect to various perturbations) representations.

Examples of applications in computer vision include DeepDream and robot navigation. They have wide applications in image and video recognition, recommender systems and natural language processing.

Deep Stacking Network

A deep stacking network (DSN) (deep convex network) is based on a hierarchy of blocks of simplified neural network modules. It was introduced in 2011 by Deng and Dong. It formulates the learning as a convex optimization problem with a closed-form solution, emphasizing the mechanism's similarity to stacked generalization. Each DSN block is a simple module that is easy to train by itself in a supervised fashion without backpropagation for the entire blocks.

Each block consists of a simplified multi-layer perceptron (MLP) with a single hidden layer. The hidden layer h has logistic sigmoidal units, and the output layer has linear units. Connections between these layers are represented by weight matrix U; input-to-hidden-layer connections have weight matrix W. Target vectors t form the columns of matrix T, and the input data vectors x form the columns of matrix X. The matrix of hidden units is $H = \sigma(W^T X)$. Modules are trained in order, so lower-layer weights W are known at each stage. The function performs the element-wise logistic sigmoid operation. Each block estimates the same final label class y, and its estimate is concatenated with original input X to form the expanded input for the next block. Thus, the input to the first block contains the original data only, while downstream blocks' input adds the output of preceding blocks. Then learning the upper-layer weight matrix U given other weights in the network can be formulated as a convex optimization problem:

$$\min_{U^T} f = \| U^T H - T \|_F^2,$$

which has a closed-form solution.

Unlike other deep architectures, such as DBNs, the goal is not to discover the transformed feature representation. The structure of the hierarchy of this kind of architecture makes parallel learning straightforward, as a batch-mode optimization problem. In purely discriminative tasks, DSNs outperform conventional DBNs.

Tensor Deep Stacking Networks

This architecture is a DSN extension. It offers two important improvements: it uses higher-order information from covariance statistics, and it transforms the non-convex problem of a lower-layer to a convex sub-problem of an upper-layer. TDSNs use covariance statistics in a bilinear mapping from each of two distinct sets of hidden units in the same layer to predictions, via a third-order tensor.

While parallelization and scalability are not considered seriously in conventional DNNs, all learning for DSNs and TDSNs is done in batch mode, to allow parallelization. Parallelization allows scaling the design to larger (deeper) architectures and data sets.

The basic architecture is suitable for diverse tasks such as classification and regression.

Regulatory Feedback

Regulatory feedback networks started as a model to explain brain phenomena found during recognition including network-wide bursting and difficulty with similarity found universally in sensory recognition. A mechanism to perform optimization during recognition is created using inhibitory feedback connections back to the same inputs that activate them. This reduces requirements during learning and allows learning and updating to be easier while still being able to perform complex recognition.

Radial Basis Function (RBF)

Radial basis functions are functions that have a distance criterion with respect to a center. Radial basis functions have been applied as a replacement for the sigmoidal hidden layer transfer characteristic in multi-layer perceptrons. RBF networks have two layers: In the first, input is mapped onto each RBF in the 'hidden' layer. The RBF chosen is usually a Gaussian. In regression problems the output layer is a linear combination of hidden layer values representing mean predicted output. The interpretation of this output layer value is the same as a regression model in statistics. In classification problems the output layer is typically a sigmoid function of a linear combination of hidden layer values, representing a posterior probability. Performance in both cases is often improved by shrinkage techniques, known as ridge regression in classical statistics. This corresponds to a prior belief in small parameter values (and therefore smooth output functions) in a Bayesian framework.

RBF networks have the advantage of avoiding local minima in the same way as multi-layer perceptrons. This is because the only parameters that are adjusted in the learning process are the linear mapping from hidden layer to output layer. Linearity ensures that the error surface is quadratic and therefore has a single easily found minimum. In regression problems this can be found in one matrix operation. In classification problems the fixed non-linearity introduced by the sigmoid output function is most efficiently dealt with using iteratively re-weighted least squares.

RBF networks have the disadvantage of requiring good coverage of the input space by radial basis functions. RBF centres are determined with reference to the distribution of the input data, but without reference to the prediction task. As a result, representational resources may be wasted on areas of the input space that are irrelevant to the task. A common solution is to associate each data point with its own centre, although this can expand the linear system to be solved in the final layer and requires shrinkage techniques to avoid overfitting.

Associating each input datum with an RBF leads naturally to kernel methods such as support vector machines (SVM) and Gaussian processes (the RBF is the kernel function). All three approaches use a non-linear kernel function to project the input data into a space where the learning problem can be solved using a linear model. Like Gaussian processes, and unlike SVMs, RBF networks are typically trained in a maximum likelihood framework by maximizing the probability (minimizing the error). SVMs avoid overfitting by maximizing instead a margin. SVMs outperform RBF networks in most classification applications. In regression applications they can be competitive when the dimensionality of the input space is relatively small.

How RBF Networks Work

RBF neural networks are conceptually similar to K-Nearest Neighbor (k-NN) models.

The basic idea is that similar inputs produce similar outputs.

In the case in of a training set has two predictor variables, x and y and the target variable has two categories, positive and negative. Given a new case with predictor values x=6, y=5.1, how is the target variable computed?

The nearest neighbor classification performed for this example depends on how many neighboring points are considered. If 1-NN is used and the closest point is negative, then the new point should be classified as negative. Alternatively, if 9-NN classification is used and the closest 9 points are considered, then the effect of the surrounding 8 positive points may outweigh the closest 9 (negative) point.

An RBF network positions neurons in the space described by the predictor variables (x,y in this example). This space has as many dimensions as predictor variables. The Euclidean distance is computed from the new point to the center of each neuron, and a radial basis function (RBF) (also called a kernel function) is applied to the distance to compute the weight (influence) for each neuron. The radial basis function is so named because the radius distance is the argument to the function.

   Weight = RBF(*distance*)

Radial Basis Function

The value for the new point is found by summing the output values of the RBF functions multiplied by weights computed for each neuron.

The radial basis function for a neuron has a center and a radius (also called a spread). The radius may be different for each neuron, and, in RBF networks generated by DTREG, the radius may be different in each dimension.

With larger spread, neurons at a distance from a point have a greater influence.

Architecture

RBF networks have three layers:

- Input layer: One neuron appears in the input layer for each predictor variable. In the case of categorical variables, N-1 neurons are used where N is the number of categories. The input neurons standardizes the value ranges by subtracting the median and dividing by the interquartile range. The input neurons then feed the values to each of the neurons in the hidden layer.

- Hidden layer: This layer has a variable number of neurons (determined by the training process). Each neuron consists of a radial basis function centered on a point with as many dimensions as predictor variables. The spread (radius) of the RBF function may be different for each dimension. The centers and spreads are determined by training. When presented with the x vector of input values from the input layer, a hidden neuron computes the Euclidean distance of the test case from the neuron's center point and then applies the RBF kernel function to this distance using the spread values. The resulting value is passed to the summation layer.

- Summation layer: The value coming out of a neuron in the hidden layer is multiplied by a weight associated with the neuron and adds to the weighted values of other neurons. This sum becomes the output. For classification problems, one output is produced (with a separate set of weights and summation unit) for each target category. The value output for a category is the probability that the case being evaluated has that category.

Training

The following parameters are determined by the training process:

- The number of neurons in the hidden layer.
- The coordinates of the center of each hidden-layer RBF function.
- The radius (spread) of each RBF function in each dimension.
- The weights applied to the RBF function outputs as they pass to the summation layer.

Various methods have been used to train RBF networks. One approach first uses K-means clustering to find cluster centers which are then used as the centers for the RBF functions. However, K-means clustering is computationally intensive and it often does not generate the optimal number of centers. Another approach is to use a random subset of the training points as the centers.

DTREG uses a training algorithm that uses an evolutionary approach to determine the optimal center points and spreads for each neuron. It determines when to stop adding neurons to the network by monitoring the estimated leave-one-out (LOO) error and terminating when the LOO error begins to increase because of overfitting.

The computation of the optimal weights between the neurons in the hidden layer and the summation layer is done using ridge regression. An iterative procedure computes the optimal regularization Lambda parameter that minimizes the generalized cross-validation (GCV) error.

General Regression Neural Network

A GRNN is an associative memory neural network that is similar to the probabilistic neural network but it is used for regression and approximation rather than classification.

Deep Belief Network

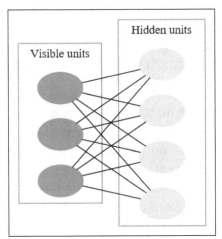

A restricted Boltzmann machine (RBM) with fully connected visible and hidden units. Note there are no hidden-hidden or visible-visible connections.

A deep belief network (DBN) is a probabilistic, generative model made up of multiple hidden layers. It can be considered a composition of simple learning modules.

A DBN can be used to generatively pre-train a deep neural network (DNN) by using the learned DBN weights as the initial DNN weights. Various discriminative algorithms can then tune these weights. This is particularly helpful when training data are limited, because poorly initialized weights can significantly hinder learning. These pre-trained weights end up in a region of the weight space that is closer to the optimal weights than random choices. This allows for both improved modeling and faster ultimate convergence.

Recurrent Neural Network

Recurrent neural networks (RNN) propagate data forward, but also backwards, from later processing stages to earlier stages. RNN can be used as general sequence processors.

Fully Recurrent

This architecture was developed in the 1980s. Its network creates a directed connection between every pair of units. Each has a time-varying, real-valued (more than just zero or one) activation (output). Each connection has a modifiable real-valued weight. Some of the nodes are called labeled nodes, some output nodes, the rest hidden nodes.

For supervised learning in discrete time settings, training sequences of real-valued input vectors become sequences of activations of the input nodes, one input vector at a time. At each time step, each non-input unit computes its current activation as a nonlinear function of the weighted sum of the activations of all units from which it receives connections. The system can explicitly activate (independent of incoming signals) some output units at certain time steps. For example, if the input sequence is a speech signal corresponding to a spoken digit, the final target output at the end of the sequence may be a label classifying the digit. For each sequence, its error is the sum of the deviations of all activations computed by the network from the corresponding target signals. For a training set of numerous sequences, the total error is the sum of the errors of all individual sequences.

To minimize total error, gradient descent can be used to change each weight in proportion to its derivative with respect to the error, provided the non-linear activation functions are differentiable. The standard method is called "backpropagation through time" or BPTT, a generalization of back-propagation for feedforward networks. A more computationally expensive online variant is called "Real-Time Recurrent Learning" or RTRL. Unlike BPTT this algorithm is local in time but not local in space. An online hybrid between BPTT and RTRL with intermediate complexity exists, with variants for continuous time. A major problem with gradient descent for standard RNN architectures is that error gradients vanish exponentially quickly with the size of the time lag between important events. The Long short-term memory architecture overcomes these problems.

In reinforcement learning settings, no teacher provides target signals. Instead a fitness function or reward function or utility function is occasionally used to evaluate performance, which influences its input stream through output units connected to actuators that affect the environment. Variants of evolutionary computation are often used to optimize the weight matrix.

Hopfield

The Hopfield network (like similar attractor-based networks) is of historic interest although it is not a general RNN, as it is not designed to process sequences of patterns. Instead it requires stationary inputs. It is an RNN in which all connections are symmetric. It guarantees that it will converge. If the connections are trained using Hebbian learning the Hopfield network can perform as robust content-addressable memory, resistant to connection alteration.

Boltzmann Machine

The Boltzmann machine can be thought of as a noisy Hopfield network. It is one of the first neural networks to demonstrate learning of latent variables (hidden units). Boltzmann machine learning was at first slow to simulate, but the contrastive divergence algorithm speeds up training for Boltzmann machines and Products of Experts.

Self-organizing Map

The self-organizing map (SOM) uses unsupervised learning. A set of neurons learn to map points in an input space to coordinates in an output space. The input space can have different dimensions and topology from the output space, and SOM attempts to preserve these.

Learning Vector Quantization

Learning vector quantization (LVQ) can be interpreted as a neural network architecture. Prototypical representatives of the classes parameterize, together with an appropriate distance measure, in a distance-based classification scheme.

Simple Recurrent

Simple recurrent networks have three layers, with the addition of a set of "context units" in the input layer. These units connect from the hidden layer or the output layer with a fixed weight of one. At each time step, the input is propagated in a standard feedforward fashion, and then a backpropagation-like learning rule is applied (not performing gradient descent). The fixed back connections leave a copy of the previous values of the hidden units in the context units (since they propagate over the connections before the learning rule is applied).

Reservoir Computing

Reservoir computing is a computation framework that may be viewed as an extension of neural networks. Typically an input signal is fed into a fixed (random) dynamical system called a reservoir whose dynamics map the input to a higher dimension. A readout mechanism is trained to map the reservois to the desired output. Training is performed only at the readout stage. Liquid-state machines are two major types of reservoir computing.

Echo State

The echo state network (ESN) employs a sparsely connected random hidden layer. The weights of output neurons are the only part of the network that are trained. ESN are good at reproducing certain time series.

Long Short-term Memory

The long short-term memory (LSTM) avoids the vanishing gradient problem. It works even when with long delays between inputs and can handle signals that mix low and high frequency components. LSTM RNN outperformed other RNN and other sequence learning methods such as HMM in applications such as language learning and connected handwriting recognition.

Bi-directional

Bi-directional RNN, or BRNN, use a finite sequence to predict or label each element of a sequence based on both the past and future context of the element. This is done by adding the outputs of two RNNs: one processing the sequence from left to right, the other one from right to left. The combined outputs are the predictions of the teacher-given target signals. This technique proved to be especially useful when combined with LSTM.

Hierarchical

Hierarchical RNN connects elements in various ways to decompose hierarchical behavior into useful subprograms.

Stochastic

A stochastic neural network introduces random variations into the network. Such random variations can be viewed as a form of statistical sampling, such as Monte Carlo sampling.

Genetic Scale

A RNN (often a LSTM) where a series is decomposed into a number of scales where every scale informs the primary length between two consecutive points. A first order scale consists of a normal RNN, a second order consists of all points separated by two indices and so on. The Nth order RNN connects the first and last node. The outputs from all the various scales are treated as a Committee of Machines and the associated scores are used genetically for the next iteration.

Modular

Biological studies have shown that the human brain operates as a collection of small networks. This realization gave birth to the concept of modular neural networks, in which several small networks cooperate or compete to solve problems.

Committee of Machines

A committee of machines (CoM) is a collection of different neural networks that together "vote" on a given example. This generally gives a much better result than individual networks. Because neural networks suffer from local minima, starting with the same architecture and training but using randomly different initial weights often gives vastly different results. A CoM tends to stabilize the result.

The CoM is similar to the general machine learning *bagging* method, except that the necessary variety of machines in the committee is obtained by training from different starting weights rather than training on different randomly selected subsets of the training data.

Associative

The associative neural network (ASNN) is an extension of committee of machines that combines multiple feedforward neural networks and the k-nearest neighbor technique. It uses the correlation between ensemble responses as a measure of distance amid the analyzed cases for the kNN. This corrects the bias of the neural network ensemble. An associative neural network has a memory that can coincide with the training set. If new data become available, the network instantly improves its predictive ability and provides data approximation (self-learns) without retraining. Another important feature of ASNN is the possibility to interpret neural network results by analysis of correlations between data cases in the space of models.

Physical

A physical neural network includes electrically adjustable resistance material to simulate artificial synapses. Examples include the ADALINE memristor-based neural network. An optical neural network is a physical implementation of an artificial neural network with optical components.

Other Types

Instantaneously Trained

Instantaneously trained neural networks (ITNN) were inspired by the phenomenon of short-term learning that seems to occur instantaneously. In these networks the weights of the hidden and the output layers are mapped directly from the training vector data. Ordinarily, they work on binary data, but versions for continuous data that require small additional processing exist.

Spiking

Spiking neural networks (SNN) explicitly consider the timing of inputs. The network input and output are usually represented as a series of spikes (delta function or more complex shapes). SNN can process information in the time domain (signals that vary over time). They are often implemented as recurrent networks. SNN are also a form of pulse computer.

Spiking neural networks with axonal conduction delays exhibit polychronization, and hence could have a very large memory capacity.

SNN and the temporal correlations of neural assemblies in such networks—have been used to model figure/ground separation and region linking in the visual system.

Regulatory Feedback

A regulatory feedback network makes inferences using negative feedback. The feedback is used to find the optimal activation of units. It is most similar to a non-parametric method but is different from K-nearest neighbor in that it mathematically emulates feedforward networks.

Neocognitron

The neocognitron is a hierarchical, multilayered network that was modeled after the visual cortex. It uses multiple types of units, (originally two, called simple and complex cells), as a cascading model for use in pattern recognition tasks. Local features are extracted by S-cells whose deformation is tolerated by C-cells. Local features in the input are integrated gradually and classified at higher layers. Among the various kinds of neocognitron are systems that can detect multiple patterns in the same input by using back propagation to achieve selective attention. It has been used for pattern recognition tasks and inspired convolutional neural networks.

Compound Hierarchical-deep Models

Compound hierarchical-deep models compose deep networks with non-parametric Bayesian models. Features can be learned using deep architectures such as DBNs, deep Boltzmann machines (DBM), deep auto encoders, convolutional variants, ss-RBMs, deep coding networks, DBNs with sparse feature learning, RNNs, conditional DBNs, de-noising auto encoders. This provides a better representation, allowing faster learning and more accurate classification with high-dimensional data. However, these architectures are poor at learning novel classes with few examples, because all network units are involved in representing the input (a *distributed representation*) and must be adjusted together (high degree of freedom). Limiting the degree of freedom reduces the number of parameters to learn, facilitating learning of new classes from few examples. *Hierarchical Bayesian (HB)* models allow learning from few examples, for example for computer vision, statistics and cognitive science.

Compound HD architectures aim to integrate characteristics of both HB and deep networks. The compound HDP-DBM architecture is a *hierarchical Dirichlet process (HDP)* as a hierarchical model, incorporating DBM architecture. It is a full generative model, generalized from abstract concepts flowing through the model layers, which is able to synthesize new examples in novel classes that look "reasonably" natural. All the levels are learned jointly by maximizing a joint log-probability score.

In a DBM with three hidden layers, the probability of a visible input "v" is:

$$p(\boldsymbol{i},\psi) = \frac{1}{Z}\sum_{h}\exp(\sum_{ij}W_{ij}^{(1)}v_i h_j^1 + \sum_{j\ell}W_{j\ell}^{(2)}h_j^1 h_\ell^2 + \sum_{\ell m}W_{\ell m}^{(3)}h_\ell^2 h_m^3),$$

where $\boldsymbol{h} = \{\boldsymbol{h}^{(1)}, \boldsymbol{h}^{(2)}, \boldsymbol{h}^{(3)}\}$ is the set of hidden units, and $\psi = \{\boldsymbol{W}^{(1)}, \boldsymbol{W}^{(2)}, \boldsymbol{W}^{(3)}\}$ are the model parameters, representing visible-hidden and hidden-hidden symmetric interaction terms.

A learned DBM model is an undirected model that defines the joint distribution $P(v, h^1, h^2, h^3)$. One way to express what has been learned is the conditional model $P(v, h^1, h^2 \mid h^3)$ and a prior term $P(h^3)$.

Here $P(v,h^1,h^2 \mid h^3)$ represents a conditional DBM model, which can be viewed as a two-layer DBM but with bias terms given by the states of h^3:

$$P(v,h^1,h^2 \mid h^3) = \frac{1}{Z(\psi,h^3)} \exp(\sum_{ij} W_{ij}^{(1)} v_i h_j^1 + \sum_{j\ell} W_{j\ell}^{(2)} h_j^1 h_\ell^2 + \sum_{\ell m} W_{\ell m}^{(3)} h_\ell^2 h_m^3).$$

Deep Predictive Coding Networks

A deep predictive coding network (DPCN) is a predictive coding scheme that uses top-down information to empirically adjust the priors needed for a bottom-up inference procedure by means of a deep, locally connected, generative model. This works by extracting sparse features from time-varying observations using a linear dynamical model. Then, a pooling strategy is used to learn invariant feature representations. These units compose to form a deep architecture and are trained by greedy layer-wise unsupervised learning. The layers constitute a kind of Markov chain such that the states at any layer depend only on the preceding and succeeding layers.

DPCNs predict the representation of the layer, by using a top-down approach using the information in upper layer and temporal dependencies from previous states. DPCNs can be extended to form a convolutional network.

Multilayer Kernel Machine

Multilayer kernel machines (MKM) are a way of learning highly nonlinear functions by iterative application of weakly nonlinear kernels. They use kernel principal component analysis (KPCA), as a method for the unsupervised greedy layer-wise pre-training step of deep learning.

Layer $\ell + 1$ learns the representation of the previous layer I, extracting the n_i principal component (PC) of the projection layer I output in the feature domain induced by the kernel. To reduce the dimensionaliity of the updated representation in each layer, a supervised strategy selects the best informative features among features extracted by KPCA. The process is:

- Rank the n_ℓ features according to their mutual information with the class labels;

- For different values of K and $m_\ell \in \{1,\dots,n_\ell\}$, compute the classification error rate of a *K-nearest neighbor (K-NN)* classifier using only the m_ℓ most informative features on a validation set;

- The value of m_ℓ with which the classifier has reached the lowest error rate determines the number of features to retain.

Some drawbacks accompany the KPCA method for MKMs.

A more straightforward way to use kernel machines for deep learning was developed for spoken language understanding. The main idea is to use a kernel machine to approximate a shallow neural net with an infinite number of hidden units, then use stacking to splice the output of the kernel machine and the raw input in building the next, higher level of the kernel machine. The number of levels in the deep convex network is a hyper-parameter of the overall system, to be determined by cross validation.

Dynamic

Dynamic neural networks address nonlinear multivariate behaviour and include (learning of) time-dependent behaviour, such as transient phenomena and delay effects. Techniques to estimate a system process from observed data fall under the general category of system identification.

Cascading

Cascade correlation is an architecture and supervised learning algorithm. Instead of just adjusting the weights in a network of fixed topology, Cascade-Correlation begins with a minimal network, then automatically trains and adds new hidden units one by one, creating a multi-layer structure. Once a new hidden unit has been added to the network, its input-side weights are frozen. This unit then becomes a permanent feature-detector in the network, available for producing outputs or for creating other, more complex feature detectors. The Cascade-Correlation architecture has several advantages: It learns quickly, determines its own size and topology, retains the structures it has built even if the training set changes and requires no backpropagation.

Neuro-fuzzy

A neuro-fuzzy network is a fuzzy inference system in the body of an artificial neural network. Depending on the FIS type, several layers simulate the processes involved in a fuzzy inference-like fuzzification, inference, aggregation and defuzzification. Embedding an FIS in a general structure of an ANN has the benefit of using available ANN training methods to find the parameters of a fuzzy system.

Compositional Pattern-producing

Compositional pattern-producing networks (CPPNs) are a variation of artificial neural networks which differ in their set of activation functions and how they are applied. While typical artificial neural networks often contain only sigmoid functions (and sometimes Gaussian functions), CPPNs can include both types of functions and many others. Furthermore, unlike typical artificial neural networks, CPPNs are applied across the entire space of possible inputs so that they can represent a complete image. Since they are compositions of functions, CPPNs in effect encode images at infinite resolution and can be sampled for a particular display at whatever resolution is optimal.

Memory Networks

Memory networks incorporate long-term memory. The long-term memory can be read and written to, with the goal of using it for prediction. These models have been applied in the context of question answering (QA) where the long-term memory effectively acts as a (dynamic) knowledge base and the output is a textual response.

In sparse distributed memory or hierarchical temporal memory, the patterns encoded by neural networks are used as addresses for content-addressable memory, with "neurons" essentially serving as address encoders and decoders. However, the early controllers of such memories were not differentiable.

One-shot Associative Memory

This type of network can add new patterns without re-training. It is done by creating a specific memory structure, which assigns each new pattern to an orthogonal plane using adjacently connected hierarchical arrays. The network offers real-time pattern recognition and high scalability; this requires parallel processing and is thus best suited for platforms such as wireless sensor networks, grid computing, and GPGPUs.

Hierarchical Temporal Memory

Hierarchical temporal memory (HTM) models some of the structural and algorithmic properties of the neocortex. HTM is a biomimetic model based on memory-prediction theory. HTM is a method for discovering and inferring the high-level causes of observed input patterns and sequences, thus building an increasingly complex model of the world.

HTM combines existing ideas to mimic the neocortex with a simple design that provides many capabilities. HTM combines and extends approaches used in Bayesian networks, spatial and temporal clustering algorithms, while using a tree-shaped hierarchy of nodes that is common in neural networks.

Holographic Associative Memory

Holographic Associative Memory (HAM) is an analog, correlation-based, associative, stimulus-response system. Information is mapped onto the phase orientation of complex numbers. The memory is effective for associative memory tasks, generalization and pattern recognition with changeable attention. Dynamic search localization is central to biological memory. In visual perception, humans focus on specific objects in a pattern. Humans can change focus from object to object without learning. HAM can mimic this ability by creating explicit representations for focus. It uses a bi-modal representation of pattern and a hologram-like complex spherical weight state-space. HAMs are useful for optical realization because the underlying hyper-spherical computations can be implemented with optical computation.

LSTM-related Differentiable Memory Structures

Apart from long short-term memory (LSTM), other approaches also added differentiable memory to recurrent functions. For example:

- Differentiable push and pop actions for alternative memory networks called neural stack machines.

- Memory networks where the control network's external differentiable storage is in the fast weights of another network.

- LSTM forget gates.

- Self-referential RNNs with special output units for addressing and rapidly manipulating the RNN's own weights in differentiable fashion (internal storage).

- Learning to transduce with unbounded memory.

Neural Turing Machines

Neural Turing machines couple LSTM networks to external memory resources, with which they can interact by attentional processes. The combined system is analogous to a Turing machine but is differentiable end-to-end, allowing it to be efficiently trained by gradient descent. Preliminary results demonstrate that neural Turing machines can infer simple algorithms such as copying, sorting and associative recall from input and output examples.

Differentiable neural computers (DNC) are an NTM extension. They out-performed Neural turing machines, long short-term memory systems and memory networks on sequence-processing tasks.

Semantic Hashing

Approaches that represent previous experiences directly and use a similar experience to form a local model are often called nearest neighbour or k-nearest neighbors methods. Deep learning is useful in semantic hashing where a deep graphical model the word-count vectors obtained from a large set of documents. Documents are mapped to memory addresses in such a way that semantically similar documents are located at nearby addresses. Documents similar to a query document can then be found by accessing all the addresses that differ by only a few bits from the address of the query document. Unlike sparse distributed memory that operates on 1000-bit addresses, semantic hashing works on 32 or 64-bit addresses found in a conventional computer architecture.

Pointer Networks

Deep neural networks can be potentially improved by deepening and parameter reduction, while maintaining trainability. While training extremely deep (e.g., 1 million layers) neural networks might not be practical, CPU-like architectures such as pointer networks and neural random-access machines overcome this limitation by using external random-access memory and other components that typically belong to a computer architecture such as registers, ALU and pointers. Such systems operate on probability distribution vectors stored in memory cells and registers. Thus, the model is fully differentiable and trains end-to-end. The key characteristic of these models is that their depth, the size of their short-term memory, and the number of parameters can be altered independently.

Hybrids

Encoder–decoder Networks

Encoder–decoder frameworks are based on neural networks that map highly structured input to highly structured output. The approach arose in the context of machine translation, where the input and output are written sentences in two natural languages. In that work, an LSTM RNN or CNN was used as an encoder to summarize a source sentence, and the summary was decoded using a conditional RNN language model to produce the translation. These systems share building blocks: gated RNNs and CNNs and trained attention mechanisms.

EXTENSION NEURAL NETWORK

Extension neural network is a pattern recognition method found by M. H. Wang and C. P. Hung to classify instances of data sets. Extension neural network is composed of artificial neural network and extension theory concepts. It uses the fast and adaptive learning capability of neural network and correlation estimation property of extension theory by calculating extension distance. ENN was used in:

- Failure detection in machinery.

- Tissue classification through MRI.

- Fault recognition in automotive engine.

- State of charge estimation in lead-acid battery.

- Classification with incomplete survey data.

Extension Theory

Extension theory was first proposed by Cai in 1983 to solve contradictory problems. While classical mathematic is familiar with quantity and forms of objects, extension theory transforms these objects to matter-element model.

$$R = (N, C, V)$$

where in matter R, N is the name or type, C is its characteristics and V is the corresponding value for the characteristic. There is a corresponding example in equation.

$$R = \begin{bmatrix} Yusuf & Height, & 178cm \\ & Weight & 98kg \end{bmatrix}$$

where *Height* and *Weight* characteristics form extension sets. These extension sets are defined by the V values which are range values for corresponding characteristics. Extension theory concerns with the extension correlation function between matter-element models like shown in equation 2 and extension sets. Extension correlation function is used to define extension space which is composed of pairs of elements and their extension correlation functions. The extension space formula is shown in equation.

$$A = \{(x, y) \mid x \in U, y = K(x)\}$$

where, A is the extension space, U is the object space, K is the extension correlation function, x is an element from the object space and y is the corresponding extension correlation function output of element x. $K(x)$ maps x to a membership interval $[-\infty, \infty]$. Negative region represents an element not belonging membership degree to a class and positive region vice versa. If x is mapped to $[0,1]$, extension theory acts like fuzzy set theory. The correlation function can be shown with the equation.

$$\rho(x, X_{in}) = \left| x - \frac{a+b}{2} \right| - \frac{b-a}{2}$$

$$\rho(x, X_{out}) = \left| x - \frac{c+d}{2} \right| - \frac{d-c}{2}$$

where, X_{in} and X_{out} are called concerned and neighborhood domain and their intervals are (a,b) and (c,d) respectively. The extended correlation function used for estimation of membership degree between x and X_{in}, X_{out} is shown in equation.

$$K(x) = \begin{cases} -\rho(x, X_{in}) & x \in X_{in} \\ \dfrac{\rho(x, X_{in})}{\rho(x, X_{out}) - \rho(x, X_{in})} & x \notin X_{in} \end{cases}$$

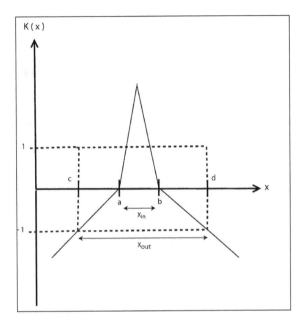

Extension Neural Network

Extension neural network has a neural network like appearance. Weight vector resides between the input nodes and output nodes. Output nodes are the representation of input nodes by passing them through the weight vector.

There are total number of input and output nodes are represented by n and n_c, respectively. These numbers depend on the number of characteristics and classes. Rather than using one weight value between two layer nodes as in neural network, extension neural network architecture has two weight values. In extension neural network architecture, for instance i, x_{ij}^p is the input which belongs to class p and o_{ik} is the corresponding output for class k. The output o_{ik} is calculated by using extension distance as shown in equation.

$$ED_{ik} = \sum_{j=0}^{n} \left(\frac{|x_{ij}^p - z_{kj}| - \dfrac{w_{kj}^U - w_{kj}^L}{2}}{|\dfrac{w_{kj}^U - w_{kj}^L}{2}|} + 1 \right)$$

$$k = 1, 2, ..., n_c$$

Estimated class is found through searching for the minimum extension distance among the calculated extension distance for all classes as summarized in equation, where k^* is the estimated class:

$$k^* = arg \min_k(o_{ik})$$

Learning Algorithm

Each class is composed of ranges of characteristics. These characteristics are the input types or names which come from matter-element model. Weight values in extension neural network represent these ranges. In the learning algorithm, first weights are initialized by searching for the maximum and minimum values of inputs for each class as shown in equation:

$$w_{kj}^U = \max_i\{x_{ij}^k\}$$
$$w_{kj}^L = \min_i\{x_{ij}^k\}, i = 1,...,N_p k = 1,...,n_c j = 1,2,....,n$$

where, I is the instance number and j is represents number of input. This initialization provides classes' ranges according to given training data.

After maintaining weights, center of clusters are found through the equation:

$$Z_k = \{z_{k1}, z_{k2},..., z_{kn}\}$$
$$z_{kj} = \frac{w_{kj}^U + w_{kj}^L}{2} k = 1,2,....,n_c, j = 1,2,....,n$$

Before learning process begins, predefined learning performance rate is given as shown in equation:

$$E_\tau = \frac{N_m}{N_p}$$

where, N_m is the misclassified instances and N_p is the total number of instances. Initialized parameters are used to classify instances. If the initialization is not sufficient due to the learning performance rate, training is required. In the training step weights are adjusted to classify training data more accurately, therefore reducing learning performance rate is aimed. In each iteration, E_τ is checked to control if required learning performance is reached. In each iteration every training instance is used for training. Instance i, belongs to class P is shown by:

$$X_i^P = \{x_{i1}^P, x_{i2}^P,..., x_{in}^P\}$$
$$1 \le p \le n_c$$

Every input data point of X_i^p is used in extension distance calculation to estimate the class of X_i^p. If the estimated class $k^* = p$ then update is not needed. Whereas, if $k^* \neq p$ then update is done. In update case, separators which show the relationship between inputs and classes, are shifted proportional to the distance between the center of clusters and the data points. The update formula:

$$z_{k^*j}^{new} = z_{k^*j}^{old} - \eta(x_{ij}^p - z_{k^*j}^{old})$$

$$z_{k^*j}^{new} = z_{k^*j}^{old} - \eta(x_{ij}^p - z_{k^*j}^{old})$$

$$w_{pj}^{L(new)} = w_{pj}^{L(old)} + \eta(x_{ij}^p - z_{pj}^{old})$$

$$w_{pj}^{U(new)} = w_{pj}^{U(old)} + \eta(x_{ij}^p - z_{pj}^{old})$$

$$w_{k^*j}^{L(new)} = w_{k^*j}^{L(old)} - \eta(x_{ij}^p - z_{k^*j}^{old})$$

$$w_{k^*j}^{U(new)} = w_{k^*j}^{U(old)} - \eta(x_{ij}^p - z_{k^*j}^{old})$$

To classify the instance i accurately, separator of class p for input j moves close to data-point of instance i, whereas separator of class k^* for input j moves far away. In the above image, an update example is given. Assume that instance I belongs to class A, whereas it is classified to class B because extension distance calculation gives out $ED_A > ED$. After the update, separator of class A moves close to the data-point of instance i whereas separator of class B moves far away. Consequently, extension distance gives out $ED_B > ED_A$, therefore after update instance I is classified to class A.

TIME DELAY NEURAL NETWORK

Time delay neural network (TDNN) is a multilayer artificial neural network architecture whose purpose is to 1) classify patterns with shift-invariance, and 2) model context at each layer of the network.

Shift-invariant classification means that the classifier does not require explicit segmentation prior to classification. For the classification of a temporal pattern (such as speech), the TDNN thus avoids having to determine the beginning and end points of sounds before classifying them.

For contextual modelling in a TDNN, each neural unit at each layer receives input not only from activations/features at the layer below, but from a pattern of unit output and its context. For time signals each unit receives as input the activation patterns over time from units below. Applied to two-dimensional classification (images, time-frequency patterns), the TDNN can be trained with shift-invariance in the coordinate space and avoids precise segmentation in the coordinate space.

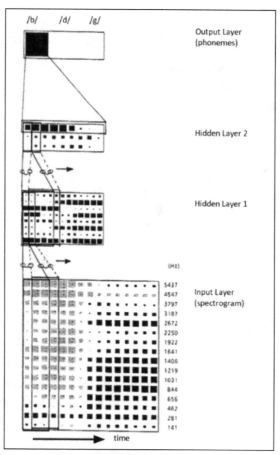

TDNN Diagram.

The Time Delay Neural Network, like other neural networks, operates with multiple interconnected layers of perceptrons, and is implemented as a feedforward neural network. All neurons (at each layer) of a TDNN receive inputs from the outputs of neurons at the layer below but with two differences:

1. Unlike regular Multi-Layer perceptrons, all units in a TDNN, at each layer, obtain inputs from a contextual *window* of outputs from the layer below. For time varying signals (e.g. speech), each unit has connections to the output from units below but also to the time-delayed (past) outputs from these same units. This models the units' temporal pattern/trajectory. For two-dimensional signals (e.g. time-frequency patterns or images), a 2-D context window is observed at each layer. Higher layers have inputs from wider context windows than lower layers and thus generally model coarser levels of abstraction.

2. Shift-invariance is achieved by explicitly removing position dependence during backpropagation training. This is done by making time-shifted copies of a network across the dimension of invariance. The error gradient is then computed by backpropagation through all these networks from an overall target vector,

but before performing the weight update, the error gradients associated with shifted copies are averaged and thus shared and constraint to be equal. Thus, all position dependence from backpropagation training through the shifted copies is removed and the copied networks learn the most salient hidden features shift-invariantly, i.e. independent of their precise position in the input data. Shift-invariance is also readily extended to multiple dimensions by imposing similar weight-sharing across copies that are shifted along multiple dimensions.

In the case of a speech signal, inputs are spectral coefficients over time. In order to learn critical acoustic-phonetic features (for example formant transitions, bursts, frication, etc.) without first requiring precise localization, the TDNN is trained time-shift-invariantly. Time-shift invariance is achieved through weight sharing across time during training: Time shifted copies of the TDNN are made over the input range (from left to right in figure). Backpropagation is then performed from an overall classification target vector resulting in gradients that will generally vary for each of the time-shifted network copies. Since such time-shifted networks are only copies, however, the position dependence is removed by weight sharing. In this example, this is done by averaging the gradients from each time-shifted copy before performing the weight update. In speech, time-shift invariant training was shown to learn weight matrices that are independent of precise positioning of the input. The weight matrices could also be shown to detect important acoustic-phonetic features that are known to be important for human speech perception, such as formant transitions, bursts, etc. TDNNs could also be combined or grown by way of pre-training.

Implementation

The precise architecture of TDNNs (time-delays, number of layers) is mostly determined by the designer depending on the classification problem and the most useful context sizes. The delays or context windows are chosen specific to each application. Work has also been done to create adaptable time-delay TDNNs where this manual tuning is eliminated.

State of the Art

TDNN-based phoneme recognizers compared favourably in early comparisons with HMM-based phone models. Modern deep TDNN architectures include many more hidden layers and sub-sample or pool connections over broader contexts at higher layers. They achieve up to 50% word error reduction over GMM-based acoustic models. While the different layers of TDNNs are intended to learn features of increasing context width, they do model local contexts. When longer-distance relationships and pattern sequences have to be processed, learning states and state-sequences is important and TDNNs can be combined with other modelling techniques.

Applications

Speech Recognition

TDNNs used to solve problems in speech recognition that were introduced in 1987 and initially focused on shift-invariant phoneme recognition. Speech lends itself nicely to TDNNs as spoken sounds are rarely of uniform length and precise segmentation is difficult or impossible. By scanning a sound over past and future, the TDNN is able to construct a model for the key elements of that sound in a time-shift invariant manner. This is particularly useful as sounds are smeared out through reverberation. Large phonetic TDNNs can be constructed modularly through pre-training and combining smaller networks.

Large Vocabulary Speech Recognition

Large vocabulary speech recognition requires recognizing sequences of phonemes that make up words subject to the constraints of a large pronunciation vocabulary. Integration of TDNNs into large vocabulary speech recognizers is possible by introducing state transitions and search between phonemes that make up a word. The resulting Multi-State Time-Delay Neural Network (MS-TDNN) can be trained discriminative from the word level, thereby optimizing the entire arrangement toward word recognition instead of phoneme classification.

Speaker Independence

Two-dimensional variants of the TDNNs were proposed for speaker independence. Here, shift-invariance is applied to the time as well as to the frequency axis in order to learn hidden features that are independent of precise location in time and in frequency (the latter being due to speaker variability).

Reverberation

One of the persistent problems in speech recognition is recognizing speech when it is corrupted by echo and reverberation (as is the case in large rooms and distant microphones). Reverberation can be viewed as corrupting speech with delayed versions of itself. In general, it is difficult, however, to de-reverberate a signal as the impulse response function (and thus the convolutional noise experienced by the signal) is not known for any arbitrary space. The TDNN was shown to be effective to recognize speech robustly despite different levels of reverberation.

Lip-reading – Audio-visual Speech

TDNNs were also successfully used in early demonstrations of audio-visual speech, where the sounds of speech are complemented by visually reading lip movement.

Here, TDNN-based recognizers used visual and acoustic features jointly to achieve improved recognition accuracy, particularly in the presence of noise, where complementary information from an alternate modality could be fused nicely in a neural net.

Handwriting Recognition

TDNNs have been used effectively in compact and high-performance handwriting recognition systems. Shift-invariance was also adapted to spatial patterns (x/y-axes) in image offline handwriting recognition.

Video Analysis

Video has a temporal dimension that makes a TDNN an ideal solution to analysing motion patterns. An example of this analysis is a combination of vehicle detection and recognizing pedestrians. When examining videos, subsequent images are fed into the TDNN as input where each image is the next frame in the video. The strength of the TDNN comes from its ability to examine objects shifted in time forward and backward to define an object detectable as the time is altered. If an object can be recognized in this manner, an application can plan on that object to be found in the future and perform an optimal action.

Image Recognition

Two-dimensional TDNNs were later applied to other image-recognition tasks under the name of "Convolutional Neural Networks", where shift-invariant training is applied to the x/y axes of an image.

Common Libraries

- TDNNs can be implemented in virtually all machine-learning frameworks using one-dimensional convolutional neural networks, due to the equivalence of the methods.

- Matlab: The neural network toolbox has explicit functionality designed to produce a time delay neural network give the step size of time delays and an optional training function. The default training algorithm is a Supervised Learning back-propagation algorithm that updates filter weights based on the Levenberg-Marquardt optimizations. The function is timedelaynet(delays, hidden_layers, train_fnc) and returns a time-delay neural network architecture that a user can train and provide inputs to.

- The Kaldi ASR Toolkit has an implementation of TDNNs with several optimizations for speech recognition.

NEOCOGNITRON

The neocognitron, proposed by Fukushima, is a hierarchical multilayered neural network capable of robust visual pattern recognition through learning.

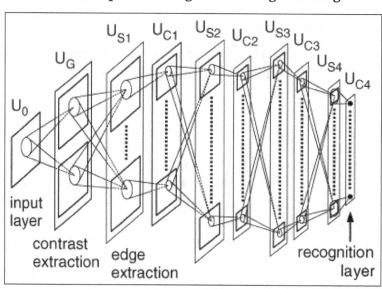

A typical architecture of the neocognitron.

Figure shows a typical architecture of the network. The lowest stage is the input layer consisting of two-dimensional array of cells, which correspond to photoreceptors of the retina. There are retinotopically ordered connections between cells of adjoining layers. Each cell receives input connections that lead from cells situated in a limited area on the preceding layer. Layers of "S-cells" and "C-cells" are arranged alternately in the hierarchical network. (In the network shown in figure, a contrast-extracting layer is inserted between the input layer and the S-cell layer of the first stage).

S-cells work as feature-extracting cells. They resemble simple cells of the primary visual cortex in their response. Their input connections are variable and are modified through learning. After having finished learning, each S-cell come to respond selectively to a particular feature presented in its receptive field. The features extracted by S-cells are determined during the learning process. Generally speaking, *local* features, such as edges or lines in particular orientations, are extracted in lower stages. More *global* features, such as parts of learning patterns, are extracted in higher stages.

C-cells, which resembles complex cells in the visual cortex, are inserted in the network to allow for positional errors in the features of the stimulus. The input connections of C-cells, which come from S-cells of the preceding layer, are fixed and invariable. Each C-cell receives excitatory input connections from a group of S-cells that extract the same feature, but from slightly different positions. The C-cell responds if at least one of these S-cells yield an output. Even if the stimulus feature shifts in position and another S-cell comes to respond instead of the first one, the same C-cell keeps responding. Thus, the C-cell's response is less sensitive to shift in position of the input pattern. We can also express that C-cells make a blurring operation, because the response of a layer of S-cells is spatially blurred in the response of the succeeding layer of C-cells.

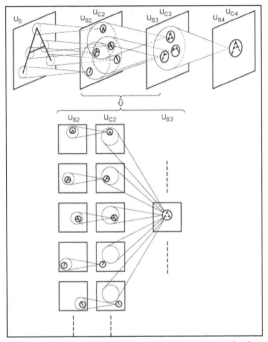

The process of pattern recognition in the neocognitron. The lower half of the figure is an enlarged illustration of a part of the network.

Each layer of S-cells or C-cells is divided into sub-layers, called "cell-planes", according to the features to which the cells responds. The cells in each cell-plane are arranged in a two-dimensional array. A cell-plane is a group of cells that are arranged retinotopically and share the same set of input connections. In other words, the connections to a cell-plane have a translational symmetry. As a result, all the cells in a cell-plane have receptive fields of an identical characteristic, but the locations of the receptive fields differ from cell to cell. The modification of variable connections during the learning progresses also under the restriction of shared connections.

Principles of Deformation-Resistant Recognition

In the whole network, with its alternate layers of S-cells and C-cells, the process of feature-extraction by S-cells and toleration of positional shift by C-cells is repeated. During this process, local features extracted in lower stages are gradually integrated into more global features, as illustrated in figure.

Since small amounts of positional errors of local features are absorbed by the blurring operation by C-cells, an S-cell in a higher stage comes to respond robustly to a specific feature even if the feature is slightly deformed or shifted.

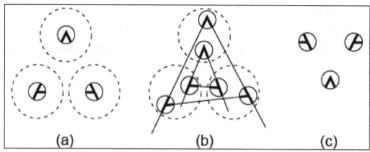

The principle for recognizing deformed patterns.

Figure illustrates this situation. Let an S-cell in an intermediate stage of the network have already been trained to extract a global feature consisting of three local features of a training pattern 'A' as illustrated in figure. The cell tolerates a positional error of each local feature if the deviation falls within the dotted circle. Hence, the S-cell responds to any of the deformed patterns shown in figure. The toleration of positional errors should not be too large at this stage. If large errors are tolerated at any one step, the network may come to respond erroneously, such as by recognizing a stimulus like figure as an 'A' pattern.

Thus, tolerating positional error a little at a time at each stage, rather than all in one step, plays an important role in endowing the network with the ability to recognize even distorted patterns.

An example of the response of a neocognitron that has been trained to recognize handwritten digits. The input pattern is recognized correctly as '5'.

The C-cells in the highest stage work as recognition cells, which indicate the result of the pattern recognition. Each C-cell of the recognition layer at the highest stage integrates all the information of the input pattern, and responds only to one specific pattern. Since errors in the relative position of local features are tolerated in the process of extracting and integrating features, the same C-cell responds in the recognition layer at the highest stage, even if the input pattern is deformed, changed in size, or shifted in position. In other words, after having finished learning, the neocognitron can recognize input patterns robustly, with little effect from deformation, change in size, or shift in position.

Self-organization of the Network

The neocognitron can be trained to recognize patterns through learning. Only S-cells in the network have their input connections modified through learning. Various training methods, including unsupervised learning and supervised learning, have been proposed so far.

In the case of unsupervised learning, the self-organization of the network is performed using two principles. The first principle is a kind of winner-take-all rule: among the cells situated in a certain small area, which is called a hypercolumn, only the one responding most strongly becomes the winner. The winner has its input connections strengthened. The amount of strengthening of each input connection to the winner is proportional to the intensity of the response of the cell from which the relevant connection leads.

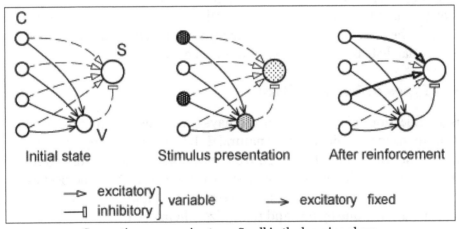

Connections converging to an S-cell in the learning phase.

To be more specific, an S-cell receives variable excitatory connections from a group of C-cells of the preceding stage as illustrated in figure. Each S-cell is accompanied with an inhibitory cell, called a V-cell. The S-cell also receives a variable inhibitory connection from the V-cell. The V-cell receives fixed excitatory connections from the same group of C-cells as does the S-cell, and always responds with the average intensity of the output of the C-cells.

The initial strength of the variable connections is very weak and nearly zero. Suppose the S-cell responds most strongly among the S-cells in its vicinity when a training stimulus is presented. According to the winner-take-all rule described above, variable connections leading from activated C-cells are strengthened. The variable excitatory connections to the S-cell grow into a template that exactly matches the spatial distribution of the response of the cells in the preceding layer. The inhibitory variable connection from the V-cell is also strengthened at the same time to the average strength of the excitatory connections.

After the learning, the S-cell acquires the ability to extract a feature of the stimulus presented during the learning period. Through the excitatory connections, the S-cell receives signals indicating the existence of the relevant feature to be extracted. If an irrelevant feature is presented, the inhibitory signal from the V-cell becomes stronger than the direct excitatory signals from the C-cells, and the response of the S-cell is suppressed.

Once an S-cell is thus selected and has learned to respond to a feature, the cell usually loses its responsiveness to other features. When a different feature is presented, a different cell usually yields the maximum output and learns the second feature. Thus, a "division of labor" among the cells occurs automatically.

The second principle for the learning is introduced in order that the connections being strengthened always preserving translational symmetry, or the condition of shared connections. The maximum-output cell not only grows by itself, but also controls the growth of neighboring cells, working, so to speak, like a seed in crystal growth. To be more specific, all of the other S-cells in the cell-plane, from which the "seed cell" is selected, follow the seed cell, and have their input connections strengthened by having the same spatial distribution as those of the seed cell.

Various Types of Neocognitron

Various modifications of the neocognitron have been proposed to improve the recognition rate or to make biologically more natural. If backward (i.e., top-down) connections are added to the conventional neocognitron, for example, the network come to have an ability to recognize occluded patterns correctly and can restore the occluded parts of the patterns. Even if many patterns are presented simultaneously, it focuses attention to individual patterns one by one and recognizes them correctly.

NEUROTECHNOLOGY

Neurotechnology is any technology that has a fundamental influence on how people understand the brain and various aspects of consciousness, thought, and higher order activities in the brain. It also includes technologies that are designed to improve and repair brain function and allow researchers and clinicians to visualize the brain.

The field of neurotechnology has been around for nearly half a century but has only reached maturity in the last twenty years. The advent of brain imaging revolutionized the field, allowing researchers to directly monitor the brain's activities during experiments. Neurotechnology has made significant impact on society, though its presence is so commonplace that many do not realize its ubiquity. From pharmaceutical drugs to brain scanning, neurotechnology affects nearly all industrialized people either directly or indirectly, be it from drugs for depression, sleep, ADD, or anti-neurotics to cancer scanning, stroke rehabilitation, and much more.

As the field's depth increases it will potentially allow society to control and harness more of what the brain does and how it influences lifestyles and personalities. Commonplace technologies already attempt to do this; games like Brain age, and programs like Fast ForWord that aim to improve brain function, are neurotechnologies.

Currently, modern science can image nearly all aspects of the brain as well as control a degree of the function of the brain. It can help control depression, over-activation, sleep deprivation, and many other conditions. Therapeutically it can help improve stroke victims' motor coordination, improve brain function, reduce epileptic episodes, improve patients with degenerative motor diseases (Parkinson's disease, Huntington's disease, ALS), and can even help alleviate phantom pain perception. Advances in the field promise many new enhancements and rehabilitation methods for patients suffering from neurological problems. The neurotechnology revolution has given rise to the Decade of the Mind initiative, which was started in 2007. It also offers the possibility of revealing the mechanisms by which mind and consciousness emerge from the brain.

Current Technologies

Live Imaging

Magnetoencephalography is a functional neuroimaging technique for mapping brain activity by recording magnetic fields produced by electrical currents occurring naturally in the brain, using very sensitive magnetometers. Arrays of SQUIDs (superconducting quantum interference devices) are the most common magnetometer. Applications of MEG include basic research into perceptual and cognitive brain processes, localizing regions affected by pathology before surgical removal, determining the function of various parts of the brain, and neurofeedback. This can be applied in a clinical setting to find locations of abnormalities as well as in an experimental setting to simply measure brain activity.

Magnetic resonance imaging (MRI) is used for scanning the brain for topological and landmark structure in the brain, but can also be used for imaging activation in the brain. While detail about how MRI works is reserved for the actual MRI article, the uses of MRI are far reaching in the study of neuroscience. It is a cornerstone technology in studying the mind, especially with the advent of functional MRI (fMRI). Functional MRI measures the oxygen levels in the brain upon activation (higher oxygen content = neural activation) and allows researchers to understand what loci are responsible for activation under a given stimulus. This technology is a large improvement to single cell or loci activation by means of exposing the brain and contact stimulation. Functional MRI allows researchers to draw associative relationships between different loci and regions of the brain and provides a large amount of knowledge in establishing new landmarks and loci in the brain.

Computed tomography (CT) is another technology used for scanning the brain. It has been used since the 1970s and is another tool used by neuroscientists to track brain structure and activation. While many of the functions of CT scans are now done using MRI, CT can still be used as the mode by which brain activation and brain injury are detected. Using an X-ray, researchers can detect radioactive markers in the brain that indicate brain activation as a tool to establish relationships in the brain as well as detect many injuries/diseases that can cause lasting damage to the brain such as aneurysms, degeneration, and cancer.

Positron emission tomography (PET) is another imaging technology that aids researchers. Instead of using magnetic resonance or X-rays, PET scans rely on positron emitting markers that are bound to a biologically relevant marker such as glucose. The more activation in the brain the more that region requires nutrients, so higher activation appears more brightly on an image of the brain. PET scans are becoming more frequently used by researchers because PET scans are activated due to metabolism whereas MRI is activated on a more physiological basis (sugar activation versus oxygen activation).

Transcranial Magnetic Stimulation

Transcranial magnetic stimulation (TMS) is essentially direct magnetic stimulation to the brain. Because electric currents and magnetic fields are intrinsically related, by stimulating the brain with magnetic pulses it is possible to interfere with specific loci in the brain to produce a predictable effect. This field of study is currently receiving a large amount of attention due to the potential benefits that could come out of better understanding this technology. Transcranial magnetic movement of particles in the brain shows promise for drug targeting and delivery as studies have demonstrated this to be noninvasive on brain physiology.

Transcranial Direct Current Stimulation

Transcranial direct current stimulation (tDCS) is a form of neurostimulation which uses constant, low current delivered via electrodes placed on the scalp. The mechanisms underlying tDCS effects are still incompletely understood, but recent advances in neurotechnology allowing for in vivo assessment of brain electric activity during tDCS promise to advance understanding of these mechanisms. Research into using tDCS on healthy adults have demonstrated that tDCS can increase cognitive performance on a variety of tasks, depending on the area of the brain being stimulated. tDCS has been used to enhance language and mathematical ability (though one form of tDCS was also found to inhibit math learning), attention span, problem solving, memory, and coordination.

Cranial Surface Measurements

Electroencephalography (EEG) is a method of measuring brainwave activity non-invasively. A number of electrodes are placed around the head and scalp and electrical signals are measured. Typically EEGs are used when dealing with sleep, as there are characteristic wave patterns associated with different stages of sleep. Clinically EEGs are used to study epilepsy as well as stroke and tumor presence in the brain. EEGs are a different method to understand the electrical signaling in the brain during activation.

Magnetoencephalography (MEG) is another method of measuring activity in the brain by measuring the magnetic fields that arise from electrical currents in the brain. The benefit to using MEG instead of EEG is that these fields are highly localized and give rise to better understanding of how specific loci react to stimulation or if these regions over-activate (as in epileptic seizures).

Implant Technologies

Neurodevices are any devices used to monitor or regulate brain activity. Currently there are a few available for clinical use as a treatment for Parkinson's disease. The most common neurodevices are deep brain stimulators (DBS) that are used to give electrical stimulation to areas stricken by inactivity. Parkinson's disease is known to be caused by an inactivation of the basal ganglia (nuclei) and recently DBS has become the more preferred form of treatment for Parkinson's disease, although current research questions the efficiency of DBS for movement disorders.

Neuromodulation is a relatively new field that combines the use of neurodevices and neurochemistry. The basis of this field is that the brain can be regulated using a number of different factors (metabolic, electrical stimulation, physiological) and that all these can be modulated by devices implanted in the neural network. While currently this field is still in the researcher phase, it represents a new type of technological integration in the field of neurotechnology. The brain is a very sensitive organ, so in addition to researching the amazing things that neuromodulation and implanted neural devices can produce, it is important to research ways to create devices that elicit as few negative responses from the body as possible. This can be done by modifying the material surface chemistry of neural implants.

Cell Therapy

Researchers have begun looking at uses for stem cells in the brain, which recently have been found in a few loci. A large number of studies are being done to determine if this form of therapy could be used in a large scale. Experiments have successfully used stem cells in the brains of children who suffered from injuries in gestation and elderly people with degenerative diseases in order to induce the brain to produce new cells and to make more connections between neurons.

Pharmaceuticals

Pharmaceuticals play a vital role in maintaining stable brain chemistry, and are the most commonly used neurotechnology by the general public and medicine. Drugs like sertraline, methylphenidate, and zolpidem act as chemical modulators in the brain, and they allow for normal activity in many people whose brains cannot act normally under physiological conditions. While pharmaceuticals are usually not mentioned and have their own field, the role of pharmaceuticals is perhaps the most far-reaching and commonplace in modern society. Movement of magnetic particles to targeted brain regions for drug delivery is an emerging field of study and causes no detectable circuit damage.

Low Field Magnetic Stimulation

Stimulation with low-intensity magnetic fields is currently under study for depression at Harvard Medical School, and has previously been explored by Bell. It has FDA approval for treatment of depression. It is also being researched for other applications such as autism. One issue is that no two brains are alike and stimulation can cause either polarization or depolarization.

Ethics

Stem Cells

The ethical debate about use of embryonic stem cells has stirred controversy both in the United States and abroad; although more recently these debates have lessened due to modern advances in creating induced pluripotent stem cells from adult cells. The greatest advantage for use of embryonic stem cells is the fact that they can differentiate (become) nearly any type of cell provided the right conditions and signals. However, recent advances by Shinya Yamanaka et al. have found ways to create pluripotent cells without the use of such controversial cell cultures. Using the patient's own cells and re-differentiating them into the desired cell type bypasses both possible patient rejection of the embryonic stem cells and any ethical concerns associated with using them, while also providing researchers a larger supply of available cells. However, induced pluripotent cells have the potential to form benign (though potentially malignant) tumors, and tend to have poor survivability in vivo (in the living body) on damaged tissue. Much of the ethics concerning use of stem cells has subsided from the embryonic/adult stem cell debate due to its rendered moot, but now societies find themselves debating whether or not this technology can be ethically used. Enhancements of traits, use of animals for tissue scaffolding, and even arguments for moral degeneration have been made with the fears that if this technology reaches its full potential a new paradigm shift will occur in human behavior.

Military Application

New neurotechnologies have always garnered the appeal of governments, from lie detection technology and virtual reality to rehabilitation and understanding the psyche. Due to the Iraq War and War on Terror, American soldiers coming back from Iraq and Afghanistan are reported to have percentages up to 12% with PTSD. There are many researchers hoping to improve these peoples' conditions by implementing new strategies for recovery. By combining pharmaceuticals and neurotechnologies, some researchers have discovered ways of lowering the "fear" response and theorize that it may be applicable to PTSD. Virtual reality is another technology that has drawn much attention in the military. If improved, it could be possible to train soldiers how to deal with complex situations in times of peace, in order to better prepare and train a modern army.

Privacy

Finally, when these technologies are being developed society must understand that these neurotechnologies could reveal the one thing that people can always keep secret: what they are thinking. While there are large amounts of benefits associated with these technologies, it is necessary for scientists, citizens and policy makers alike to consider implications for privacy. This term is important in many ethical circles concerned with the state and goals of progress in the field of neurotechnology. Current improvements such as "brain fingerprinting" or lie detection using EEG or fMRI could give rise to a set fixture of loci/emotional relationships in the brain, although these technologies are still years away from full application. It is important to consider how all these neurotechnologies might affect the future of society, and it is suggested that political, scientific, and civil debates are heard about the implementation of these newer technologies that potentially offer a new wealth of once-private information. Some ethicists are also concerned with the use of TMS and fear that the technique could be used to alter patients in ways that are undesired by the patient.

Cognitive Liberty

Cognitive liberty refers to a suggested right to self-determination of individuals to control their own mental processes, cognition, and consciousness including by the use of various neurotechnologies and psychoactive substances. This perceived right is relevant for reformation and development of associated laws.

NEURAL BACKPROPAGATION

Backpropagation is the central mechanism by which neural networks learn. It is the messenger telling the network whether or not the net made a mistake when it made a prediction.

To propagate is to transmit something (light, sound, motion or information) in a particular direction or through a particular medium. When we discuss backpropagation in deep learning, we are talking about the transmission of information, and that information relates to the error produced by the neural network when it makes a guess about data.

Untrained neural network models are like new-born babies: They are created ignorant of the world, and it is only through exposure to the world, experiencing it, that their ignorance is slowly relieved. Algorithms experience the world through data. So by training a neural network on a relevant dataset, we seek to decrease its ignorance. The way we measure progress is by monitoring the error produced by the network each time it makes a prediction.

The knowledge of a neural network with regard to the world is captured by its weights, the parameters that alter input data as its signal flows through the neural network towards the net's final layer, which will make a decision about that input. Those decisions are often wrong, because the parameters transforming the signal into a decision are poorly calibrated; they haven't learned enough yet. Forward propagation is when a data instance sends its signal through a network's parameters toward the prediction at the end. Once that prediction is made, its distance from the ground truth (error) can be measured.

So the parameters of the neural network have a relationship with the error the net produces, and when the parameters change, the error does, too. We change the parameters using optimization algorithms. A very popular optimization method is called gradient descent, which is useful for finding the minimum of a function. We are seeking to minimize the error, which is also known as the loss function or the objective function.

A neural network propagates the signal of the input data forward through its parameters towards the moment of decision, and then backpropagates information about the error, in reverse through the network, so that it can alter the parameters. This happens step by step:

- The network makes a guess about data, using its parameters.
- The network's is measured with a loss function.
- The error is backpropagated to adjust the wrong-headed parameters.

You could compare a neural network to a large piece of artillery that is attempting to strike a distant object with a shell. When the neural network makes a guess about an instance of data, it fires, a cloud of dust rises on the horizon, and the gunner tries to make out where the shell struck, and how far it was from the target. That distance from the target is the measure of error. The measure of error is then applied to the angle and direction of the gun (parameters), before it takes another shot.

Backpropagation takes the error associated with a wrong guess by a neural network, and uses that error to adjust the neural network's parameters in the direction of less error. How does it know the direction of less error?

Gradient Descent

A gradient is a slope whose angle we can measure. Like all slopes, it can be expressed as a relationship between two variables: "y over x", or rise over run. In this case, the y is the error produced by the neural network, and x is the parameter of the neural network. The parameter has a relationship to the error, and by changing the parameter, we can increase or decrease the error. So the gradient tells us the change we can expect in y with regard to x.

To obtain this information, we must use differential calculus, which enables us to measure instantaneous rates of change, which in this case is the tangent of a changing slope expressed the relationship of the parameter to the neural network's error. As the parameter changes, the error changes, and we want to move both variables in the direction of less error.

Obviously, a neural network has many parameters, so what we're really measuring are the partial derivatives of each parameter's contribution to the total change in error.

What's more, neural networks have parameters that process the input data sequentially, one after another. Therefore, backpropagation establishes the relationship between the neural network's error and the parameters of the net's last layer; then it establishes the relationship between the parameters of the neural net's last layer those the parameters of the second-to-last layer, and so forth, in an application of the chain rule of calculus.

It is of interest to note that backpropagation in artificial neural networks has echoes in the functioning of biological neurons, which respond to rewards such as dopamine to reinforce how they fire; i.e. how they interpret the world. Dopaminergenic behavior tends to strengthen the ties between the neurons involved, and helps those ties last longer.

References

- Martin Anthony (January 2001). Discrete Mathematics of Neural Networks: Selected Topics. SIAM. Pp. 3–. ISBN 978-0-89871-480-7

- Time Series and Dynamic Systems - MATLAB & Simulink". Mathworks.com. Retrieved 21 June 2016

- Hinton, G.E. (2009). "Deep belief networks". Scholarpedia. 4 (5): 5947. Bibcode:2009schpj...4. 5947 H Doi 10 4249/scholarpedia:5947

- Charu C. Aggarwal (25 July 2014). Data Classification: Algorithms and Applications. CRC Press. Pp. 209–. ISBN 978-1-4665-8674-1

- Rodriguez, Abel; Dunson, David (2008). "The Nested Dirichlet Process". Journal of the American Statistical Association. 103 (483): 1131–1154. Citeseerx 10.1.1.70.9873. Doi:10.1198/016214508000000553

- Convolutional Neural Networks (lenet) – deeplearning 0.1 documentation". Deeplearning 0.1. LISA Lab. Retrieved 31 August 2013

- Artificial-intelligence-ai, definition: techopedia.com, Retrieved 16 January, 2019

- How-neuroscience-enables-better-artificial-intelligence-design: medium.com, Retrieved 30 April, 2019

- JHU – Institute for Computational Medicine | Computational Anatomy". Icm.jhu.edu. Retrieved 2018-01-01

- Carlson, Neil R. (2013). Physiology of Behavior. Upper Saddle River, NJ: Pearson Education Inc. ISBN 9780205239399 pp 152-153

5

Softwares and Technologies used in Computational Neuroscience

Various software and technologies are used in computational neuroscience. The most common of them are GENESIS, NEURON, BRIAN, neurocomputational speech processing and artificial brain. The topics elaborated in this chapter will help in gaining a better perspective about these software and technologies used in computational neuroscience.

GENESIS

GENESIS (the General Neural Simulation System) is a general purpose software platform that was developed to support the biologically realistic simulation of neural systems, ranging from subcellular components and biochemical reactions to complex models of single neurons, simulations of large networks, and systems-level models. The object-oriented approach taken by GENESIS and its high-level simulation language allows modelers to easily extend the capabilities of the simulator, and to exchange, modify, and reuse models or model components.

Purpose and Modeling Philosophy

GENESIS (the General Neural Simulation System) was designed as an extensible general simulation system for the realistic modeling of neural and biological systems, based on the known anatomical and physiological organization of neurons, circuits and networks . Thus, single cell models in GENESIS usually include dendritic morphology and a variety of ionic conductances, whereas realistic network models attempt to duplicate known efferent and afferent projection patterns. Models of this type at all levels of analysis require that finer scale single components be linked together into larger structures whose emergent behavior is then predicted numerically.

Thus, from the outset, the design of GENESIS has been premised on the assumption that advancement in understanding neural function requires the ability to build computer models based on the actual anatomy and physiology of the nervous system itself

Further, both the software design and support for the GENESIS project has assumed that such a system should:

1. Support the construction of models at many different levels of scale from sub-cellular to systems (Thus GENESIS was the first broad scale modeling system in computational biology).

2. Be organized in such a way as to allow modelers to continue to develop and share model features and components.

3. Have minimal dependence on any particular computer (Our commitment to Unix, C and open graphics standards has facilitated very broad-based use of the system).

4. Include a graphical interface that supported users with a range of computer expertise (thus the success of GENESIS is engaging real neurobiologists in modeling).

5. For success, have to foster and support the educational use of the system to build modeling expertise within the neuroscience community (thus, GENESIS has been involved in many international courses in computational neuroscience, and the project has supported use of the system in university courses at both the graduate and undergraduate levels).

6. Have to commit considerable time and resources to user support (accordingly, GENESIS was the first computational modeling effort to make extensive use of the World Wide Web).

Features

GENESIS is an object-orient simulation system in which simulations and their Graphical User Interfaces are based on a "building block" approach. Simulations are constructed from modules that receive inputs, perform calculations on them, and then generate outputs. Model neurons are constructed from these basic components, such as compartments. and variable conductance ion channels. Compartments are linked to their channels and are then linked together to form multi-compartmental neurons of any desired level of complexity. Neurons may be linked together to form neural circuits. This object-oriented approach is central to the generality and flexibility of the system, as it allows modelers to easily exchange and reuse models or model components. In addition, it makes it possible to extend the functionality of GENESIS by adding new commands or simulation components to the simulator, without having to modify the GENESIS base code.

GENESIS uses a high-level simulation language to construct neurons and their networks. Commands may be issued either interactively to a command prompt, by use of simulation scripts, or through the graphical interface. A particular simulation is set up by writing a sequence of commands in the scripting language that creates the network itself and the graphical interface for a particular simulation. The scripting language and the modules are powerful enough that only a few lines of script are needed to specify a sophisticated simulation. The principal components of the simulation system and the various modes of interacting with GENESIS are illustrated below:

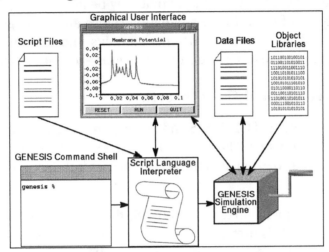

The underlying level of the GENESIS user interface is the Script Language Interpreter (SLI). This is a command interpreter similar to a Unix system shell with an extensive set of commands related to building, monitoring and controlling simulations. GENE-SIS simulation objects and graphical objects are linked together using the scripting language. The interpreter can read SLI commands either interactively from the keyboard (allowing interactive debugging, inspection, and control of the simulation), or from files containing simulation scripts.

The GENESIS Simulation Engine consists of the simulator base code that provides the common control and support routines for the system, including those for input/output and for the numerical solution of the differential equations obeyed by the various neural simulation objects.

In addition to receiving commands from the SLI and the GUI, the simulation engine can construct simulations using information from data files and from the pre-compiled GENESIS object libraries. For example, the GENESIS cell reader allows one to build complex model neurons by reading their specifications from a data file, instead of from a lengthy series of GENESIS commands delivered to the SLI. Similarly, network connection specifications may be read from a data file with the fileconnect command.

The GENESIS object libraries contain the building blocks from which many different simulations can be constructed. These include the spherical and cylindrical compartments from which the physical structure of neurons are constructed, voltage and/or concentration activated channels, dendro-dendritic channels, and synaptically-activated channels with synapses of several types including Hebbian and facilitating synapses. In addition, there are objects for computing intracellular ionic concentrations from channel currents, for modeling the diffusion of ions within cells (e.g., concentration pools, ionic pumps, and buffers), modeling biochemical reactions, and for allowing ligand gating of ion channels (e.g., magnesium blocking for NMDA channels).

There are also a number of device objects that may be interfaced to the simulation to provide various types of input to the simulation (pulse and spike generators, voltage clamp circuitry, etc.) or measurements (peristimulus and interspike interval histograms, spike frequency measurements, auto- and cross-correlation histograms, etc.).

The GENESIS Graphical User Interface

The object-oriented design of GENESIS and its scripting language are among the greatest strengths of the simulator. The ease with which existing simulations can be modified for new purposes also extends to the graphical user interface (GUI) for a GENESIS simulation as well.

A GENESIS GUI is implemented with XODUS, the X-windows Output and Display Utility for Simulations. This provides a higher level and user-friendly means for developing simulations and monitoring their execution. XODUS consists of a set of graphical objects that are the same as the computational modules from the user's point of view, except that they perform graphical functions. As with the computational modules, XODUS modules can be set up in any manner that the user chooses to display or enter data. Furthermore, the graphical modules can call functions from the script language, so the full power of the SLI is available through the graphical interface. This makes it possible to interactively change simulation parameters in real time to directly observe the effects of parameter variations. The mouse may also be used to plant recording or injection electrodes into a graphical representation of the cell. In addition to provisions for plotting the usual quantities of interest (membrane potentials, channel conductances, etc.), XODUS has visualization features that permit such things as using color to display the propagation of action potentials or other variables throughout a multi-compartmental model, and to display connections and cell activity in a network model.

GENESIS also offers general purpose graphical environments for the construction, running, and visualization of single cell models (Neurokit) and biochemical reactions (Kinetikit) with little or no script programming. Nevertheless, most GENESIS modelers prefer the control and flexibility that the scripting language provides for constructing custom GUIs. These are typically based on simple modifications of the many examples provided with GENESIS, or with the GENESIS Modeling Tutorials package.

The figure below shows a customizable GUI that was constructed for network simulations. This simulation is one of the examples provided in the GENESIS Modeling Tutorial, and consists of a grid of simplified neocortical regular spiking pyramidal cells, each one coupled with excitory synaptic connections to its four nearest neighbors. The example simulation script was designed to be easily modified to allow one to use other cell models, implement other patterns of connectivity, or to augment with a population of inhibitory interneurons and the several other types of connections found in a realistic cortical network.

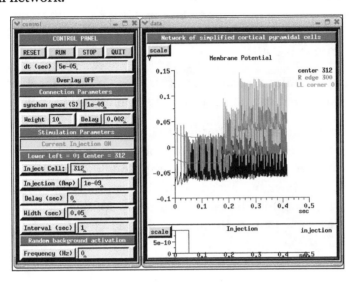

This animated image of the network activity visualization display shows repeating sequences from the view widget that represents the membrane potentials for each of the cells in the network, using a cold to hot color scale. Here, one can see propagating waves of action potentials.

GENESIS as an Educational Tool

The GENESIS project has a particular commitment to the use of simulation technology in education. GENESIS tutorials have been used for education in neuroscience and computational neuroscience in more than 50 universities around the world. "The Book of GENESIS" provides an introduction both to GENESIS and to its use in education and modeling, and is now available for free from the GENESIS web site. Several GENESIS-based tutorials are available at the GENESIS website, and several others have recently been published in association with the new on-line journal, Brains, Minds, and Media.

Over the last 19 years, the GENESIS project has witnessed and contributed to a major growth in the use of realistic modeling in computational biology. During this time, GENESIS use has grown until it is now one of the two most widely used modeling systems for realistic models (NEURON being the other).

User Support and Documentation

The Sourceforge GENESIS development site contains the CVS Repository for the latest GENESIS 2 versions, as well as public forums for reporting bugs or compiling problems, and for discussing issues related to GENESIS use.

Members of BABEL are entitled to access the BABEL directories and email newsgroup. These are used as a repository for the latest contributions by GENESIS users and developers. These include new simulations, libraries of cells and channels, additional simulator components, new documentation and tutorials, bug reports and fixes, and the posting of questions and hints for setting up GENESIS simulations. As the results of GENESIS research simulations are published, many of these simulations are being made available through BABEL.

The GENESIS user community comes together in an annual meeting in San Antonio specifically focused on realistic modeling and its application to biology.

The GENESIS Neural Modeling Tutorials are an evolving package of HTML tutorials intended to teach the process of constructing biologically realistic neural models with the GENESIS simulator. The GENESIS Neural Modeling Tutorials, and others from WAM-BAMM*05, have been published in article form (both in browseable HTML and downloadable PDF format) in the November 2005 special issue on Realistic Neural Modeling in the electronic journal Brains, Minds, and Media.

NEURON

Neuron is a simulation environment for modeling individual and networks of neurons. It was primarily developed by Michael Hines, John W. Moore, and Ted Carnevale at Yale and Duke.

Neuron models individual neurons via the use of sections that are automatically subdivided into individual compartments, instead of requiring the user to manually create compartments. The primary scripting language is hoc but a Python interface is also available. Programs can be written interactively in a shell, or loaded from a file. Neuron supports parallelization via the MPI protocol.

Neuron is capable of handling diffusion-reaction models, and integrating diffusion functions into models of synapses and cellular networks. Parallelization is possible via internal multithreaded routines, for use on multi-core computers. The properties of the membrane channels of the neuron are simulated using compiled mechanisms written using the NMODL language or by compiled routines operating on internal data structures that are set up with Channel Builder.

Along with the analogous software platform GENESIS, Neuron is the basis for instruction in computational neuroscience in many courses and laboratories around the world.

User Interface

Neuron features a graphical user interface (GUI), for use by individuals with minimal programming experience. The GUI comes equipped with a builder for single and multiple compartment cells, networks, network cells, channels and linear electric circuits. Single and multiple compartment cells differ in that multiple compartment cells features several "sections", each with potentially distinct parameters for dimensions and kinetics. Tutorials are available on the Neuron website, including for getting basic models out of the cell, channel and network builders. With these builders, the user can form the basis of all simulations and models.

Cell Builder

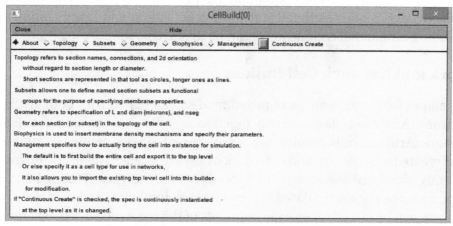

The cell builder menu with the six options visible.

Cell Builder allows the user to generate and modify stick figure cell structures. These sections form the basis of functionally distinct areas of the neuron.

The user can define functionally distinct groups of sections. Sections branching from one another can be labeled "dendrites," while another, single section that projects from the same central one can be labeled as the "axon." The user can define parameters along which certain values are variable as a function across a section. For instance, path length along a subset can be defined as a domain, the functions along which can then be defined later.

The user can select either individual sections, or groups and set precise parameters for length, diameter, area and length for that group or section. Any of these values can be set as a function of length or some other parameter of the corresponding section. The user can set the number of functional segments in a section, which is a strategy for spatial resolution. The higher the number of segments, the more precisely Neuron can handle a function in a section. Segments are the points where point process managers can be associated.

Users can define kinetic and electro-physiological functions across both subsets and sections. Neuron comes equipped with a probabilistic model of Hodgkin-Huxley Model giant squid axon kinetics, as well as a function to model passive leak channel kinetics. Both of these functions, and the features they describe, can be added to the membrane of the constructed cell. Values for leak rate, sodium conductance and potassium conductance can be set for modeling these kinetics can be set as functions over a parameterized domain. Channels become available for implementation in a cell membrane.

Channel Builder

The user can generate both voltage and ligand-gated channel models. Channel Builder supports local point channels, generally used for single, large channels whose function is to be modeled, and general channels whose density across the cell can be defined. Maximum conductance, reversal potential, ligand sensitivity, ion permeability, as well as precise dynamics of transitional states using activation and inactivation variables, and including differential conductance, can be defined.

Network and Network Cell Builder

Neuron allows for the generation of mixed models, populated with both artificial cells and neurons. Artificial cells essentially function as point processes, implemented into the network. Artificial cells require only a point process, with defined parameters. The user can create the structure and dynamics of network cells. The user can create synapses, using simulated synapse point processes as archetypes. Parameters on these point processes can be manipulated to simulate both inhibitory and excitatory responses. Synapses can be placed on specific segments of the constructed cell, wherein, again, they will behave as point processes, except that they are sensitive to the activity of a pre-synaptic element. Cells can be managed. The user creates the basic grid of network cells, taking previously completed network cells as archetypes. Connections can be defined between source cells and target synapses on other cells. The cell containing the target synapse becomes the post-synaptic element, whereas the source cells function as pre-synaptic elements. Weights can be added to define strength of activation of a synapse by the pre-synaptic cell. A plot option can be activated to open a graph of spikes across time for individual neurons.

Simulation and Recording

Neuron comes equipped with a slew of simulation tools. Most notably, it includes several "point processes," which are simple functions at a particular segment of a cell. Point processes include simulations of voltage, patch, single electrode and current clamps, as well as several simulated synapses. Synapse point processes are distinct for their ability to model stimulation intensities that vary non-linearly across time. These can be placed on any segment of any section of a built cell, individual or network, and their precise values, including amplitude and duration of stimulation, delay time of activation in a run and time decay parameters (for synapses), can be defined from the point process manager module. When implemented into a network as synapses, point process parameters are defined in the synapse builder for a particular network cell. Graphs describing voltage, conductance, and current axes over time can be used to describe changes in electrical state at the location of any segment on the cell. Neuron allows for graphs of change at both individual points over time, and across an entire section through time. Duration of run can be set. All point processes, including those standing for cells or synapses of artificial neurons, and all graphs reflect the duration.

BLUE GENE SUPERCOMPUTER

Blue Gene is an IBM project aimed at designing supercomputers that can reach operating speeds in the petaFLOPS (PFLOPS) range, with low power consumption.

The project created three generations of supercomputers, Blue Gene/L, Blue Gene/P, and Blue Gene/Q. Blue Gene systems have often led the TOP500 and Green500 rankings of the most powerful and most power efficient supercomputers, respectively. Blue Gene systems have also consistently scored top positions in the Graph500 list. The project was awarded the 2009 National Medal of Technology and Innovation.

As of 2015, IBM seems to have ended the development of the Blue Gene family though no public announcement has been made. IBM's continuing efforts of the supercomputer scene seems to be concentrated around OpenPower, using accelerators such as FPGAs and GPUs to battle the end of Moore's law.

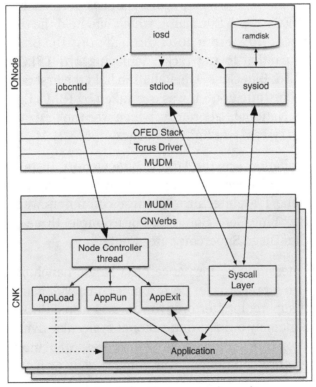

Hierarchy of Blue Gene processing units.

In December 1999, IBM announced a US$100 million research initiative for a five-year effort to build a massively parallel computer, to be applied to the study of bio-molecular phenomena such as protein folding. The project had two main goals: to advance our understanding of the mechanisms behind protein folding via large-scale simulation, and to explore novel ideas in massively parallel machine architecture and software. Major areas of investigation included: how to use this novel platform to effectively meet its scientific goals, how to make such massively parallel machines more usable, and how to achieve performance targets at a reasonable cost, through novel machine architectures. The initial design for Blue Gene was based on an early version of the Cyclops64 architecture, designed by Monty Denneau. The initial research and development work was pursued at IBM T.J. Watson Research Center and led by William R. Pulleyblank.

At IBM, Alan Gara started working on an extension of the QCDOC architecture into a more general-purpose supercomputer: The 4D nearest-neighbor interconnection network was replaced by a network supporting routing of messages from any node to any other; and a parallel I/O subsystem was added. DOE started funding the development of this system and it became known as Blue Gene/L (L for Light); development of the original Blue Gene system continued under the name Blue Gene/C (C for Cyclops) and, later, Cyclops64.

In November 2004 a 16-rack system, with each rack holding 1,024 compute nodes, achieved first place in the TOP500 list, with a Linpack performance of 70.72 TFLOPS. It thereby overtook NEC's Earth Simulator, which had held the title of the fastest computer in the world since 2002. From 2004 through 2007 the Blue Gene/L installation at LLNL gradually expanded to 104 racks, achieving 478 TFLOPS Linpack and 596 TFLOPS peak. The LLNL BlueGene/L installation held the first position in the TOP500 list for 3.5 years, until in June 2008 it was overtaken by IBM's Cell-based Roadrunner system at Los Alamos National Laboratory, which was the first system to surpass the 1 PetaFLOPS mark. The system was built in Rochester, MN IBM plant.

While the LLNL installation was the largest Blue Gene/L installation, many smaller installations followed. In November 2006, there were 27 computers on the TOP500 list using the Blue Gene/L architecture. All these computers were listed as having an architecture of eServer Blue Gene Solution. For example, three racks of Blue Gene/L were housed at the San Diego Supercomputer Center.

While the TOP500 measures performance on a single benchmark application, Linpack, Blue Gene/L also set records for performance on a wider set of applications. Blue Gene/L was the first supercomputer ever to run over 100 TFLOPS sustained on a real-world application, namely a three-dimensional molecular dynamics code (ddcMD), simulating solidification (nucleation and growth processes) of molten metal under high pressure and temperature conditions. This achievement won the 2005 Gordon Bell Prize.

In June 2006, NNSA and IBM announced that Blue Gene/L achieved 207.3 TFLOPS on a quantum chemical application (Qbox). At Supercomputing 2006, Blue Gene/L was awarded the winning prize in all HPC Challenge Classes of awards. In 2007, a team from the IBM Almaden Research Center and the University of Nevada ran an artificial neural network almost half as complex as the brain of a mouse for the equivalent of a second.

Name

The name Blue Gene comes from what it was originally designed to do, help biologists understand the processes of protein folding and gene development. "Blue" is a traditional moniker that IBM uses for many of its products and the company itself. The original Blue Gene design was renamed "Blue Gene/C" and eventually Cyclops64. The "L" in Blue Gene/L comes from "Light" as that design's original name was "Blue Light". The "P" version was designed to be a petascale design. "Q" is just the letter after "P". There is no Blue Gene/R. The computer is not named after Gene Amdahl.

Major Features

The Blue Gene/L supercomputer was unique in the following aspects:

- Trading the speed of processors for lower power consumption. Blue Gene/L used low frequency and low power embedded PowerPC cores with floating point accelerators. While the performance of each chip was relatively low, the system could achieve better power efficiency for applications that could use large numbers of nodes.

- Dual processors per node with two working modes: co-processor mode where one processor handles computation and the other handles communication; and virtual-node mode, where both processors are available to run user code, but the processors share both the computation and the communication load.

- System-on-a-chip design. All node components were embedded on one chip, with the exception of 512 MB external DRAM.

- A large number of nodes (scalable in increments of 1024 up to at least 65,536).

- Three-dimensional torus interconnect with auxiliary networks for global communications (broadcast and reductions), I/O, and management.

- Lightweight OS per node for minimum system overhead (system noise).

Architecture

The Blue Gene/L architecture was an evolution of the QCDSP and QCDOC architectures. Each Blue Gene/L Compute or I/O node was a single ASIC with associated

DRAM memory chips. The ASIC integrated two 700 MHz PowerPC 440 embedded processors, each with a double-pipeline-double-precision Floating Point Unit (FPU), a cache sub-system with built-in DRAM controller and the logic to support multiple communication sub-systems. The dual FPUs gave each Blue Gene/L node a theoretical peak performance of 5.6 GFLOPS (gigaFLOPS). The two CPUs were not cache coherent with one another.

Compute nodes were packaged two per compute card, with 16 compute cards plus up to 2 I/O nodes per node board. There were 32 node boards per cabinet/rack. By the integration of all essential sub-systems on a single chip, and the use of low-power logic, each Compute or I/O node dissipated low power (about 17 watts, including DRAMs). This allowed aggressive packaging of up to 1024 compute nodes, plus additional I/O nodes, in a standard 19-inch rack, within reasonable limits of electrical power supply and air cooling. The performance metrics, in terms of FLOPS per watt, FLOPS per m^2 of floorspace and FLOPS per unit cost, allowed scaling up to very high performance. With so many nodes, component failures were inevitable. The system was able to electrically isolate faulty components, down to a granularity of half a rack (512 compute nodes), to allow the machine to continue to run.

Each Blue Gene/L node was attached to three parallel communications networks: a 3D toroidal network for peer-to-peer communication between compute nodes, a collective network for collective communication (broadcasts and reduce operations), and a global interrupt network for fast barriers. The I/O nodes, which run the Linux operating system, provided communication to storage and external hosts via an Ethernet network. The I/O nodes handled filesystem operations on behalf of the compute nodes. Finally, a separate and private Ethernet network provided access to any node for configuration, booting and diagnostics. To allow multiple programs to run concurrently, a Blue Gene/L system could be partitioned into electronically isolated sets of nodes. The number of nodes in a partition had to be a positive integer power of 2, with at least $2^5 = 32$ nodes. To run a program on Blue Gene/L, a partition of the computer was first to be reserved. The program was then loaded and run on all the nodes within the partition, and no other program could access nodes within the partition while it was in use. Upon completion, the partition nodes were released for future programs to use.

Blue Gene/L compute nodes used a minimal operating system supporting a single user program. Only a subset of POSIX calls was supported, and only one process could run at a time on node in co-processor mode or one process per CPU in virtual mode. Programmers needed to implement green threads in order to simulate local concurrency. Application development was usually performed in C, C++, or Fortran using MPI for communication. However, some scripting languages such as Ruby and Python have been ported to the compute nodes.

Blue Gene/P

A Blue Gene/P node card.

IBM unveiled Blue Gene/P, the second generation of the Blue Gene series of supercomputers and designed through a collaboration that included IBM, LLNL, and Argonne National Laboratory's Leadership Computing Facility.

Design

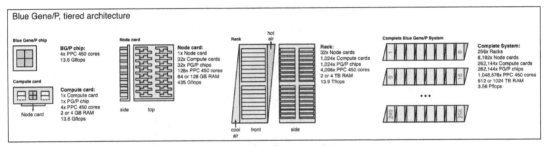

A schematic overview of a Blue Gene/P supercomputer.

The design of Blue Gene/P is a technology evolution from Blue Gene/L. Each Blue Gene/P Compute chip contains four PowerPC 450 processor cores, running at 850 MHz. The cores are cache coherent and the chip can operate as a 4-way symmetric multiprocessor (SMP). The memory subsystem on the chip consists of small private L2 caches, a central shared 8 MB L3 cache, and dual DDR2 memory controllers. The chip also integrates the logic for node-to-node communication, using the same network topologies as Blue Gene/L, but at more than twice the bandwidth. A compute card contains a Blue Gene/P chip with 2 or 4 GB DRAM, comprising a "compute node". A single compute node has a peak performance of 13.6 GFLOPS. 32 Compute cards are plugged into an air-cooled node board. A rack contains 32 node boards (thus 1024 nodes, 4096 processor cores). By using many small, low-power, densely packaged chips, Blue Gene/P exceeded the power efficiency of other supercomputers of its generation, and at 371 MFLOPS/W Blue Gene/P installations ranked at or near the top of the Green500 lists in 2007-2008.

Installations

The following is an incomplete list of Blue Gene/P installations. Per November 2009, the TOP500 list contained 15 Blue Gene/P installations of 2-racks (2048 nodes, 8192 processor cores, 23.86 TFLOPS Linpack) and larger.

- On November 12, 2007, the first Blue Gene/P installation, JUGENE, with 16 racks (16,384 nodes, 65,536 processors) was running at Forschungszentrum Jülich in Germany with a performance of 167 TFLOPS. When inaugurated it was the fastest supercomputer in Europe and the sixth fastest in the world. In 2009, JUGENE was upgraded to 72 racks (73,728 nodes, 294,912 processor cores) with 144 terabytes of memory and 6 petabytes of storage, and achieved a peak performance of 1 PetaFLOPS. This configuration incorporated new air-to-water heat exchangers between the racks, reducing the cooling cost substantially. JUGENE was shut down in July 2012 and replaced by the Blue Gene/Q system JUQUEEN.

- The 40-rack (40960 nodes, 163840 processor cores) "Intrepid" system at Argonne National Laboratory was ranked #3 on the June 2008 Top 500 list. The Intrepid system is one of the major resources of the INCITE program, in which processor hours are awarded to "grand challenge" science and engineering projects in a peer-reviewed competition.

- Lawrence Livermore National Laboratory installed a 36-rack Blue Gene/P installation, "Dawn", in 2009.

- The King Abdullah University of Science and Technology (KAUST) installed a 16-rack Blue Gene/P installation, "Shaheen", in 2009.

- In 2012, a 6-rack Blue Gene/P was installed at Rice University and will be jointly administered with the University of Sao Paulo.

- A 2.5 rack Blue Gene/P system is the central processor for the Low Frequency Array for Radio astronomy (LOFAR) project in the Netherlands and surrounding European countries. This application uses the streaming data capabilities of the machine.

- A 2-rack Blue Gene/P was installed in September 2008 in Sofia, Bulgaria, and is operated by the Bulgarian Academy of Sciences and Sofia University.

- In 2010, a 2-rack (8192-core) Blue Gene/P was installed at the University of Melbourne for the Victorian Life Sciences Computation Initiative.

- In 2011, a 2-rack Blue Gene/P was installed at University of Canterbury in Christchurch, New Zealand.

- In 2012, a 2-rack Blue Gene/P was installed at Rutgers University in Piscataway, New Jersey. It was dubbed "Excalibur" as an homage to the Rutgers mascot, the Scarlet Knight.

- In 2008, a 1-rack (1024 nodes) Blue Gene/P with 180 TB of storage was installed at the University of Rochester in Rochester, New York.

- The first Blue Gene/P in the ASEAN region was installed in 2010 at the Universiti of Brunei Darussalam's research centre, the UBD-IBM Centre. The installation has prompted research collaboration between the university and IBM research on climate modeling that will investigate the impact of climate change on flood forecasting, crop yields, renewable energy and the health of rainforests in the region among others.

- In 2013, a 1-rack Blue Gene/P was donated to the Department of Science and Technology for weather forecasts, disaster management, precision agriculture, and health it is housed in the National Computer Center, Diliman, Quezon City, under the auspices of Philippine Genome Center (PGC) Core Facility for Bioinformatics (CFB) at UP Diliman, Quezon City.

Applications

- Veselin Topalov, the challenger to the World Chess Champion title in 2010, confirmed in an interview that he had used a Blue Gene/P supercomputer during his preparation for the match.

- The Blue Gene/P computer has been used to simulate approximately one percent of a human cerebral cortex, containing 1.6 billion neurons with approximately 9 trillion connections.

- The IBM Kittyhawk project team has ported Linux to the compute nodes and demonstrated generic Web 2.0 workloads running at scale on a Blue Gene/P. Their paper, published in the ACM Operating Systems Review, describes a kernel driver that tunnels Ethernet over the tree network, which results in all-to-all TCP/IP connectivity. Running standard Linux software like MySQL, their performance results on SpecJBB rank among the highest on record.

- In 2011, a Rutgers University / IBM / University of Texas team linked the KAUST Shaheen installation together with a Blue Gene/P installation at the IBM Watson Research Center into a "federated high performance computing cloud", winning the IEEE SCALE 2011 challenge with an oil reservoir optimization application.

Blue Gene/Q

The third supercomputer design in the Blue Gene series, Blue Gene/Q has a peak performance of 20 Petaflops, reaching LINPACK benchmarks performance of 17 Petaflops. Blue Gene/Q continues to expand and enhance the Blue Gene/L and /P architectures.

The IBM Blue Gene/Q installed at Argonne National Laboratory, near Chicago, Illinois.

Design

The Blue Gene/Q Compute chip is an 18 core chip. The 64-bit A2 processor cores are 4-way simultaneously multithreaded, and run at 1.6 GHz. Each processor core has a SIMD Quad-vector double precision floating point unit (IBM QPX). 16 Processor cores are used for computing, and a 17th core for operating system assist functions such as interrupts, asynchronous I/O, MPI pacing and RAS. The 18th core is used as a redundant spare, used to increase manufacturing yield. The spared-out core is shut down in functional operation. The processor cores are linked by a crossbar switch to a 32 MB eDRAM L2 cache, operating at half core speed. The L2 cache is multi-versioned, supporting transactional memory and speculative execution, and has hardware support for atomic operations. L2 cache misses are handled by two built-in DDR3 memory controllers running at 1.33 GHz. The chip also integrates logic for chip-to-chip communications in a 5D torus configuration, with 2GB/s chip-to-chip links. The Blue Gene/Q chip is manufactured on IBM's copper SOI process at 45 nm. It delivers a peak performance of 204.8 GFLOPS at 1.6 GHz, drawing about 55 watts. The chip measures 19×19 mm (359.5 mm²) and comprises 1.47 billion transistors. The chip is mounted on a compute card along with 16 GB DDR3 DRAM (i.e., 1 GB for each user processor core).

A Q32 compute drawer contains 32 compute cards, each water cooled. A "midplane" (crate) contains 16 Q32 compute drawers for a total of 512 compute nodes, electrically interconnected in a 5D torus configuration (4×4×4×4×2). Beyond the midplane level, all connections are optical. Racks have two midplanes, thus 32 compute drawers, for a total of 1024 compute nodes, 16,384 user cores and 16 TB RAM.

Separate I/O drawers, placed at the top of a rack or in a separate rack, are air cooled and contain 8 compute cards and 8 PCIe expansion slots for Infiniband or 10 Gigabit Ethernet networking.

Performance

At the time of the Blue Gene/Q system announcement in November 2011, an initial 4-rack Blue Gene/Q system (4096 nodes, 65536 user processor cores) achieved 17 in the TOP500 list with 677.1 TeraFLOPS Linpack, outperforming the original 2007

104-rack BlueGene/L installation. The same 4-rack system achieved the top position in the Graph500 list with over 250 GTEPS (giga traversed edges per second). Blue Gene/Q systems also topped the Green500 list of most energy efficient supercomputers with up to 2.1 GFLOPS/W.

In June 2012, Blue Gene/Q installations took the top positions in all three lists: TOP500, Graph500 and Green500.

Installations

The following is an incomplete list of Blue Gene/Q installations. Per June 2012, the TOP500 list contained 20 Blue Gene/Q installations of 1/2-rack (512 nodes, 8192 processor cores, 86.35 TFLOPS Linpack) and larger. At a (size-independent) power efficiency of about 2.1 GFLOPS/W, all these systems also populated the top of the June 2012 Green 500 list.

- A Blue Gene/Q system called Sequoia was delivered to the Lawrence Livermore National Laboratory (LLNL) beginning in 2011 and was fully deployed in June 2012. It is part of the Advanced Simulation and Computing Program running nuclear simulations and advanced scientific research. It consists of 96 racks (comprising 98,304 compute nodes with 1.6 million processor cores and 1.6 PB of memory) covering an area of about 3,000 square feet (280 m²). In June 2012, the system was ranked as the world's fastest supercomputer. at 20.1 PFLOPS peak, 16.32 PFLOPS sustained (Linpack), drawing up to 7.9 megawatts of power. In June 2013, its performance is listed at 17.17 PFLOPS sustained (Linpack).

- A 10 PFLOPS (peak) Blue Gene/Q system called *Mira* was installed at Argonne National Laboratory in the Argonne Leadership Computing Facility in 2012. It consist of 48 racks (49,152 compute nodes), with 70 PB of disk storage (470 GB/s I/O bandwidth).

- JUQUEEN at the Forschungzentrum Jülich is a 28-rack Blue Gene/Q system, and was from June 2013 to November 2015 the highest ranked machine in Europe in the Top500.

- Vulcan at Lawrence Livermore National Laboratory (LLNL) is a 24-rack, 5 PFLOPS (peak), Blue Gene/Q system that was commissioned in 2012 and decommissioned in 2019. Vulcan served Lab-industry projects through Livermore's High Performance Computing (HPC) Innovation Center as well as academic collaborations in support of DOE/National Nuclear Security Administration (NNSA) missions.

- Fermi at the CINECA Supercomputing facility, Bologna, Italy, is a 10-rack, 2 PFLOPS (peak), Blue Gene/Q system.

- A five rack Blue Gene/Q system with additional compute hardware called *AMOS* was installed at Rensselaer Polytechnic Institute in 2013. The system was rated at 1048.6 teraflops, the most powerful supercomputer at any private university, and third most powerful supercomputer among all universities in 2014.

- An 838 TFLOPS (peak) Blue Gene/Q system called *Avoca* was installed at the Victorian Life Sciences Computation Initiative in June, 2012. This system is part of a collaboration between IBM and VLSCI, with the aims of improving diagnostics, finding new drug targets, refining treatments and furthering our understanding of diseases. The system consists of 4 racks, with 350 TB of storage, 65,536 cores, 64 TB RAM.

- A 209 TFLOPS (peak) Blue Gene/Q system was installed at the University of Rochester in July, 2012. This system is part of the Health Sciences Center for Computational Innovation, which is dedicated to the application of high-performance computing to research programs in the health sciences. The system consists of a single rack (1,024 compute nodes) with 400 TB of high-performance storage.

- A 209 TFLOPS peak (172 TFLOPS LINPACK) Blue Gene/Q system called Lemanicus was installed at the EPFL in March 2013. This system belongs to the Center for Advanced Modeling Science CADMOS which is a collaboration between the three main research institutions on the shore of the Geneva Lake in the French speaking part of Switzerland : Université de Lausanne, Université de Genève and EPFL. The system consists of a single rack (1,024 compute nodes) with 2.1 PB of IBM GPFS-GSS storage.

- A half-rack Blue Gene/Q system, with about 100 TFLOPS (peak), called Cumulus was installed at A*STAR Computational Resource Centre, Singapore, at early 2011.

- As part of DiRAC, the EPCC hosts a 6144-node Blue Gene/Q system at the University of Edinburgh.

Applications

Record-breaking science applications have been run on the BG/Q, the first to cross 10 petaflops of sustained performance. The cosmology simulation framework HACC achieved almost 14 petaflops with a 3.6 trillion particle benchmark run, while the Cardioid code, which models the electrophysiology of the human heart, achieved nearly 12 petaflops with a near real-time simulation, both on Sequoia. A fully compressible flow solver has also achieved 14.4 PFLOP/s (originally 11 PFLOP/s) on Sequoia, 72% of the machine's nominal peak performance.

BRIAN

Brian is an open source Python package for developing simulations of networks of spiking neurons.

Brian is aimed at researchers developing models based on networks of spiking neurons. The general design is aimed at maximising flexibility, simplicity and users' development time. Users specify neuron models by giving their differential equations in standard mathematical form as strings, create groups of neurons and connect them via synapses. This is in contrast to the approach taken by many neural simulators in which users select from a predefined set of neuron models.

Brian is written in Python. Computationally, it is based around the concept of code generation: users specify the model in Python but behind the scenes Brian generates, compiles and runs code in one of several languages (including Python, Cython and C++). In addition there is a "standalone" mode in which Brian generates an entire C++ source code tree with no dependency on Brian, allowing models to be run on platforms where Python is not available.

Example of Brian

The following code defines, runs and plots a randomly connected network of leaky integrate and fire neurons with exponential inhibitory and excitatory currents.

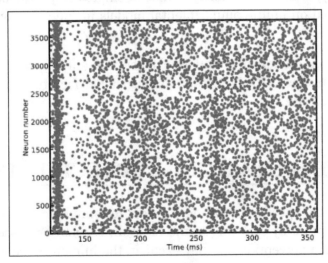

Sample raster plot from randomly connected network of integrate and fire neurons with exponential inhibitory and excitatory currents.

```
from brian2 import *

eqs = '''
dv/dt  = (ge+gi-(v+49*mV))/(20*ms) : volt
```

```
dge/dt = -ge/(5*ms)                    : volt
dgi/dt = -gi/(10*ms)                   : volt
''' ''
P = NeuronGroup(4000, eqs, threshold='v>-50*mV', reset='v=-60*mV')
P.v = -60*mV
Pe = P[:3200]
Pi = P[3200:]
Ce = Synapses(Pe, P, on_pre='ge+=1.62*mV')
Ce.connect(p=0.02)
Ci = Synapses(Pi, P, on_pre='gi-=9*mV')
Ci.connect(p=0.02)
M = SpikeMonitor(P)
run(1*second)
plot(M.t/ms, M.i, '.')
show()
```

Comparison to other Simulators

Brian is primarily, although not solely, aimed at single compartment neuron models. Simulators focused on multi-compartmental models include Neuron, GENESIS, and its derivatives.

The focus of Brian is on flexibility and ease of use, and only supports simulations running on a single machine. The NEST simulator includes facilities for distributing simulations across a cluster.

NEUROCOMPUTATIONAL SPEECH PROCESSING

Neurocomputational speech processing is computer-simulation of speech production and speech perception by referring to the natural neuronal processes of speech production and speech perception, as they occur in the human nervous system (central nervous system and peripheral nervous system).

Neurocomputational models of speech processing are complex. They comprise at least a cognitive part, a motor part and a sensory part.

The cognitive or linguistic part of a neurocomputational model of speech processing comprises the neural activation or generation of a phonemic representation on the side of speech production (e.g. neurocomputational and extended version of the Levelt model developed by Ardi Roelofs: WEAVER++ as well as the neural activation or generation of an intention or meaning on the side of speech perception or speech comprehension.

The motor part of a neurocomputational model of speech processing starts with a phonemic representation of a speech item, activates a motor plan and ends with the articulation of that particular speech item.

The sensory part of a neurocomputational model of speech processing starts with an acoustic signal of a speech item (acoustic speech signal), generates an auditory representation for that signal and activates a phonemic representations for that speech item.

Neurocomputational Speech Processing Topics

Neurocomputational speech processing is speech processing by artificial neural networks. Neural maps, mappings and pathways, are model structures, i.e. important structures within artificial neural networks.

Neural Maps

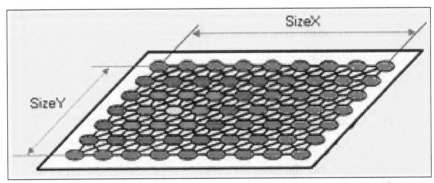

Neuronal map with a local activation pattern. magenta: neuron with highest degree of activation; blue: neurons with no activation.

An artificial neural network can be separated in three types of neural maps, also called "layers":

1. Input maps (in the case of speech processing: primary auditory map within the auditory cortex, primary somatosensory map within the somatosensory cortex).

2. Output maps (primary motor map within the primary motor cortex).

3. Higher level cortical maps (also called "hidden layers").

The term "neural map" is favoured here over the term "neural layer", because a cortial neural map should be modeled as a 2D-map of interconnected neurons. Thus, each "model neuron" or "artificial neuron" within this 2D-map is physiologically represented by a cortical column since the cerebral cortex anatomically exhibits a layered structure.

Neural Representations (Neural States)

A neural representation within an artificial neural network is a temporarily activated (neural) state within a specific neural map. Each neural state is represented by a specific neural activation pattern. This activation pattern changes during speech processing (e.g. from syllable to syllable).

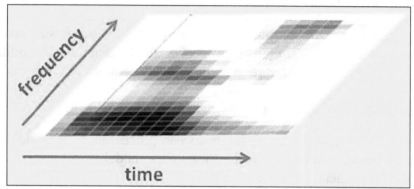

Neuronal map with a distributed activation pattern. Example: "neural spectrogram"
(This auditory neural representation is speculative).

In the ACT model, it is assumed that an auditory state can be represented by a "neural spectrogram" within an auditory state map. This auditory state map is assumed to be located in the auditory association cortex.

A somatosensory state can be divided in a tactile and proprioceptive state and can be represented by a specific neural activation pattern within the somatosensory state map. This state map is assumed to be located in the somatosensory association cortex.

A motor plan state can be assumed for representing a motor plan, i.e. the planning of speech articulation for a specific syllable or for a longer speech item (e.g. word, short phrase). This state map is assumed to be located in the premotor cortex, while the instantaneous (or lower level) activation of each speech articulator occurs within the primary motor cortex.

The neural representations occurring in the sensory and motor maps are distributed representations: Each neuron within the sensory or motor map is more or less activated, leading to a specific activation pattern.

The neural representation for speech units occurring in the speech sound map is a punctual or local representation. Each speech item or speech unit is represented here by a specific neuron.

Neural Mappings Synaptic Projections

A neural mapping connects two cortical neural maps. Neural mappings (in contrast to neural pathways) store training information by adjusting their neural link weights.

Neural mappings are capable of generating or activating a distributed representation of a sensory or motor state within a sensory or motor map from a punctual or local activation within the other map (see for example the synaptic projection from speech sound map to motor map, to auditory target region map, or to somatosensory target region map in the DIVA model, explained below; or see for example the neural mapping from phonetic map to auditory state map and motor plan state map in the ACT model).

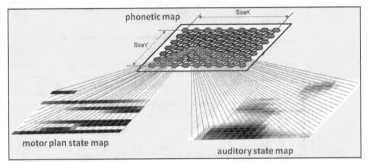

Neural mapping between phonetic map (local activation pattern for a specific phonetic state), motor plan state map (distributed activation pattern) and auditory state map (distributed activation pattern) as part of the ACT model. Only neural connections with the winner neuron within the phonetic map are shown.

Neural mapping between two neural maps are compact or dense: Each neuron of one neural map is interconnected with (nearly) each neuron of the other neural map. Because of this density criterion for neural mappings, neural maps which are interconnected by a neural mapping are not far apart from each other.

Neural Pathways

In contrast to neural mappings neural pathways can connect neural maps which are far apart (e.g. in different cortical lobes, see cerebral cortex). From the functional or modeling viewpoint, neural pathways mainly forward information without processing this information. A neural pathway in comparison to a neural mapping need much less neural connections. A neural pathway can be modelled by using a one-to-one connection of the neurons of both neural maps (see topographic mapping and see somatotopic arrangement).

Example: In the case of two neural maps, each comprising 1,000 model neurons, a neural mapping needs up to 1,000,000 neural connections (many-to-many-connection), while only 1,000 connections are needed in the case of a neural pathway connection.

Furthermore, the link weights of the connections within a neural mapping are adjusted during training, while the neural connections in the case of a neural pathway need not to be trained (each connection is maximal exhibitory).

DIVA Model

The leading approach in neurocomputational modeling of speech production is the DIVA model developed by Frank H. Guenther and his group at Boston University. The model accounts for a wide range of phonetic and neuroimaging data but - like each neurocomputational model - remains speculative to some extent.

Structure of the Model

The organization or structure of the DIVA model is shown in figure.

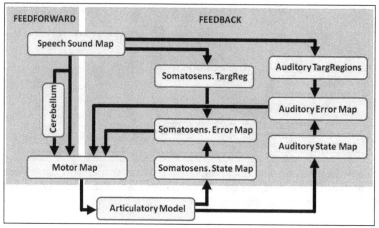

Organization of the DIVA model.

Speech Sound Map: The Phonemic Representation as a Starting Point

The speech sound map - assumed to be located in the inferior and posterior portion of Broca's area (left frontal operculum) - represents (phonologically specified) language-specific speech units (sounds, syllables, words, short phrases). Each speech unit is represented by a specific model cell within the speech sound map. Each model cell corresponds to a small population of neurons which are located at close range and which fire together.

Feedforward Control: Activating Motor Representations

Each neuron (model cell, artificial neuron) within the speech sound map can be activated and subsequently activates a forward motor command towards the motor map, called articulatory velocity and position map. The activated neural representation on the level of that motor map determines the articulation of a speech unit, i.e. controls all articulators (lips, tongue, velum, glottis) during the time interval for producing that speech unit. Forward control also involves subcortical structures like the cerebellum, not modelled in detail here.

A speech unit represents an amount of speech items which can be assigned to the same phonemic category. Thus, each speech unit is represented by one specific neuron within the speech sound map, while the realization of a speech unit may exhibit some articulatory and acoustic variability. This phonetic variability is the motivation to define sensory target regions in the DIVA model.

Articulatory Model: Generating Somatosensory and Auditory Feedback Information

The activation pattern within the motor map determines the movement pattern of all model articulators (lips, tongue, velum, glottis) for a speech item. In order not to overload the model, no detailed modeling of the neuromuscular system is done. The Maeda articulatory speech synthesizer is used in order to generate articulator movements, which allows the generation of a time-varying vocal tract form and the generation of the acoustic speech signal for each particular speech item.

In terms of artificial intelligence the articulatory model can be called plant (i.e. the system, which is controlled by the brain); it represents a part of the embodiement of the neuronal speech processing system. The articulatory model generates sensory output which is the basis for generating feedback information for the DIVA model.

Feedback Control: Sensory Target Regions, State Maps and Error Maps

On the one hand the articulatory model generates sensory information, i.e. an auditory state for each speech unit which is neurally represented within the auditory state map (distributed representation), and a somatosensory state for each speech unit which is neurally represented within the somatosensory state map (distributed representation as well). The auditory state map is assumed to be located in the superior temporal cortex while the somatosensory state map is assumed to be located in the inferior parietal cortex.

On the other hand, the speech sound map, if activated for a specific speech unit (single neuron activation; punctual activation), activates sensory information by synaptic projections between speech sound map and auditory target region map and between speech sound map and somatosensory target region map. Auditory and somatosensory target regions are assumed to be located in higher-order auditory cortical regions and in higher-order somatosensory cortical regions respectively. These target region sensory activation patterns which exist for each speech unit are learned during speech acquisition.

Consequently, two types of sensory information are available if a speech unit is activated at the level of the speech sound map: (i) learned sensory target regions (i.e. intended sensory state for a speech unit) and (ii) sensory state activation patterns resulting from a possibly imperfect execution (articulation) of a specific speech unit (i.e. current sensory state, reflecting the current production and articulation of that particular speech unit). Both types of sensory information is projected to sensory error maps, i.e. to an auditory error map which is assumed to be located in the superior temporal cortex (like the auditory state map) and to a somatosensosry error map which is assumed to be located in the inferior parietal cortex (like the somatosensory state map).

If the current sensory state deviates from the intended sensory state, both error maps are generating feedback commands which are projected towards the motor map and which are capable to correct the motor activation pattern and subsequently the articulation of a speech unit under production. Thus, in total, the activation pattern of the motor map is not only influenced by a specific feedforward command learned for a speech unit (and generated by the synaptic projection from the speech sound map) but also by a feedback command generated at the level of the sensory error maps.

Learning (Modeling Speech Acquisition)

While the structure of a neuroscientific model of speech processing (given in figure for the DIVA model) is mainly determined by evolutionary processes, the (language-specific) knowledge as well as the (language-specific) speaking skills are learned and trained during speech acquisition. In the case of the DIVA model it is assumed that the newborn has not available an already structured (language-specific) speech sound map; i.e. no neuron within the speech sound map is related to any speech unit. Rather the organization of the speech sound map as well as the tuning of the projections to the motor map and to the sensory target region maps is learned or trained during speech acquisition. Two important phases of early speech acquisition are modeled in the DIVA approach: Learning by babbling and by imitation.

Babbling

During babbling the synaptic projections between sensory error maps and motor map are tuned. This training is done by generating an amount of semi-random feedforward commands, i.e. the DIVA model "babbles". Each of these babbling commands leads to the production of an "articulatory item", also labeled as "pre-linguistic (i.e. non language-specific) speech item" (i.e. the articulatory model generates an articulatory movement pattern on the basis of the babbling motor command). Subsequently, an acoustic signal is generated.

On the basis of the articulatory and acoustic signal, a specific auditory and somatosensory state pattern is activated at the level of the sensory state maps for each (pre-linguistic) speech item. At this point the DIVA model has available the sensory and associated motor activation pattern for different speech items, which enables the model to tune the synaptic projections between sensory error maps and motor map. Thus, during babbling the DIVA model learns feedback commands (i.e. how to produce a proper (feedback) motor command for a specific sensory input).

Imitation

During imitation the DIVA model organizes its speech sound map and tunes the synaptic projections between speech sound map and motor map i.e. tuning of forward motor commands as well as the synaptic projections between speech sound map and sensory target regions. Imitation training is done by exposing the model to an amount of acoustic speech signals representing realizations of language-specific speech units (e.g. isolated speech sounds, syllables, words, short phrases).

The tuning of the synaptic projections between speech sound map and auditory target region map is accomplished by assigning one neuron of the speech sound map to the phonemic representation of that speech item and by associating it with the auditory representation of that speech item, which is activated at the auditory target region map. Auditory regions (i.e. a specification of the auditory variability of a speech unit) occur, because one specific speech unit (i.e. one specific phonemic representation) can be realized by several (slightly) different acoustic (auditory) realizations.

The tuning of the synaptic projections between speech sound map and motor map (i.e. tuning of forward motor commands) is accomplished with the aid of feedback commands, since the projections between sensory error maps and motor map were already tuned during babbling training. Thus the DIVA model tries to "imitate" an auditory speech item by attempting to find a proper feedforward motor command. Subsequently, the model compares the resulting sensory output (current sensory state following the articulation of that attempt) with the already learned auditory target region (intended sensory state) for that speech item. Then the model updates the current feedforward motor command by the current feedback motor command generated from the auditory error map of the auditory feedback system. This process may be repeated several times (several attempts). The DIVA model is capable of producing the speech item with a decreasing auditory difference between current and intended auditory state from attempt to attempt.

During imitation the DIVA model is also capable of tuning the synaptic projections from speech sound map to somatosensory target region map, since each new imitation attempt produces a new articulation of the speech item and thus produces a somatosensory state pattern which is associated with the phonemic representation of that speech item.

Perturbation Experiments

- Real-time Perturbation of F1: The Influence of Auditory Feedback.

While auditory feedback is most important during speech acquisition, it may be activated less if the model has learned a proper feedforward motor command for each speech unit. But it has been shown that auditory feedback needs to be strongly coactivated in the case of auditory perturbation (e.g. shifting a formant frequency). This is comparable to the strong influence of visual feedback on reaching movements during visual perturbation (e.g. shifting the location of objects by viewing through a prism).

- Unexpected Blocking of the Jaw: The Influence of Somatosensory Feedback.

In a comparable way to auditory feedback, also somatosensory feedback can be strongly coactivated during speech production, e.g. in the case of unexpected blocking of the jaw.

ACT Model

A further approach in neurocomputational modeling of speech processing is the ACT model developed by Bernd J. Kröger and his group at RWTH Aachen University, Germany. The ACT model is in accord with the DIVA model in large parts. The ACT model focuses on the action repository, which is not spelled out in detail in the DIVA model. Moreover, the ACT model explicitly introduces a level of motor plans, i.e. a high-level motor description for the production of speech items. The ACT model like any neurocomputational model remains speculative to some extent.

Structure

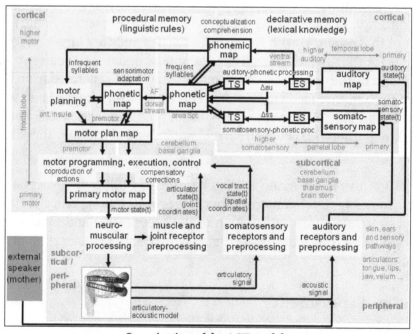

Organization of the ACT model.

The organization or structure of the ACT model is given in figure. For speech production, the ACT model starts with the activation of a phonemic representation of a speech item (phonemic map). In the case of a frequent syllable, a co-activation occurs at the level of the phonetic map, leading to a further co-activation of the intended sensory state at the level of the sensory state maps and to a co-activation of a motor plan state at the level of the motor plan map. In the case of an infrequent syllable, an attempt for a motor plan is generated by the motor planning module for that speech item by activating motor plans for phonetic similar speech items via the phonetic map. The motor plan or vocal tract action score comprises temporally overlapping vocal tract actions, which are programmed and subsequently executed by the motor programming, execution, and control module. This module gets real-time somatosensory feedback information for controlling the correct execution of the (intended) motor plan. Motor programing leads to activation pattern at the level lof the primary motor map and subsequently activates neuromuscular processing. Motoneuron activation patterns generate muscle forces and subsequently movement patterns of all model articulators (lips, tongue, velum, glottis). The Birkholz 3D articulatory synthesizer is used in order to generate the acoustic speech signal.

Articulatory and acoustic feedback signals are used for generating somatosensory and auditory feedback information via the sensory preprocessing modules, which is forwarded towards the auditory and somatosensory map. At the level of the sensory-phonetic processing modules, auditory and somatosensory information is stored in short-term memory and the external sensory signal (ES, figure, which are activated via the sensory feedback loop) can be compared with the already trained sensory signals (TS, figure, which are activated via the phonetic map). Auditory and somatosensory error signals can be generated if external and intended (trained) sensory signals are noticeably different (DIVA model).

The light green area in figure indicates those neural maps and processing modules, which process a syllable as a whole unit (specific processing time window around 100 ms and more). This processing comprises the phonetic map and the directly connected sensory state maps within the sensory-phonetic processing modules and the directly connected motor plan state map, while the primary motor map as well as the (primary) auditory and (primary) somatosensory map process smaller time windows (around 10 ms in the ACT model).

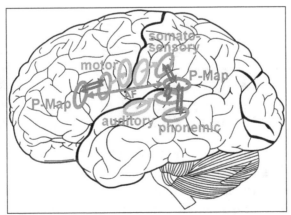

Hypothetical location of brain regions for neural maps of the ACT model.

The hypothetical cortical location of neural maps within the ACT model is shown in figure. The hypothetical locations of primary motor and primary sensory maps are given in magenta, the hypothetical locations of motor plan state map and sensory state maps (within sensory-phonetic processing module, comparable to the error maps in DIVA) are given in orange, and the hypothetical locations for the mirrored phonetic map is given in red. Double arrows indicate neuronal mappings. Neural mappings connect neural maps, which are not far apart from each other. The two mirrored locations of the phonetic map are connected via a neural pathway, leading to a (simple) one-to-one mirroring of the current activation pattern for both realizations of the phonetic map. This neural pathway between the two locations of the phonetic map is assumed to be a part of the fasciculus arcuatus.

For speech perception, the model starts with an external acoustic signal (e.g. produced by an external speaker). This signal is preprocessed, passes the auditory map, and leads to an activation pattern for each syllable or word on the level of the auditory-phonetic processing module. The ventral path of speech perception would directly activate a lexical item, but is not implemented in ACT. Rather, in ACT the activation of a phonemic state occurs via the phonemic map and thus may lead to a coactivation of motor representations for that speech item (i.e. dorsal pathway of speech perception).

Action Repository

Visualization of synaptic link weights for a section of the phonetic map, trained for the 200 most frequent syllables of Standard German. Each box represents a neuron within the self-organizing phonetic map. Each of the three link weight representations refers to the same section within the phonetic map and thus refers to the same 10×10 neurons.

The phonetic map together with the motor plan state map, sensory state maps (occurring within the sensory-phonetic processing modules), and phonemic (state) map form the action repository. The phonetic map is implemented in ACT as a self-organizing neural map and different speech items are represented by different neurons within this map. The phonetic map exhibits three major characteristics:

- More than one phonetic realization may occur within the phonetic map for one phonemic state.

- Phonetotopy: The phonetic map exhibits an ordering of speech items with respect to different phonetic features.

- The phonetic map is hypermodal or multimodal: The activation of a phonetic item at the level of the phonetic map coactivates, (i) a phonemic state (ii) a motor plan state, (iii) an auditory state and (iv) a somatosensory state. All these states are learned or trained during speech acquisition by tuning the synaptic link weights between each neuron within the phonetic map, representing a particular phonetic state and all neurons within the associated motor plan and sensory state maps.

The phonetic map implements the action-perception-link within the ACT model.

Motor Plans

A motor plan is a high level motor description for the production and articulation of a speech items. In our neurocomputational model ACT a motor plan is quantified as a vocal tract action score. Vocal tract action scores quantitatively determine the number of vocal tract actions (also called articulatory gestures), which need to be activated in order to produce a speech item, their degree of realization and duration, and the temporal organization of all vocal tract actions building up a speech item. The detailed realization of each vocal tract action (articulatory gesture) depends on the temporal organization of all vocal tract actions building up a speech item and especially on their temporal overlap. Thus the detailed realization of each vocal tract action within an speech item is specified below the motor plan level in our neurocomputational model ACT.

Integrating Sensorimotor and Cognitive Aspects: The Coupling of Action Repository and Mental Lexicon

A severe problem of phonetic or sensorimotor models of speech processing (like DIVA or ACT) is that the development of the phonemic map during speech acquisition is not modeled. A possible solution of this problem could be a direct coupling of action repository and mental lexicon without explicitly introducing a phonemic map at the beginning of speech acquisition.

Experiments: Speech Acquisition

A very important issue for all neuroscientific or neurocomputational approaches is to separate structure and knowledge. While the structure of the model (i.e. of the human neuronal network, which is needed for processing speech) is mainly determined by evolutionary processes, the knowledge is gathered mainly during speech acquisition by processes of learning. Different learning experiments were carried out with the model ACT in order to learn (i) a five-vowel system /i, e, a, o, u/, (ii) a small consonant system (voiced plosives /b, d, g/ in combination with all five vowels acquired earlier as CV syllables (ibid.), (iii) a small model language comprising the five-vowel system, voiced and unvoiced plosives /b, d, g, p, t, k/, nasals /m, n/ and the lateral /l/ and three syllable types (V, CV, and CCV) and (iv) the 200 most frequent syllables of Standard German for a 6-year-old child. In all cases, an ordering of phonetic items with respect to different phonetic features can be observed.

Experiments: Speech Perception

Despite the fact that the ACT model in its earlier versions was designed as a pure speech production model (including speech acquisition), the model is capable of exhibiting important basic phenomena of speech perception, i.e. categorical perception and the McGurk effect. In the case of categorical perception, the model is able to exhibit that categorical perception is stronger in the case of plosives than in the case of vowels. Furthermore, the model ACT was able to exhibit the McGurk effect, if a specific mechanism of inhibition of neurons of the level of the phonetic map was implemented.

ARTIFICIAL BRAIN

Given the considerable progress made in our understanding of the brain and the way in which neurons function, it seems possible to develop an artificial brain system. The idea does not consist of copying the biological components which have technical constraints linked to metabolic necessities (anabolic and catabolic) justifying complex circuits for the distribution of nutriments such as oxygen. Their miniaturization is at the nanometer scale level and data transmission and storage is well achieved through neurochemical synaptic gates using activation or inhibition. Modern neurosciences give us increasingly precise images and information about these biological components thanks to the steady improvement of imaging and signal processing tools. At the same time, electronics and modern computer sciences provide us with components that look increasingly closer to the miniaturization of living things, and therefore it seems possible to create an entirely artificial structure capable of mimicking the cerebral functions, without copying them.

The Architecture

The human brain's communication functions receive input from two sources: on the one hand, sensory inputs such as vision, touch, hearing, olfaction-taste, and on the other hand, a central black box where almost unconscious recognition occurs by accessing the brain's memory zones. It processes multimedia information producing expressive responses mainly in the form of spoken and written languages, but also mimicry and gestures, as well as behavioral responses. The back box constitutes the realm of thoughts with its multiple facets which are nowadays better understood such as cognition, memory, intelligence, speculation, conceptualization, consciousness, emotions, mental calculation, artistic creation, and more. The challenge of the Big Artificial Brain's is therefore to find the technological solutions to create inputs, process them and effectively transmit the appropriate responses in the shortest possible time.

The Entries

When it comes to communication, vision and hearing are two essential inputs. Today, we have access to very sophisticated two-dimensional or three-dimensional image acquisition systems, capable of capturing shapes, colors, and motion with a resolution and frame rate higher than the human eye. HFR tools (Hyper Fast Reading) can scan and generate text at a speed much greater than the fastest human reader. Similarly, miniaturized radars can measure distances and speed with greater precision than the human eye. On the topic of hearing, we have at our disposal high-performance systems capturing sounds from greater distances and within a broader range of frequencies that can be perceived by the human ear (20 to 20000 Hz). In summary, the BAB can receive extremely large amount of valuable data in a very short time and the NeuroMem chips can learn and recognize this data at high speed. Note that the maximum speed of data transfer in the nervous system is 120 m / sec for the largest nerve fibers of 25µ, when the BAB works at the speed light. In fact, the reaction time of the BAB is independent of the number of neuromorphic memory cells involved in the decision and will be in the order of 10µs.

The Black Box

This is the equivalent of our biological Black Box, where memory occupies a prominent place. Patients who suffer from Alzheimer's disease live only in the present and loose memory functions while keeping some cognitive remnants of the past. In electronics, memory components have made considerable progress both in term of capacity and performance and we can envision their use for the development of cognitive modules resembling the cortical columns of the human brain. The production of such modules (for text, image, sound recognition) can become pervasive in many domains including scientific, artistic, cultural, sporting, gastronomic, ecological. Unlike the human brain, they waive the risk of loss of information. Another essential attribute of neuromorphic memories must be the comprehension of the unknown which is necessary to trigger learning. This is possible with a topology implementing an RBF network (Radial Basis Function) instead of a k Nearest Neighbors type of classifier (k-NN). The neuromorphic memories recall stimuli by comparing their similarity to their own influence fields.

This involves a processing unit built into each memory cell and adjusting an acceptable range of similarity dynamically each time a new stimulus is taught.

The concept of intelligence which can be expressed as speculative and / or praxis, is the ability to solve a problem once stimuli and contextual information are comprehended and understood. Artificial inputs can be recognized and converted to keywords in any language describing the nature of the problem and activating the corresponding cognitive module to get an answer. Decision-making algorithms can also be stored in the BAB, allowing it to recognize a situation and take a decision. At this stage, we are describing a highly non-linear classifier simply trained by examples as opposed to complex conventional analytical tools which must solve problems, considering numerous variables.

There is also the problem of consciousness, whose emergence does not coincide with the arrival of mankind as some still believe. Indeed, any animal with a nervous system has some form of consciousness: The fly being chased quickly goes away; The dog recognizing his master wags its tail; The carnivore awaiting its prey and preparing his attack has a strategy. On the other hand, the chimpanzee throwing a stick to catch a banana out of his reach uses it as a tool, and unlike the human, does not seek to improve it or keep it with him. Indeed, consciousness features many levels and the most complex level, only granted to humans, is abstraction. In the brain, there is not a central location for consciousness, but the need for many activated neuronal columns. One can wonder what level of consciousness can the BAB have through the instantiation of numerous interactive components. It is likely that it could free itself from the tutelage of its authors and go on with its life. This is certainly an interesting aspect of our research as well as its artistic creativity which is expressed with brushes, scissors, paint, and other tools very easy to simulate by software installed in the BAB.

Note that in a specific operating mode of the BAB called RBF mode, the network can learn, recognize, and generalize. It can recognize even if the stimulus is different than the examples used during training. Such ability of the BAB is like our own biology which can adapt and match elements that have evolved. The difficulty for the BAB machine will be to find the best set of parameters describing the event to help its identification and proper discrimination from other elements (feature extraction process). For example, we can all recognize, even after several years, a friend or loved one because we are able to generalize.

Finally, come the subject of emotions. They play a considerable role in human and animal behavior. We know quite well the circuit of emotions in the brain which is in fact largely linked to the memory as demonstrated by Papez. We also know that all kinds of visual, auditory, or tactile emotions are experienced by the body in its entirety through the connections of the limbic system to the hypothalamus, which manage the always present vegetative reactions (palms, sweating, acceleration of heart rate, intestinal tract, etc.) and neuroendocrine (adrenal system). Of course, the BAB, which does not have a physical body and especially no sympathetic or parasympathetic neuro-vegetative system, will not have any emotions. This becomes an advantage when it comes to solving a complex intellectual problem, but a disadvantage when it comes to appreciating a painting or experiencing an emotional situation. The great director Stephen Spielberg has remarkably explored this problem in his film A. I.

Expressive Exits

Synthetic spoken languages are now commonly accepted in most industrialized countries. They have considerably improved and feature rich intonations resembling human voices. The BAB will be able to speak and even sing if necessary.

With regards to writing, multiple technologies are available, including our modern printers, speech to text translators, FMW (Fast Multilingual Writing) software, etc. So, the answer to a question could easily appear in a form we are familiar with. It is a technical aspect related to the human-machine interface which does not present any major difficulties.

References

- Sur, M.; Rubenstein, J. L. R. (2005). "Patterning and Plasticity of the Cerebral Cortex". Science. 310 (5749): 805–10. Bibcode:2005Sci...310..805S. Doi:10.1126/science.1112070. PMID 16272112

- Doidge, Norman (2007). The Brain That Changes Itself: Stories of Personal Triumph from the Frontiers of Brain Science. Viking Adult. ISBN 978-0-670-03830-5

- Farwell, LA; Smith, SS (2001). "Using brain MERMER testing to detect knowledge despite efforts to conceal". Journal of Forensic Sciences. 46 (1): 135–43. Doi:10.1520/JFS14925J. PMID 11210899

- Harris, Mark (September 18, 2009). "Obama honours IBM supercomputer". Techradar.com. Retrieved 2009-09-18

- Goodman, D. And Brette, R. (2008). "Brian: a simulator for spiking neural networks in Python", Front. Neuroinform. 2:5. Doi:10.3389/neuro.11.005.2008 PMID 19115011

Permissions

Index

CPSIA information can be obtained
at www.ICGtesting.com
Printed in the USA
LVHW061634090222
710692LV00006B/487